"In lyrically elegant prose, *The Memory Palace* explores not just relationships but the slippery nature of memory itself."

—*O, the Oprah Magazine*

"Bartók juggles a handful of profound themes: how to undertake a creative life . . . how we remember . . . how one says good-bye to a loved one in a manner that might redeem in some small way a life and a relationship blighted by psychosis; and, most vividly and harrowingly, how our society and institutions throw mental illness back in the hands of family members, who are frequently helpless to deal with the magnitude of the terrifying problems it generates. On all counts, it's an engrossing read."

—*Elle* magazine

"[L]ike the cabinet of wonders that is a frequent motif here, Bartok's memory palace contains some rare, distinctive and genuinely imaginative treasures. "

—*The New York Times Book Review*

"*The Memory Palace* is not so much a palace of memories as a complex web of bewitching verbal and visual images, memories, dreams, true stories, and rambling excerpts from the author's mentally ill mother's notebooks. It is an extraordinary mix."

—*The Washington Post*

unforgettable memoir of loss and recovery, love and forgiveness." —*Booklist*

Praise for
The Memory Palace

"In lyrically elegant prose, *The Memory Palace* explores not just relationships but the slippery nature of memory itself."

—*O, THE OPRAH MAGAZINE*

"Bartók juggles a handful of profound themes: how to undertake a creative life ... how we remember ... how one says goodbye to a loved one in a manner that might redeem in some small way a life and a relationship blighted by psychosis; and, most vividly and harrowingly, how our society and institutions throw mental illness back in the hands of family members, who are frequently helpless to deal with the magnitude of the terrifying problems it generates. On all counts, it's an engrossing read."

—*ELLE* magazine

"*The Memory Palace* is not so much a palace of memories as a complex web of bewitching verbal and visual images, memories, dreams, true stories and rambling excerpts from the author's mentally ill mother's notebooks. It is an extraordinary mix."

—*THE WASHINGTON POST*

"Bartók's story overcame my memoir phobia with a page-turning plot, sophisticated writing and, as a bonus, vivid illustrations from the author. It does indeed deserve to be mentioned in the same breath as *The Glass Castle* and *The Liars' Club*, and readers of those memoirs will find *The Memory Palace* richly rewarding."

—*BOOKPAGE*

"The ineffable functioning of memory and the brain itself is integral to Bartók's complex story. She brilliantly teases out the emotional and physical fallout of her mother's brain, damaged by illness ... The fact that Bartók can convey how and why she still loves her mother is perhaps the book's greatest triumph."

—*THE BOSTON GLOBE*

"This is a book so strong, so powerful, so richly and dangerously evocative that the pages seem to quiver almost imperceptivity, as if at any moment they might leap to life."

—*MORE* magazine

"A disturbing, mesmerizing personal narrative about growing up with a brilliant but schizophrenic mother ... Richly textured, compassionate and heartbreaking."

—*KIRKUS*, starred review

"Neither sensational nor cagily sentimental nor self pitying, this grounded, exquisitely written work ... requires reading."
—*LIBRARY JOURNAL*

"Poignant, powerful, disturbing, and exceedingly well-written, this is an unforgettable memoir of loss and recovery, love and forgiveness."
—*BOOKLIST*, starred review

"... like the cabinet of wonders that is a frequent motif here, Bartók's memory palace contains some rare, distinctive, and genuinely imaginative treasures."
—*THE NEW YORK TIMES BOOK REVIEW*

"*The Memory Palace* is almost a fairy tale: two little girls grow up under the spell of their mother's madness. But it really did happen, once upon a time, and Mira Bartók uses her considerable powers of recollection and compassion to understand her family and to present them to readers as complete, loved human beings. This is an extraordinary book."
—AUDREY NIFFENEGGER, author of *The Time Traveler's Wife* and *Her Fearful Symmetry*

"A haunting, almost patchwork, narrative that lyrically chronicles a complex mother-daughter relationship."
—*PUBLISHERS WEEKLY*, starred review

"In this often gorgeous and often disturbing memoir ... the palace Bartók builds in this book is as beautiful as it is full of devastating damage."
—*NEW YORK JOURNAL OF BOOKS*

"The intertwined voices of grief-stricken, articulate sanity and not-so-sane but often quite poetic illness make a duet both wonderful and terrible."
—*THE NEW YORK TIMES*

"Mira Bartók's memoir will haunt you with its compassion for people who have mental illness and for the tender vulnerability of their children. Bartók's writing is at times spare and at times lyrical as she struggles in the unpredictable and unsafe world of being the child of a paranoid schizophrenic. 'How heavy is a dresser when you're the only one pushing it against the door?' she asks, distilling years of nights of fear. Beautifully written, touchingly told, *The Memory Palace* lingers, radiating with pain and fear, love and freedom."
—JANINE LATUS, author of *If I Am Missing or Dead*

"*The Memory Palace* is a stunning meditation on the tenacity of familial bonds, even in the face of extreme adversity, and an artist's struggle to claim her own creative life. Bartók carries us, room to luminous room, through her memory palace, filling it with stories that link loss to grace, guilt to love, the natural world's great beauty to the creative act, and tragic beginnings to quietly triumphant closings. This extraordinary book, with its beautiful illuminated images, will stay with me."
—MEREDITH HALL, author of *Without A Map*

"Schizophrenia is more than a thief of the mind and Mira Bartók gives us the layered understanding to see the illness for all its cruel manifestations when the illness hijacks her mother. The best memoirs illuminate us all, and *The Memory Palace* left me illuminated with Bartók's courage and unwavering belief in artistic expression in the midst of a shattered family. The writing is spectacular."
—JACQUELINE SHEEHAN, Ph.D., *New York Times* bestselling author of *Lost & Found*, and *Now & Then*

"In *The Memory Palace*, Bartók's gilded prose and encyclopedic mind lead the reader through her life's darkest chambers where debilitating mental illness sends the author's mother spiraling from a promising career as a concert pianist to years of madness. But Bartók does not merely decorate her palace with humanistic portraits of the mentally ill and the seemingly insurmountable challenges they and their families face. She takes the reader up secret staircases illuminated by her own irrepressible creativity and struggle to survive, her mother's flashpoints of lucidity, and their equally ravishing intellects. From this great height Bartók shows us that art's healing powers affect even those that illness has pushed to the shadowiest extremes of the human experience. *The Memory Palace* is a grand, unforgettable estate."
—ELYSSA EAST, author of *Dogtown: Death and Enchantment in a New England Ghost Town*

"All you'd need is to see my copy to know—I have Post-it notes marking phrases and sentences I wanted to repeat because they were so good. About one-third of the way through, I thought that if this book were a person, I'd consider making out with it."
—*LIBRARY JOURNAL BOOK SMACK!*, starred review

"Some books you carry with you while you're reading them—in your purse, your e-reader, whatever—but this is one you also carry along well after the last page, on a small mantel in your own memory palace . . . It's an arresting, compassionate, and unforgettable memoir."
—*BUST* magazine

"A book of aching beauty and compassion, that circles around the essence of what it is to be alive."

    —NICK FLYNN, author of *Another Bullshit Night in Suck City* and *The Ticking is the Bomb: A Memoir*

"Among the plethora of books now available by the children of parents with schizophrenia, *The Memory Palace* stands out. Elegantly written, the book details what it is like to grow up with a mother with schizophrenia and sensitively assesses the long-term effects her mother's illness had on both her and her sister. Strongly recommended."

    —E. FULLER TORREY, M.D., author of *The Insanity Offense*

"Mira Bartók's harrowing and beautiful tale of growing up with her paranoid schizophrenic mother is in some ways a memoir about memory itself. For Bartók—suffering from a brain injury and raised by someone who had tenuous contact with the external world—the question "what really happened" takes on a particular urgency. She answers it with painstaking honesty, weaving deft parallels between domestic and institutional abuse, individual and national trauma. And as she recalls the shattering experiences of her childhood, literally illuminating them with her haunting mnemonic paintings, something that was never intact is made resonantly whole again."

    —ALISON BECHDEL, author of *Fun Home: A Family Tragicomic*

"Mira Bartók's *The Memory Palace* is a beautifully crafted tale of life with an absent father and a mentally ill mother. As the story unfolds, you'll see how fine the line is between gentle artistic creativity and debilitating madness. With each new vignette, Mira reveals the wonder and the horror of life in a house ruled by insanity. As the daughters get older, the mother devolves, making her way from world-class musician to paranoid homeless schizophrenic. Despite that tragedy, Mira's spirit never fails to shine through. You'll wish you could pick her up, like a little lost kitten, but in the end, she makes it on her own."

    —JOHN ELDER ROBISON, author of *Look Me in the Eye*

The Memory Palace

MIRA BARTÓK

Free Press
New York London Sydney
Toronto

Author's Note

Nearly all the names of those who appear in this book have remained intact. However, I have changed the names of a couple people so as to protect their privacy. I have also reconstructed various conversations and condensed certain moments from my life.

This is a book about memory itself as much as it is a book about my relationship with my mother and I have tried my best to follow my own memory's capricious and meandering path along the way. As for my mother's diary entries between each chapter—they are her words but my headings.

***ƒ*P**

Free Press
A Division of Simon & Schuster, Inc.
1230 Avenue of the Americas
New York, NY 10020

First Free Press trade paperback edition August 2011

FREE PRESS and colophon are trademarks of Simon & Schuster, Inc.

For information about special discounts for bulk purchases, please contact Simon & Schuster Special Sales at 1-866-506-1949 or business@simonandschuster.com.

The Simon & Schuster Speakers Bureau can bring authors to your live event. For more information or to book an event contact the Simon & Schuster Speakers Bureau at 1-866-248-3049 or visit our website at www.simonspeakers.com.

Illustrations by Mira Bartók
Art photography by Adam Laipson
Book design by Ellen R. Sasahara

Manufactured in the United States of America

7   9   10   8

Library of Congress Cataloging-in-Publication Data

Bartók, Mira.
The memory palace / by Mira Bartók.
p. cm.
1. Herr, Norma Kurap, 1926–2007. 2. Bartók, Mira. 3. Children of the mentally ill—United States—Biography. 4. Mentally ill parents—United States—Biography.
I. Herr, Norma Kurap, 1926–2007. II. Title.
RC464.H47 2011
362.2085092—dc22
[B]   2010008399
ISBN 978-1-4391-8331-1
ISBN 978-1-4391-8332-8 (pbk)
ISBN 978-1-4391-8333-5 (ebook)

Contents

For my mother

Norma Kurap Herr
November 17, 1926 – January 6, 2007

☙

And dedicated to the women
at the Norma Herr Women's Center of Cleveland, Ohio
(Formerly the Community Women's Shelter)

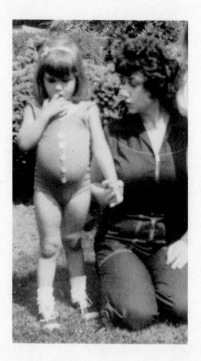

Child, knowledge is a treasury and your heart its strongbox.

Hugo of St. Victor, from *The Three Best Memory Aids for Learning History*

Homeless

A homeless woman, let's call her my mother for now, or yours, sits on a window ledge in late afternoon in a working-class neighborhood in Cleveland, or it could be Baltimore or Detroit. She is five stories up, and below the ambulance is waiting, red lights flashing in the rain. The woman thinks they're the red eyes of a leopard from her dream last night. The voices below tell her not to jump, but the ones in her head are winning. In her story there are leopards on every corner, men with wild teeth and cat bodies, tails as long as rivers. If she opens her arms into wings she must cross a bridge of fire, battle four horses and riders. *I am a swan, a spindle, a falcon, a bear.* The men below call up to save her, cast their nets to lure her down, but she knows she cannot reach the garden without the distant journey. She opens her arms to enter the land of birds and fire. *I will become wind, bone, blood, and memory.* And the red eyes below are amazed to see just how perilously she balances on the ledge—like a leaf or a delicate lock of hair.

Every passion borders on chaos, that of the collector
on the chaos of memory.

Walter Benjamin, *"Ich packe meine Bibliothek aus"*

Part I

The Order of Things

1

. . . Climb the mountains, search the valleys, the deserts, the seashores . . .
the deep recesses of the earth . . . for in this way and no other will you arrive at . . .
the true nature of things.

Petrus Severinus, 16th century Danish alchemist

The Subterranean World

Even now, when the phone rings late at night, I think it's her. I stumble out of bed ready for the worst. Then I realize—it's a wrong number, or a friend calling from the other side of the ocean. The last time my mother called was in 1990. I was thirty-one and living in Chicago. She said if I didn't come home right away she'd kill herself. After she hung up, she climbed onto the second-floor balcony of my grandmother's house in Cleveland, boosted herself onto the banister, and opened her arms to the wind. Below, our neighbor Ruth Armstrong and two paramedics tried to coax her back inside. When the call came the next time, almost seventeen years later, it was right before Christmas 2006, and I didn't even hear the phone ring.

The night before, I had a dream: I was in an empty apartment with my mother. She looked like she had that winter of 1990—her brown and gray hair unwashed and wild, her blouse stained and torn. She held a cigarette in her right hand, fingers crossed over it as if for good luck. She never looked like a natural-born smoker, even though she smoked four packs a day. The walls of the apartment were covered in dirt. I heard a knock. "What do you want?" I asked the stranger behind the door. He whispered, "Make

3

this place as clean as it was in the beginning." I scrubbed the floors and walls, then I lifted into the air, sailing feet-first through the empty rooms. I called out to my mother, "Come back! You can fly too!" but she had already disappeared.

When I awoke there was a message on my machine from my friend Mark in Vermont. He had been keeping a post office box for me in Burlington, about three hours from my home in Western Massachusetts. The only person who wrote me there was my mother. "A nurse from a hospital in Cleveland called about a Mrs. Norma Herr," he said. "She said it was an emergency." How did they find me? For years, I had kept my life secret from my schizophrenic and homeless mother. So had my sister, Natalia. We both had changed our names, had unpublished phone numbers and addresses.

The story unfolded over the next couple days. After the ambulance rushed my mother to the hospital, the red sweater I had sent her for the holidays arrived at the women's shelter where she had been living for the last three years. Tim, her social worker, brought the package to her in ICU to cheer her up after surgery. He noticed the return address was from me, care of someone in Vermont. He knew I was her daughter. A nurse called information to get Mark's number and left the message on his machine. How easy it was to find me after all those years. When I called a friend to tell her I was going to see my mother, she said, "I hope you can forgive her for what she did to you." "Forgive her?" I said. "The question is—will she ever forgive *me?*"

The night before I left for Cleveland, while Doug, my fiancé, was making dinner, I went to my studio above our barn to gather some things for my trip. I did what I always do when I enter: I checked the small table to the left of my desk to see if I had written any notes to myself the day before. It's there, on my memory table, that I keep an ongoing inventory of what I'm afraid I'll forget. Ever since I suffered a brain injury from a car accident a few years ago, my life has become a palimpsest—a piece of parchment from which someone had rubbed off the words, leaving only a ghost image behind.

Above my desk are lists of things I can't remember anymore, the meaning of words I used to know, ideas I'll forget within an hour or a day. My computer is covered in Post-its, reminding me of which books I lent out to whom, memories I'm afraid I'll forget, songs from the past I suddenly recall.

I was forty when, in 1999, a semi hurtled into my car while a friend and I were stopped at a construction site on the New York Thruway. The car was old and had no airbag—my body was catapulted back and forth in the passenger's seat, my head smashing against the headrest and dashboard. *Coupcontrècoup* it's called, blow against blow, when your brain goes flying against the surface of your skull. This kind of impact causes contusions in the front and back areas of the brain and can create microscopic bleeding and shearing of neural pathways, causing synapses to misfire, upsetting the applecart of your brain, sometimes forever. Even if you don't lose consciousness, or, as in my case, don't lose it for very long.

The next days and months that followed I couldn't remember the words for things or they got stuck in my head and wouldn't come out. Simple actions were arduous—tipping a cabbie, reading an e-mail, and listening to someone talk. On good days, I acted normal, sounded articulate. I still do. I work hard to process the bombardment of stimuli that surrounds me. I work hard not to let on that for me, even the sound of a car radio is simply too much, or all those bright lights at the grocery store. We children of schizophrenics are the great secret-keepers, the ones who don't want you to think that anything is wrong.

Outside the glass door of my studio, the moon was just a sliver in the clear obsidian sky. Soon I'd be in the city again, where it's hard to see the stars. Hanging from a wooden beam to the right of my desk is a pair of reindeer boots I made when I lived in the Arctic, before my brain injury, when I could still travel with ease. What to bring to show my mother the last seventeen years of my life? How long would I stay in Cleveland? One month? Five? The doctor had said on the phone that she had less than six months to live—but he didn't know my mother.

What would she think of the cabinet of curiosities I call my studio: the mouse skeleton, the petrified bat, the pictures of co-joined twins, the shelves of seedpods and lichen, the deer skull and bones? Would she think that aliens had put them there or would she want to draw them, like me? I fantasized about kidnapping her from the hospital. I would open the couch bed and let her spend her last days among the plants, the paints, and the books; let her play piano anytime she wanted. I'd even let her smoke. She could stay up all night drawing charts of tornadoes, hurricanes, and other future disasters, like the ones she used to send me through my post office box. But she would never see this place. She probably would never leave her bed.

Lining the walls in my studio was evidence of a life intersecting art and science: books on art history and evolution, anthropology, polar exploration, folklore, poetry, and neuroscience. If I brought her here, would my mother really be happy? There was a cabinet of art supplies, an antique globe, a map of Lapland. I had star charts, bird charts, and a book of maps from the Age of Discovery. Had my mother ever been truly happy? Had she ever passed a day unafraid, without a chorus of voices in her head?

The questions I wrote down before I left for Cleveland: How long does she have to live? Does she have a coat? Will she remember me? How will I remember her, after she is gone?

ↄ৲

The next day I flew into Cleveland Hopkins International Airport. I almost always travel with Doug now: he is my compass, my driver, my word-finder and guide. How would I fare in this place without him? When I collected my suitcase from baggage claim, I half expected my mother to appear. She had slept on one of the benches off and on for years. Sometimes people came up to her and gave her money but she never understood why. Once she wrote to say: *A kind man offered me five dollars at the airport for some reason. A bright moment in a storm-ridden day. I bought a strawberry milkshake at Micky D's then pocketed the rest.*

I had flown to Cleveland just two months before to go to my thirtieth high school reunion. The day after the reunion, Doug and I drove to Payne

Avenue near downtown Cleveland to see the shelter where my mother lived. She had given me her address in 2004, not a post office box number like she had in the past. I had no idea she had cancer then, nor did she, even though her body was showing signs that something was seriously wrong. *I live in pain on Payne*, she had written to me several times. *I am bleeding a lot from below*. But how to know what was real? *Are you sick?* I'd write her; she would respond: *Sometimes I am taken out of the city and given enemas in my sleep. It's what they do to Jews*. In her last few letters, she always ended with: *If you come to see me, I'll make sure they find you a bed*. Doug and I parked across the street from the shelter; I put on dark sunglasses and wouldn't get out of the car. "I just want to see where she lives," I said. "If I go in, she'll want to come home with me, and then what?" I sank low in the seat and watched the women smoke out in front, waiting for the doors to open. It was windy and trash blew around the desolate treeless road. "I wish I could take her home. It looks like a war zone," I said to Doug as we drove away. "At least I saw where she lives. It makes it more real. But now what?"

I felt worse, finally knowing where she lived, knowing exactly what the place looked like. How could I turn my back on her now when her sad life was staring me in the face? And if I didn't do something soon, what was to stop her from moving on yet again, to another shelter, another town?

I had been communicating with my mother's social worker for the past year about reuniting us, with a third party present for support. I wouldn't do it without a third party, without my mother living somewhere under close watch, in a halfway house or a nursing home. Even though she was now elderly, in my mind she was still the madwoman on the street, brandishing a knife; the woman who shouts obscenities at you in the park, who follows you down alleyways, lighting matches in your hair.

I had no idea if my sister Natalia would want to see her at all, but planned to ask her when the time came. The organization that was helping my mother, MHS (Mental Health Services for Homeless Persons, Inc.), had been trying to arrange a legal guardianship for her so she could be placed in a nursing home where she could get adequate care. She would finally have an advocate—someone to make decisions for her about finances, housing, and health. But when MHS presented my mother's case before the court, they lost. It didn't matter that she slept outside on the wet ground some nights, or that she was incontinent, nearly blind, and seriously ill, or that she had a long history of suicide attempts and hospitalizations. The judge declared my mother sane for three simple reasons: she could balance a checkbook, buy her own cigarettes, and use correct change. It was just like when my sister and I had tried to get a guardianship for her in the past.

I picked up a rental car at the airport and met my childhood friend Cathy at my hotel. We had seen each other for the first time after thirty years when I came to town two months before. Except for a few extra pounds and some faint lines etched around her blue eyes, Cathy hadn't changed. I could still picture her laughing, leaning against her locker at Newton D. Baker Junior High—a sweet, sympathetic girl in a miniskirt, straight blond hair flowing down to her waist.

As we were going up the elevator at University Hospital, I told Cathy about what the doctor had said to me earlier that day on the phone. He had said that my mother's abdomen was riddled with tumors, and that he had removed most of her stomach and colon. He explained what stomas were, how her waste was being removed through them and how they had to be kept clean. I said, "He claims she'll never go back to the shelter. They'll get her into a good nursing home and make her as comfortable as possible before she dies."

"That's a relief," she said, taking my hand.

"I don't know, Cathy. I still think she'll just get up, walk out the door, and disappear."

The door was slightly ajar when we arrived at my mother's room. I asked Cathy to wait in the hall until I called her in. The lights were off when I entered. I watched my mother sleep for a few minutes; the sun filtered through the slats in the shades, illuminating her pallid face. She looked like my grandfather when he was dying—hollow cheeks, ashen skin, breath labored and slow. Would she believe it was really me? She thought that aliens could assume the shape of her loved ones.

"Mom," I said. "It's me. Your daughter, Myra." I used my old name, the one she gave me. She opened her eyes.

"Myra? Is it really you?" Her voice was barely audible and her cadence strange.

"I brought you a little gift," I said, and placed the soft orange scarf I had knitted for her around her neck.

I sat down and took her hand. How well could she see? She had always written about her blindness, caused by glaucoma, cataracts, and "poisonous gas from enemy combatants." I wondered if she could see how I had aged. My dark brown hair was cut in a bob, like the last time I had seen her, but I had a few wrinkles now, a few more gray hairs. I still dressed like a tomboy, though, and was wearing black sweatpants and a sweater. "That's a good look for you, honey," she said. "You look sporty. Where's your sister?"

"She'll be here in a couple days," I said. "She sends her love."

I was relieved that I could say that. What if my sister couldn't bear to come? What would I have said?

When the nurse came in I asked her how much my mother weighed.

"Eighty-three pounds. Are you her daughter?"

"Yes," I said, then hesitated. "I haven't seen her in seventeen years."

I expected the nurse to reproach me, but instead she was kind. "How nice that you can be together now. I hope you two have a great reunion."

My mother brought her hand up to shield her eyes. "Turn that damn light off."

"It's off," I said.

"Shut the curtains. It's too bright in here. Where's my music? When am I going home?"

"Where do you want to go?" I asked.

"Back to my women."

Did she mean the women's shelter? Or did she want to be with my sister and me in her old house on West 148th Street?

"Where's my little radio? Did someone steal it again?"

The last time I visited my mother in a hospital, it was over twenty years ago. She was in a lockdown ward at Cleveland Psychiatric Institute (CPI) and had asked me to bring her a radio. She had always needed a radio and a certain level of darkness. In her youth, my mother had been a musical prodigy. When I was growing up, she listened to the classical radio station night and day. I always wondered if her need for a radio meant more than just a love of music. Did it help block out the voices in her head?

I pulled the curtains shut over the shades. "Is that better?"

"Yes, honey. You're a good girl."

I could smell lunch arriving down the hall—coffee, soup, and bread. Comforting smells in a world of beeping machines and gurneys—the clanking, squeaking sounds of the ICU.

"Are you hungry?" I asked.

"Not that hungry these days," she said. "You want something to eat? You're too thin. Go ask them to make you a sandwich. I'll pay. Bring me my purse."

My mother was missing all but her four front teeth. I remember her writing me several years before to say that she had had them all removed because disability wouldn't pay for dental care. *According to the Government, teeth and eyes are just accessories,* she wrote. *Like buying a belt or a brooch.*

"Where are your false teeth?" I asked. "They'll be serving lunch soon."

"Someone stole them," she whispered. "They always steal my teeth."

We sat for a while, holding hands. She drifted in and out of sleep. I put my mother's palm up to my lips. For the first time in my life, I couldn't smell cigarettes on her skin. She smelled like baby lotion. She opened her eyes.

"You should be proud of me. I quit smoking," she said.

"When did you quit?"

"A week ago. When they brought me here."

"Good for you," I said. "You know, I always loved you, Mommy."

It was the first time I had used that word since I was a child. My sister and I always called her Mother, Norma, or Normie, or, on rare occasions, Mom. It was hard to call her anything maternal, even though she tried so hard to be just that. But in the hospital, as she lay dying, *Mommy* seemed the only right word to use.

"I love you too," she said. "But you ran away from me. Far away."

"I know. I'm sorry."

"A lot happened," she said.

"A lot happened to me too. But I'm here now."

"Yes," she said. "I'm glad you came. Now let me sleep. I'm so very tired."

On Tuesday, my second day at the hospital, a nurse came in and asked me how old my mother was. "She just turned eighty in November," I said.

My mother threw me a nasty look. "It's a lie!"

"How old *are* you?" I asked.

"Not *that* old," she said.

"I was just kidding," I said. "Are you in your forties now?" I winked at the nurse.

"A little older but not much. A woman should never reveal her age."

"She's fifty-two," I said to the nurse but mouthed the word *eighty* when my mother turned away.

Later, the surgeon talked to me outside the room. He said that the pathology report had finally come in. What he originally thought was colon cancer was late-stage stomach cancer, which is more deadly and was moving fast. I bombarded him with questions: "Where else has the cancer spread? Is she too far gone for chemo? How long does she have?"

"Well, the good news is that your mother is doing remarkably well!" How can a dying person do remarkably well? I wondered. He added, "She's recovering great from the surgery but there's nothing we can really do for her anymore, just keep her comfortable."

"Can you explain what you did?" I asked.

The doctor borrowed my notepad and drew a picture. His pen flew over the paper; it was a map of what my mother looked like inside. "Here's what I did," he said. "I redirected what's left of her colon and moved this over here, so that her waste can exit through this stoma, see?"

He spoke too fast for my brain, using words like *fistula, ileostomy,* and *carcinomatosis.* I had no idea what he was talking about. It looked like he was drawing the map of a city as seen from above. Was this what is inside us, these roads and byways, these rotaries and hairpin turns?

"Thanks," I said. "That explains a lot."

"Super," said the doctor, perpetually upbeat. "We can talk more later. I want to speak with your mother now."

The doctor and I went back inside her room. "Good morning, Norma! How are you doing today?"

She smiled weakly. "All right."

He turned to me. "Her abdomen is completely diseased. We couldn't take everything out."

I glared at him and put my finger to my lips. The day before I had said on the phone that discussing this with my mother would just upset her and that she wouldn't really understand. The doctor continued anyway.

"It's much worse than we thought, Norma. People always want to know how long, but I can't tell them. I could say a few weeks, months, either way I'd be wrong." He sat down beside her, took her hand in his, and said loudly, "You have cancer, Norma. It's very bad. Do you understand?"

She looked baffled. The night before she had told me it wasn't anything serious, she just had food poisoning from bad Mexican food. "Don't eat at Taco Bell," she had warned me. "They poison the beans there."

The doctor said again, "Norma. Do you understand that you have cancer?"

"Get me a Danish," she whispered in my ear as if it were a secret. She thought for a second. "One with sweet cheese."

Later that day, my mother suddenly became concerned about her things at the shelter. "Where's my black backpack? Where's my purse? Who took them?"

I asked Tim, her shy young social worker from MHS, to retrieve her two large garbage bags from the shelter on Payne Avenue. I assumed these were the only things she owned in the world. In the years that we were apart, she often mentioned in her letters that she still had some of our family things in storage. Was it true or did she just imagine they were locked up somewhere for safekeeping? Sometimes she wrote me urgent letters, begging me to come to Cleveland and help her move her things from one place to another, but I suspected that it was just a ploy to get me to come back home.

In the hospital parking lot Tim and I rummaged through her bags to see if there was anything she might want. We found her backpack in one of them, filthy and ripped, filled with laundry detergent, toothpaste, damp cigarettes, receipts, a diary, a sketchbook, a medical dictionary, incontinence pads, and a dirty white sock filled with keys. I took the keys and counted them, seventeen in all. Most looked like they went to lockers and storage units. One was a house key. Did it unlock our old red brick house?

Back in her room I showed her the sock. "Where do these go to?" I asked.

"I'm tired. I don't know. Let me sleep." Then she motioned me to come closer. "I have Grandma's diamond rings for you girls. They're locked up in a safety-deposit box."

"Where?" I asked. "What box? What are all these keys for?"

"Tell you later. Too tired now. Shut lights. Don't let them steal my pack."

That evening, in the hotel room, I picked up the diary I had found in her backpack. It was a pocket-sized purple notebook with red hearts on the cover, like the diary of a ten-year-old girl. I wondered if she had more of them hidden somewhere. I flipped through the coffee-stained pages. The book had the same faint odor of stale smoke and mildew that her letters had. I turned to her last few entries. Two weeks before the paramedics picked her up from the Community Women's Shelter, my mother wrote: *Magma: Hot liquid rock can be three shapes: spherical, spiral or a rod. It flows out like lava or cools underground.*

They had told me at the shelter that when they called 911 that day, she couldn't stop vomiting and her stomach was distended as if she were about to give birth. "That Norma, she didn't want to go to the hospital," one woman had said to me on the phone. "She is one stubborn lady." She had been sick for months, but wouldn't see a doctor. Finally, the day the ambulance came to take her to the hospital, the women at the shelter convinced her to go.

In her diary, my mother wrote: *If lava reaches Earth's surface it turns into igneous rock. Basalt: dark gray rock forms when magma cools into a solid.* My mother had been studying geology. I turned back the pages. Before geology, she had reread all of Edgar Allan Poe. Before that she had turned to the stars:

Recently, I had a dream of a cataclysm. Was not prepared for study of the planets, which has fevered my imagination once again.

Before I left for Cleveland I had been studying geology too. I was in the middle of a book about Nicolaus Steno, the seventeenth century Danish anatomist, whom some call the grandfather of geology. Steno was fascinated by what the oceans hid and left behind. I had read about how one day, in 1666, young Steno was in an anatomical theater in Florence, Italy, dissecting the head of a shark. It wasn't just any shark but a great white. The shark was a wonder, and Steno's patron, the Grand Duke Ferdinando II de' Medici, wanted to know what was inside. This was the time when wonder and scientific inquiry were intricately entwined—when collectors collected the rare and the mysterious, the miraculous and mundane, from the bounty that explorers brought back to Europe from the New World.

When Steno peered into the monster's mouth he noticed that the shark's teeth resembled the little stones people called "tongue stones," or *glossopetrae*, the mysterious stones Pliny the Elder said fell from the heavens on dark and moonless nights, what the church said were miracle stones left from Noah's Great Flood. Steno's mind leapt from shark to sea to a question that plagued him for the rest of his life: why are seashells found on mountaintops? Even his scientific colleagues thought the fossils were signs from God. Nicolaus Steno laid the foundation for reading the archival history of the earth: How crystals are formed, how land erodes and sediment is made over time. How over centuries, seashells become fossils embedded deep inside the bedrock of mountains.

My mother would have liked Nicolaus Steno. She'd marvel at the way his mind flew from one thought to another, uncovering the truth about ancient seas, how he learned to read the memory of a landscape, one layer at a time. The earth is also a palimpsest—its history scraped away time and time again. If my mother were well enough, I would tell her this. She'd light up a cigarette, pour herself a cup of black coffee, and get out her colored pens. Then she'd draw a giant chart with a detailed geological timeline, revealing the stratification of the earth.

———

That Tuesday night I met my sister, Natalia, at the airport. I spotted her cherry-red coat in the thick throng of hurried holiday travelers. She lugged a huge suitcase behind her, walking a fast clip in high black boots. Like me, it had been close to seventeen years since she had last seen our mother, but my sister had made the painful decision never to write to her. When I had called her about our mother dying, I didn't know whether or not she would come. Her last vision of our mother was a nightmare, indelible in her mind. I was relieved when, without even deliberating, she said she'd join me in Cleveland.

"Nattie, I'm so happy you're here." I ran up to hug her. I had almost called her Rachel, her birth name before she changed it more than a decade before. Being back in Cleveland made her newer name feel strange on my tongue for the first time in years. Just as well. Around our mother, we'd have to be Myra and Rachel one last time.

"How is she?" asked Natalia.

"Don't be shocked. She looks like a survivor from the camps."

"I really want to see her. Let's go first thing in the morning."

"Before I forget, I wanted to tell you—I found some keys. And receipts from U-Haul. She must have a storage room somewhere."

"What do you think is in there?"

"I don't know. But we can go this week and see. I imagine there's a lot of junk."

The next morning Natalia woke up early to work out in the gym. She has always kept a strict regimen—a daily exercise routine, a rigorous schedule for writing, teaching, grading her students' papers before bed. While Natalia was out of the room, I skimmed through my mother's dairy. She wrote about staying up all night in the rain on a stranger's porch and trying to sleep at the bus station without getting mugged. Should I read any of this to my sister?

When we walked into our mother's room at the hospital, she looked up at Natalia and said, "Who are you?" She turned to me. "Who's this lady?"

How could my mother not recognize her? Did she look that different seventeen years ago? The last time our mother saw her, Natalia was running away from the house on West 148th Street. Maybe that was how our mother remembered her—a terrified young girl in flight, long hair flying in the cold January wind.

"It's me. Rachel," said my sister.

How could we explain that we had changed our names so she could never find us? That we had been so scared of her all these years? She was the cry of madness in the dark, the howling of wind outside our doors. I had changed my name the year after my sister did, reluctantly, giving up the name signed at the bottom of my paintings so I would be harder to find. But I could never relinquish my first name. I simply exchanged a *y* for an *i*. My sister couldn't give up her first name either and kept it sandwiched between the first and the last: Natalia Rachel Singer. She took Isaac Bashevis Singer's last name, I took Béla Bartók's.

"Rachel? I thought you were dead."

"I'm not dead," said my sister. "I'm here, right beside you."

"Is it really you?"

Natalia pulled up a chair next to the bed. "It's really me. How are you feeling?"

"You girls have got to get me out of here! We have to go back to the house. There are criminals inside."

"Don't worry, the house is fine," I lied to her. "Everything is just like you left it. You can go home as soon as you are better."

After all these years, our mother was still obsessed about her parents' house she'd sold in 1989. When she signed the papers over to the new owner, she believed that she was only renting it to him for a while. Not long after the sale, and after my sister's and my last failed attempt to get her a legal guardian and medical treatment, our mother disappeared into the streets.

"Do you have a husband?" my mother asked Natalia. "Are you wearing a ring?"

"Yes," said my sister. "I'll tell you all about him."

Natalia, who had seventeen years of stored-up conversations, began to talk. But after a few minutes, I could tell our mother was too exhausted and frail to listen anymore.

"She can't tolerate that much talking or sound," I said. "She gets over-whelmed like me. Just sit with her. That's enough; she's happy you're here."

Natalia took out a brush from her purse. "Can I brush your hair?" she asked.

"If you like," said my mother.

I looked at them, mother and eldest daughter, strangers for seventeen years. "I'll leave you two alone," I said, and left.

If you glanced in the room at that moment, you would see two women in tranquil silence, one tenderly brushing the hair of the other, as if she had been doing it her entire life.

❧

When I called U-Haul, they confirmed our mother had a storage room there. It was at Kamm's Corners in West Park, not far from our old neighborhood. Early the next day, on Thursday, before heading over to the hospital, Natalia and I drove to the U-Haul on Lorain Avenue. Natalia sat in the passenger's seat, clutching the map, nervous about getting lost. I expected to get lost. I got lost nearly every day.

When we arrived, the man at the counter said, "Norma used to change clothes in there sometimes, even in winter. There's no light or heat in the rooms. She was one tough broad."

Natalia and I wound our way through the maze of corridors. I could see my breath and regretted not having brought a hat or a pair of gloves. Fluorescent lights hummed, casting a pale, eerie glow on the high metal walls. I wondered how many other homeless men and women used these rooms to store their belongings, to change, or to catch up on sleep. Finally we came to our mother's room; it was just like all the others, eight-by-eight feet. I pulled the keys out of the sock. We tried them all. The last one fit; the padlock clicked open.

I hesitated for a moment before I looked in. I was terribly curious to know what was inside, but I also wished I never had found the key. I was afraid of what we would find, even more afraid to find out what had been lost. Wasn't it enough that we were here, now, in her final days? I shone my flashlight into the cold dark room. Things were piled up to the ceiling: furniture, boxes, trash, clothes, books, cans of soup. I imagined her changing clothes in the dark, shivering, cursing to herself, taking off one shirt and putting on another, then layering on three more for warmth. Natalia and I began to dig.

My sister and I worked fast, sorting things into piles. We needed to get back to the hospital and didn't have the luxury of taking our time. There was that familiar sense of purpose that I hadn't felt in years, that old "it's an emergency, let's just get the job done" kind of feeling. I was glad not to do it alone.

I first tried to separate all the trash from things that we needed to save. I almost tossed out one of my mother's old grimy pocketbooks when I felt something hard inside. I pulled out a butcher knife. "Jesus, look at this," I said.

"Do you think that's the one she had when the police caught her at Logan Airport?" said Natalia. "I'm sure she was on her way to find me."

Natalia and I excavated. We found a 1950s Geiger counter, and a bag of our mother's hair with a note taped to it with instructions on how to make a wig. I found a chart she had drawn showing all the nuclear power plants in the world, similar to one she had sent me when I lived in the Norwegian Arctic ten years before. There were boxes crammed with newspaper articles on cryogenics, alien abductions, radon poisoning, global warming, child abuse, train wrecks, and unsolved murders in Chicago. I discovered a huge box labeled "Scribing Books" filled with notebooks devoted to my mother's eclectic research: geometry, poetry, chemistry, botany, geography, art history, medicine, fairy tales, zoology, car mechanics, physics, and the Bible. For each subject, she made vocabulary lists with detailed definitions, something I would have done even before my brain injury. Her files could have been my files; her notes, mine.

I came across the chiffon scarf I had bought for her in New Orleans years ago. In the same box were many of my favorite books from childhood. I pulled out a collection of Jack London I'd read when I was about eleven. After reading *Call of the Wild*, I became obsessed with polar exploration. If a man could survive by boiling his boots, or walking out onto the glacial ice with nothing but a few sled dogs and a piece of seal blubber in his pocket, then certainly I could withstand whatever obstacles came my way.

At the bottom of the box were two big fairy-tale collections our father had sent us sometime after our parents divorced in 1963. I was four and my sister was five. We never saw him again. One book was a beautifully illustrated collection of Russian fairy tales inscribed, *To Rachel, from Daddy*. The other, a book of Japanese fables, was inscribed to me. It had been years since I had opened them. I stared at the handwriting. Something seemed a bit off. Then it dawned on me—both inscriptions bore my own adolescent scrawl. I had always remembered the books and our father's dedications as proof of his love for us. Yet, how malleable our memories are, even if our brains are intact. Neuroscientists now suggest that while the core meaning of a long-term memory remains, the memory transforms each time we attempt to retrieve it. In fact, anatomical changes occur in the brain every single time we remember. As Proust said, "The only paradise is paradise lost."

As I paged through the Russian fairy tale book, a piece of paper fell out—a photocopied picture of a piano keyboard. Was this how my mother played music all these years? Did my homeless mother, once a child prodigy, play Bach inside her head, her hands fluttering over imaginary keys?

What I found next took my breath away. "Nat," I said. "She saved my pony."

I took out the old palomino horse I used to call Pony from a torn moldy box. The horse's right foreleg was broken. My mother had tried to mend it with a piece of packing tape, then wrapped it in a red wool hat I had sent her for her birthday two years before. I put it in my bag to take back to the hotel. In the same box were all the letters I had written my mother over the last seventeen years. There were also photocopies she had made of her letters to me. Natalia glanced over to see what I was looking at. I wondered what she felt as she saw me sifting through the stack. We had barely spoken about our mother for years.

At the bottom of the box were thirteen pairs of scissors. Right after her divorce, when I was four, my mother tried to slit her wrists with a pair of cutting shears and was rushed to the hospital. I remember sitting at the foot of the stairs, my grandfather looming over me, puffing on a cigar. He handed me a rag and told me to wipe the blood off each and every stair. At the top of the staircase was the open door to our apartment; inside, a limp frilly blouse draped over an ironing board, on the floor a pair of scissors and a pool of blood. My sister remembers the incident too but neither of us recalls the other being there. Did it even happen? Before the age of ten, children have a kind of childhood amnesia. We lack developed language skills and a cognitive sense of self, especially when we are very young. It's hard to even know if our memories are real. Even though we feel they are, they might not be. And in family narratives, what if the person you learned your early autobiography from couldn't tell the difference from reality and a dream?

In another box were all the museum date books I had sent my mother over the years. I found a little stuffed owl, a teddy bear, and a children's book I once sent her called *Owl Babies*, about a mother owl who disappears but is reunited with her children in the end. There were nursing textbooks and lists of medical schools my mother planned to apply to. When she turned seventy-nine she wrote to tell me that although she was now legally blind she had decided to study medicine: *I am thinking of going to nursing school, maybe in a foreign country. That way, if I ever get sick or lose my sight completely, I'll know what to do.* I found a set of her teeth stuck inside an old eyeglass case. I uncovered dozens of legal claims filed by her, accusing various moving companies, housing projects, the Chicago Transit Authority and the city of Cleveland of stealing her teeth, her glasses, her house, her hair, her children, her memory, and her youth. I pulled out stacks of drawings she had made of street scenes, family members, flowers, and fairies. One was titled *Rachel Has No Flowers in Her Hair*, a desolate stretch of gray land with nothing in it but one scraggly tree.

Our mother was expecting us and we had already been at U-Haul for over two hours. My hands were so cold I could barely feel my fingers anymore. I'd been about to suggest leaving when I found the box.

"Nattie," I said. "You better take a look."

We dragged the heavy box out into the hall. It was stuffed with diaries, seventeen years of secrets: typewritten journals in bulging three-ring binders, others pocket-sized and written by hand. I skimmed through them for half an hour or more, but had to stop. It reminded me of when I was a teenager and hid in our grandparents' attic, digging through boxes, searching for a father who had disappeared, searching for a mother before she lost her mind. Then I saw several papers stapled together, stuck in between two journals. At the top of the page, my mother had written, "Life Story." It began like this:

There was danger imparted to me at birth. The street was well kept and quiet during the day. You hardly saw anyone. In 1945 I suffered a childhood nervous breakdown. I was nineteen. My father and I were supposed to go to a party at my uncle's, but instead, we went to a foreign film and as we returned home by bus on 148th Street, my father became angry and said something about not liking my uncle's associates. Leaving the bus I dropped coins in the fare box. My father was angry that I paid for myself. He became more and more enraged and I became mildly hysterical. When we were in the house, he seized a lamp and said, "I'll kill you" to parties unknown. My early childhood was deprived in some respects. I did not view television until 1963 and now I see that little bits of my life in distorted form have gotten into movie stories. I still have received no compensation for that. Ultimately, what I do know is this: I am a homemaker, my records have never been straightened out, and my need for privacy and house is greater than ever. I write this in a motel room looking out onto garbage bins.

I slumped down onto the floor and couldn't move. *I write this in a motel room looking out onto garbage bins.* How much more did I really want to know about her life on the street? My brain was done for the day.

"Nattie," I said. "Maybe we should go." My sister didn't hear me; she was lost in her own little world. She sprang up into a standing yoga posture, stretching her arms high above her head. Before my injury, I would have been just as resilient. After a few more stretches, Natalia went back in. I gathered my reserves and went back in too.

"Look at this!" she said. She pulled out something big, white, and fuzzy from deep within our mother's den. It was a teddy bear the size of a toddler, dressed in a festive red dress. The red bow around its neck said 2000.

"It's a millennium bear," I said.

I tried to remember where I was on New Year's Day 2000, but couldn't. Where was my mother that day? Who gave her this bear? Would she still be here this coming January 1?

"Let's bring the bear," said Natalia. "We better go back," she added. "You look tired. Besides, she's going to think we're not going to come."

Before we left, we made a stack of things our mother might want at the hospital. My sister placed *The Brothers Karamazov* on the pile and a torn almanac from 1992. "Definitely this," she said, holding up our mother's Glenville High School yearbook from 1945. "She loved looking at pictures of her old friends."

I flipped through the pages to find her maiden name, *Norma Kurap*. The portrait of her in a simple white blouse was sweet and demure. She was eighteen, and schizophrenia had yet to rear its ugly head. I read the list of activities below her smiling face: *Orchestra, Play Production, Choral Club, Accompanist, Student Council, Music Appreciation Club, National Honor Society,* the list went on. She was voted "Most Versatile" in the Popularity Poll. Her classmates wrote: *Good luck at Carnegie Hall! May your magic piano fingers charm all the hearts of the world.* One boy wrote, *To my dream girl, the sweetest and prettiest gal at Glenville.* Another wrote, *So when are you going to teach me how to rumba?* And another, *It will take more than a war to make me forget you.* The introduction to her yearbook, written by a boy named Marvin, is titled "War Baby." He writes at the end: *We are the class of January, 1945—a war class. We leave Glenville, determined to finish the fight.*

I never realized until then that my mother lost her mind the year we dropped the bomb. Seven months after she graduated, in August 1945, America obliterated Hiroshima and Nagasaki. Shortly afterward while on a bus coming home from a movie with her father, the voices inside my mother's head arrived unannounced, in all their terrible glory.

Our mother was wide awake when we arrived. "Where were you? I thought you weren't going to come. You girls need to help me. We have to get back to the house before it's too late."

"Don't worry," I said. "We've got everything under control."

"But I'm so worried about everything." My mother reached up and touched the back of my head. "And you. What about your little noggin? Does it still hurt?"

"My head's okay," I said. "Just some problems here and there, you know."

"You should wear a helmet," she said. "That way, they can't get you again."

When I injured my brain, I almost didn't write her about it, but changed my mind. It seemed like the kind of thing a mother should know, even if she was indigent and ill. When I wrote, I spared her the gory details, like I did with most things.

"They stole my memory too," she whispered, as I straightened out her pillows. "They have their tricks."

When the truck hit, I was in the passenger's seat, leaning over, looking for a cassette. The man driving my car, who suffered whiplash in the accident, was a guy I was dating at the time. We were on our way home from my sister's house in northern New York. The truck driver, who must have fallen asleep, swerved toward the right and tried to put on his brakes. The next thing I recall was a pair of white-gloved hands reaching in to pull me out of the car. I remember a blur of blinking lights, and the feeling of hot lava dripping down the back of my head.

When I eventually told my mother about the accident, I said that I suffered from memory loss, mostly short-term but some long-term memory as well, which isn't that common with traumatic brain injury. I didn't tell her about the strange sensations of lost time that one doctor thought might be temporal lobe seizures, or that I no longer could follow directions, that I didn't know how to leave a tip, and had trouble reading, writing, and doing just about anything that required over ten minutes of concentration. Why tell a homeless woman who slept at the airport that it felt like it was raining inside my body and ants were crawling up and down my legs? My mother thought there were rats living inside her body, aliens in her head.

Natalia and I returned to the storage room before dinner. "We should have worn headlamps," I said. "It's like going down into a cave."

"Let's not stay long," said my sister. "I want to go back tonight to see her. How are you doing, by the way? You look exhausted."

Even though I usually appear fine to the outside world, when I do too many things, say, shop for food and have coffee with a friend on the same day, I might not be able to drive home or talk to anyone for two days after that. If I'm exhausted, I stutter or shut down. If I go to a noisy dinner party, I can easily press down on the accelerator instead of the brake on my way home. Because I didn't learn how to drive until I was almost forty, the act of putting my foot on the brake isn't the same kind of habitual memory as tying my shoe. It's frightening when the part of my brain that's supposed to process all those stimuli being hurled at me won't do its job anymore. I get terribly frustrated with myself and with friends who don't understand. My judgment isn't always the best either. I think I'm able to handle much more than I really can.

"You have to drive back, you know," said Natalia. "We didn't put me down on the rental. Maybe we should do that tomorrow."

"I'm fine. Let's keep going," I said.

I was packing more journals to take back to the hotel when Natalia found a big black trunk with brass trim. We hauled it out and yanked the top open.

"Jesus," I said. "I thought these were lost."

Inside were family photos we thought we'd never see again: our mother at sixteen, smiling from a tenement window, our father's black-and-white glossy for his first book, our grandfather standing with a menacing grin in the garden, holding a pair of pruning shears. And nestled in a pile of loose photos was my sister's and my baby album. I skimmed through the pages till I came to a picture of my sister as a chubby toddler, sitting on top of a baby grand, looking at my mother, eyes closed, playing with abandon. My sister seemed frightened in the picture, as if she were about to fall. I imagined her during the fourteen months before I came into the world—an infant living with a gifted and beautiful mother who lived in an alternate universe, a brilliant father who drank himself to sleep each night. A bit like Zelda and F. Scott Fitzgerald, I thought. I put the book aside to bring back to the hotel.

Natalia and I continued mining. Inside the trunk, there were pictures I had drawn when I was small, report cards, my art and music awards. I picked up a small plastic grandfather clock to toss into the garbage pile. "Look at this crappy old thing," I said. "I can't believe the things she saved."

"There's too much here," said my sister. "I can't take it all in."

"I can come back tomorrow by myself."

"Don't exclude me. Stop thinking that you have to do everything. It's annoying."

"I'm sorry it's just . . . Nattie, there's something inside this."

I pried open the little glass window below the clock face—inside was a drawing of two little rabbits, and below the rabbits was a drawing of a tiger. "There's another picture hidden underneath!"

On the back of the picture was a list of birth dates for those born in the Chinese Year of the Tiger, which included my mother, and a detailed description of feline carnivores written in tiny script. Underneath the tiger my mother had placed a photo of my sister and me at ages five and six. I look stiff and unhappy; my sister smiles at the viewer and strikes a girlish pose. Behind the photo was yet another picture, cut from a 1960s *Life* magazine— a still life of red and green Christmas ornaments and holly. Was she trying to protect us? Did she believe a drawing could be a talisman against the forces of evil in the world?

Back at the hotel that night, as my sister and I got ready for bed, I wondered what lay ahead. The next day or the day after that, our mother would be moved to a nursing home for hospice care. How long would she hang on? Days? Weeks? My sister, who suffers from insomnia, performed her nocturnal rituals to calm her nerves. She took an aromatherapy bath, stretched, and read before inserting her earplugs. She put on her eye mask and turned off her lamp. We are both vigilant sleepers: she can't fall asleep; I wake at the slightest sound.

"Good night," she said.

"Night, Nattie. I'll turn off the light in a little bit. Sleep well."

I pulled a few of our mother's journals from the pile. As the years passed, I saw how they became smaller and more portable. She daily mulled over her dreams, trying to interpret them and discern if they were real or not. She recorded exactly what she ate each day—mostly donuts, small cups of chili, cheap black coffee, and hamburgers from McDonald's. She recorded what she spent, down to the penny. She spoke to someone in her head and struggled to understand what was an outside influence and what came from within. She wrote about how light fell on certain trees and described the delicate scents of flowers she saw in the park; she also wrote each flower's common and Latin names, and drew a picture of it. One sentence stuck in my head and I marked its place in the book. It sounded like something she had written to me in a letter once: *Of my life at the piano, I shall say nothing for the time being.*

I picked up her very last journal, the diary I had found when I looked through her backpack. In the pages I read prescient signs of her living with cancer, unaware. My mother was nauseous, dizzy, incontinent, and had blood in her stool. She doubled over with abdominal pain. She was bloated from a tumor but thought it was because she was overweight, so she tried to eat even less. She ate most meals in hospital cafeterias, the cheapest places, and rode the subway all over the city to get there, no matter how bad the weather. She recorded the weather daily, sometimes every hour. Near the end of her last diary, she wrote: *Awoke today with stronger remembrance for loved ones.*

I knew I should go to bed—it was well past midnight and we wanted to get an early start. but I couldn't stop reading. She wrote: *This A.M. I'm in a hotel I can't identify, I see so many gray closed doors. I cannot work with poor memory. To note something, a rat will find incentive to report. Caution: I've suffered as much as anyone in history. Note: Metamorphic rock means changes deep inside earth from heat and weight of other rocks.*

I cannot work with poor memory either, I thought. How will I remember these passing days? Once again, I thought of Nicolaus Steno. My mother was dying and yet I turned to history for solace, to ancient geology. I thought of when Steno made his final public appearance as a scientist. These things I remember well, these odd little facts from science, history, and art. That year, in 1673, Steno was dedicating an anatomical theater and gave a speech on the importance of scientific research. He told the audience, "Beautiful is what we see. More beautiful is what we understand. Most beautiful is what we do not comprehend."

Natalia was fast asleep in the bed next to mine, like when we were little and our names were Rachel and Myra. I read about how many nights my mother slept outside in the rain one November, hungry and cold, suffering from a bladder infection and a terrible cough. She had been sleeping in her old backyard while the owner was out of town. This was how she spent her birthday in the fall of 2001, two months after the tragedies of 9/11. I felt sick to my stomach, knowing that my own mother spent so many nights outside in the rain. Why didn't anyone help her, lead her to safety? I wanted to go back in time and be the person who took her in.

In my mother's very last diary, from the fall of 2006, she returned to the history of the earth: *The outer shell . . . is divided into about thirty large and small pieces that fit together . . . called tectonic plates. They move on hot layers of rock within the mantle. Continents sit on top of the plates; plates are also under the ocean floor. As the plates move, the continents and oceans slowly change.*

What hadn't she studied these seventeen years? I searched her journals for my name, my sister's, but she barely mentioned us at all, and even then only obliquely: *Long nightmare dream of losses. Bury the nightmare. Bury the losses. Bury the dream.*

On Friday morning, Natalia and I sat side by side next to our mother's bed. My sister graded her students' English papers while I drew in my sketchbook. It felt like old times. When we were children, Natalia sat on the bed and wrote stories while I sat next to her and made pictures—rare moments of calm in a turbulent world. I still felt at home sitting only a few inches apart, her writing, me drawing, neither of us saying a word. Soon our mother would be moved to a nursing home. We were waiting to find out where she would be placed. She still thought she was going "home."

There was a radio in the room now; one of the nurses had brought it in after I told her how my mother's favorite classical music station calmed her down, and that she listened to it twenty-four hours a day. Christmas was in three days and every radio station was playing "Jingle Bells."

"Turn that holiday crap off," said my mother. "I can't stand it anymore."

"I'll bring some CDs as soon as I can get a CD player," I said.

"What's a CD?"

"It's a little record. I'll get you some classical music. Don't worry."

"Well, hurry up. This crap is killing me."

I only came home once during Christmastime, the first year after I left for college. My Russian Orthodox grandfather was still alive then and he was the only one in the family who celebrated Christmas. After he died in

1980, our mother always spent the holidays alone, or with our grandmother, the two of them eating corned beef sandwiches, watching sitcoms on TV. I always told myself that it didn't matter anyway, that they were secular Jews who had no interest in any religious celebrations, Chanukah or otherwise. A neighbor from next door told me that my mother spent her last Thanksgiving in the family house locked up inside. When the neighbor peeked in the window, she saw piles of dishes in the sink and garbage on the floor. "I was afraid to go in but was worried your mother would starve to death." The neighbor left food in the milk chute, then came back later to retrieve the empty plates.

As my mother slept, I tried to draw her face. It was my fourth attempt since I'd arrived on December 18. It had been many years since I had drawn her. When I was in high school, I stayed home on weekend nights sometimes so she wouldn't be alone. We listened to the radio together or to records. She'd lie on the couch and smoke and I would sketch her. Now I drew her asleep and dying, head tilted back upon the pillow, her mouth open as if in song.

I took out the drawing the doctor had made of what my mother looked like inside. It reminded me of choreography, the staging of an intricate dance. It reminded me of my own inevitable demise. There is a Buddhist meditation I do sometimes. I imagine the layers of my body as I sit, mindful of my breath. I picture my flesh falling away, then the muscles and connective tissue, the organs, and finally the bones. I do this once in a while to remind myself of where I'm going. A rather macabre way to comfort myself, I suppose. Sometimes I take it a step further, into deep time—I imagine my bones beneath the earth, crumbling to gypsum, forming into chalk held by a child writing words upon a blackboard. I imagine the words erased by another child's hand, and still another, breathing in chalk dust, exhaling into air.

An aide came into the room to remove my mother's tray. She had barely touched her eggs. Little by little, we cease to consume, take in food, water, air. My sister glanced up, then jotted something down. What would she remember? What would I? Our brains are built for selective attention—we focus on some things while ignoring a vast array of other stimuli around us. It is those select things that we recall, not the rest. I couldn't take notes about what was going on around me like Natalia. Just the act of taking visual and auditory information in, processing it, then writing it down, is an act of multitasking, something I don't do well anymore. I was afraid I would miss something, something so small you can't see or sense if you are putting words to the page—the subtle twitch of a finger, a swift sideways glance, a snippet of song down the hall.

And yet, what does it matter anyway? Memory, if it is anything at all, is unreliable. Even birds, with their minute brains, have better memories than we do. Nuthatches and black-capped chickadees remember precisely where they stored food in the wild. Honeybees have "flower memory" and remember exactly where they already have been to pollinate a flower. They can even recall the colors and scents of their food sources, and the times of day when their food is at its best. We humans are different—our brains are built not to fix memories in stone but rather to transform them. Our recollections change in their retelling.

Still, I wondered if I should try to take notes. Without some kind of written record, would I remember these quiet, fleeting days? Nobel Prize–winning neuroscientist Eric Kandel says we are who we are because of what we learn and what we remember. Who am I, then, if my memory is impaired? And how will I remember my mother after she is gone?

Some of my old memories feel trapped in amber in my brain, lucid and burning, while others are like the wing beat of a hummingbird, an intangible, ephemeral blur. But neuroscientists say that is how memory works—it is complex and mercurial, a subterranean world that changes each time we drag something up from below. Every sensation, thought, or event we recall physically changes the neuroconnections in our brain. And for someone who suffers from brain trauma, synapses get crossed, forcing their dendritic branches to wander aimlessly down the wrong road.

And yet, I can still walk into a museum and name almost everything on the wall. I can recall pictures I drew, even ones I made as a child. I remember artifacts from museums, fossils, masks, and bones. The part of my brain that stores art and all the things I loved to look at and draw is for the most part intact. Perhaps the visual part of my brain can help retrieve the events that are lost. If neuroscientific research suggests that the core meaning of a memory remains, even if its details have been lost or distorted, then if I find the right pictures, the pictures could lead me to the core.

In my mother's room, while she slept and Natalia wrote, I took out one of my mother's diaries, one from 1992. That year I had gone to Israel and brought back a bag of stones. One contained an ammonite, a fossilized nautilus shell. When I got home I poured water on it to see what it might have looked like centuries ago in the sea. I wondered how long it had been hidden in the earth, a rock shifting against rocks, rising up over time from primordial sediment. Isn't that how memory works too? We look at something—a picture, a stone, a bird—and a memory surfaces, then that memory carries us to another, and another. Memory isn't just mutable, it is associative. Thomas Aquinas once said, "One arrives at the color white through milk, to air from the color white, to dampness from air and on to Autumn." How, then, would I arrive back at my own past?

"Myra?" my mother said, her eyes half shut. "Are you still here?"

I hid her journal inside the book in my lap. "I'm still here."

"Where's your sister?"

"She's here too. She just stepped out for a second but she'll be right back."

"You won't run away?"

"No," I said. "I won't run away."

"Myra?"

"Yes?"

"Would you do something for your old lady?"

"Anything."

"Brush your hair. It's really a mess."

"I'll do it right now."

"Good. Because a girl has to put her best foot forward whenever she can."

We left the hospital late that night. Most of the day had been quiet, just the sound of our mother's slow breathing and the radio purring in the background. My sister got ready for bed while I pulled out one of the photo albums we'd brought back from U-Haul, our baby book. "You coming?" she asked. She switched off her light and turned her masked face to the wall. "Soon," I said. "Good night."

I held the photo album up to my nose. It smelled like my mother used to smell—cigarettes and Tabu, her favorite perfume—our sense of smell, the strongest memory trigger of all, the only sense that travels directly to the limbic system in our brain. I thought of my mother's small white face in the hospital bed, her delicate, cold hands. Then another picture of her rose up in my mind, her hands hovering over mine at the piano—a younger Norma; my mother in the bloom of life, a dark-eyed beauty in a red silk dress, her face unreadable, listening to something no one else can hear.

I took out my mother's last diary. Her final entry was a random list: *Hyssop: plant used in bunches for purification rites by ancient Hebrews. Po River: Runs through Italy into Adriatic. Avert: to turn away or aside. Note: My white cane is missing. I dropped my sunglasses on the bus.* Then farther down, these words: *Chica—drink of Peru. Hecuba—wife of Priam. Baroque Palace—?* What palace? What did her last entry mean? A few pages back were little sketches she had made: a leaf, her hand, a shoe.

I thought of random pictures from my past—paintings from the Cleveland Museum of Art, objects from our grandparents' house, things I liked to draw. What pictures did I remember? What could I create to contain them all? Was the answer in my mother's very last page? Hadn't she herself built a memory cabinet at U-Haul to contain her beautiful, tragic, and transient life? Was there something I could build too?

A memory palace. A man named Matteo Ricci built one once. I read about him the year after my accident. Ricci, a Jesuit priest who possessed great mnemonic powers, traveled to China in 1596 and taught scholars how to build an imaginary palace to keep their memories safe. He told them that the size of the palace would depend on how much they wanted to remember. To everything they wanted to recall, they were to affix an image; to every image, a position inside a room in their mind. His idea went back to the Greek poet Simonides, who, one day while visiting friends at a palace, stepped outside for a minute to see who was at the door. As soon as he went outside, the great hall came crashing down. All the people inside were crushed to death and no one could recognize them. Simonides, however, remembered where everyone stood at the party, and recalled them one by one so their bodies could be identified.

My mind was full of so many pictures—with each one I could build a different room, each room could lead me to a memory, each memory to another. Since I knew what Ricci didn't at the time, that memories cannot be fixed, my palace would always be changing. But the foundation would stay the same.

Ricci told the scholars that the place to put each picture must be spacious, the light even and clear, but not too bright. He said that the first image they should choose for their memory palace must arouse strong emotions. It was the entranceway, after all. I closed my eyes and opened a door. I turned to the right and there, in a reception room with high arched ceilings, I placed two pictures on opposite walls. The light was clear in the room, the space free of clutter.

2

They turned their snaky heads and when they saw Perseus, they roared with fury. Flapping their great wings, they set off in pursuit. But they could not outstrip the winged sandals.

"The Gorgon's Head," *The Golden Treasury of Myths and Legends*

Medusa

The first picture in my memory palace is from the baby book my sister and I found in our mother's storage room. It's a close-up of her, taken shortly after she gave birth to me in 1959. Her face is soft and demure in the cropped photograph, and a little startled. If you could see the entire picture, you would notice me on my mother's lap looking up at her, smiling. What you can't tell from the photo is that not long after it was taken, my mother tried to fly out of a second-story window.

The other picture, hanging across from my mother's photograph, is Caravaggio's painting of the Gorgon Medusa, right after Perseus cut off her head. I remember someone reading Medusa's story to me when I was a child, about how men turned to stone when they looked at her and how the hero, Perseus, with his helmet of invisibility, his winged sandals, and sword, slayed the terrible Gorgon. Medusa's children were born from her spilled blood; one of them was Pegasus. For years I dreamed I was a winged horse, watching, from the sky, my mother's serpentine head float away from her body.

In 1964 I am five and my sister is six. We live in a second-floor flat on the west side of Cleveland, next to a church with a small crabapple orchard out back. Most of the tenants in our building are transplants from Appalachia. At dinnertime I can hear the sound of fiddle music and TV drifting through the walls. In our own apartment our mother keeps the classical radio station turned up loud. Triskett Road in the early 1960s is full of fast cars and chattering shoppers, families walking to church, the movie theater, Pick 'n Pay, or Kresge's five and dime. Off Triskett, on West 148th Street where our grandparents live, and Rainbow, Gramatan, and Tuckahoe, a quiet hush shrouds the side streets after the fathers leave in the morning and the children are hurried off to school.

Our own father, Paul Herr, had disappeared shortly after our mother divorced him in 1963, a few months after I turned four. Once in a while he sends money but has no permanent home or steady job. My mother says he's living in a South American jungle, eating snake meat and writing his second book. Sometimes she tells me he is painting pictures in Mexico; sometimes she says he is dead. His first book was called *Journey Not to End*. Does that mean my father can't find his way home?

At school, in my kindergarten class at Riverside Elementary, I run and hide in the cloakroom whenever someone asks me to play house. I don't know how to play; how would I? Mrs. Bemis comes inside to coax me out. I tell her I am a cat. I curl my hands into claws in front of my face. I'm an invisible cat. Mrs. Bemis is kind and gently leads me to the art table. She gives me paper and crayons, or fat wooden beads to string and count. "You don't have to play if you don't want to," she says. Mrs. Bemis teaches me how to plant seedlings in small pots, how to make butter from a cup of cream.

There is a boy at school who lives in our building on Triskett Road. He's not in my class at Riverside but I watch him at recess sometimes, running in wild circles by himself. When the other kids see him, they call out, "Retard!" then run away fast. One day, I am looking for my mother but can't find her anywhere inside our place. I am on the stairs leading down to the basement when the boy plunges a long pole into my face, not because I call him Retard or some other name; I am just standing in his path. I wake up in the hospital, my face covered in gauze.

For the rest of the year I wear a black patch over my left eye. It isn't easy to see. I run into furniture and trip over my feet. At home, in our apartment, I pretend I am blind. I close my good eye and walk with my arms stretched out in front of me, circumnavigating the rooms by sound and touch. I pick up random objects on the floor near my mother's bed and try to guess what they are: Cracked coffee cup. Empty perfume bottle. Cigarette lighter. Scattered pills. "You're my little Helen Keller!" she says when my fingers find her soft, cool face. She pulls the black patch up; kisses the spot above my big ugly swollen eye.

I'm in my sister's and my bedroom when I hear it one day—a low guttural sound followed by strange chattering and laughter. I am playing Helen Keller, eyes shut tight, ears open to the world. There are two small beds in our room and one old dresser with a broken drawer. My grandma told me once that when I was a baby, my mother put me in the drawer to sleep, then forgot she had left me there. Someone shut the drawer and I almost suffocated to death. My grandma had to break the handle to get me out.

I reach up and touch the objects on our dresser—an old teddy bear, a stuffed horse, and a plastic palomino I call Pony. I pick up the plastic horse, run my fingers over its hard thin legs, its pointy ears and tail. Something isn't right—the sound, the strange laughter. I feel something grab hold of my breath; I want to hide and don't know why. I clutch the little horse in my hand. Where's Rachel? She's older; she should be the one to see what's wrong, but she's not here. Maybe she's at a friend's. Rachel is more outgoing than I am. I usually tag along and she always lets me come. She does the things my mother doesn't do for some reason—fixes my hair, ties my shoes, makes me toast. Where is she now?

I walk out into the hallway, my good eye open. Who's there? Is it the man who lives across the way, Mr. Bade, the pimply man with the fat neck and bulbous red nose who leers at our mother when he passes her in the hall? Is it a stranger at the door? The police? I follow the sound to the living room. Is it the radio? The TV? I tiptoe down the hall. Who is she talking to? What is so funny?

And then I see her. She is stumbling around in her underwear as if she's drunk, but she's not. My mother never drinks. Her voice sounds familiar, but it's not her own. My mother is impersonating a drunk. I recognize the voice from TV—it's a character from *The Jackie Gleason Show* called Crazy Guggenheim. I take a step back so she can't see me and peek around the corner of the hall. Her voice changes again. I know who she is now; she's Joe the Bartender, a character Jackie Gleason plays on the show.

"The usual?" says my mother. She pantomimes Gleason wiping down the counter at the bar. "There ya go, pal!" She laughs. "There ya go, there ya go, there ya go!" She keeps repeating the line, then switches back to Crazy Guggenheim, walking in circles. That's how I remember it, her stumbling around, muttering these things, but who can say for sure? I am only five years old. The girl downstairs says that sometimes the devil crawls inside you when you're sleeping and only Jesus can get him out. Is the devil inside her body?

On the real show the joke about Crazy is that he's mentally impaired, or, as people used to say back then, retarded, like the boy who hurt my eye. He's a retarded drunk. Jackie Gleason always calls out, "Craz! Come on out here!" and Crazy totters to the bar, tripping over his feet. The audience goes wild. Gleason and Crazy tell a few jokes, Crazy gets drunker and dumber, until finally Joe says, "Hey, Craz, how 'bout a song?" "Okay, Joe," he says, and Crazy lumbers over to the jukebox every time, pushes a button, and goes back to the bar. Then he takes off his frumpy turned-up hat, places it on the counter, and transforms into someone else. He sings a heartbreaker of a song, a lovelorn Irish ballad in his rich, melodious voice. The audience explodes. He puts his hat back on, says, "'Bye, Joe," and waddles out the swinging doors. That is how it always is on the show.

My mother doesn't know I am there. She struts around the living room, mumbling and shouting, "How 'bout another, Joe?" She rolls her eyes like Crazy Guggenheim, makes her lips droopy like his. "I'm C-C-C-raaaaazy Guggenheim!" She stutters, "I'm C-c-c-c-crazy!"

To her left is the baby grand piano she had rented for a few months, which will be repossessed in a week or two because she can't pay the bill. To her right and in front of her are walls lined with the books our father left behind. Will he ever come back to get them? There are big art books—

Gauguin, Klee, Picasso, Bosch, and Brueghel, books in Spanish, Russian, Yiddish, and French, plays by Shakespeare, Ibsen, Ionesco, Beckett, and Shaw, Russian classics, books by all the Beat poets, and Chaucer, William Blake. On the top shelf is *The Golden Treasury of Myths and Legends* with the story of Medusa and Perseus inside. There's Oscar Wilde's *Salome*, on the cover a madwoman with wild snaky hair. My mother reads it over and over like she rereads Lewis Carroll's *Alice's Adventures in Wonderland*, searching for prophetic signs.

Suddenly my mother turns into someone else, someone I can't recognize from TV. She makes slicing movements in the air. She's holding something now, something long and shiny. She spins around fast as if someone has just crept up behind her. She is spinning and spinning, obscenities rolling off her tongue, words I've only heard my grandfather use. There is the smell of burnt toast and cigarettes, no music coming from anywhere, no radio or TV. The radio is always on twenty-four hours a day, but today it is silent. Behind my mother is the couch and three big open windows. Can the neighbors below us hear her? Can people see her from the street? Will she jump?

I don't know how it ends, this scene—the beginning of knowledge, the knowledge that I have a secret I must keep from the outside world. In this scene, my mother is forever spinning, wielding a knife. My sweet beautiful mother merges with Medusa—they meld into one another, pull apart, and come together again, morphing into other restless creatures—characters from TV shows, mythological monsters, demons from my dreams. She is forever spinning and I am forever watching her with my one good eye—a small child frozen behind a wall, both of us surrounded by so many beautiful books.

Dreamless Nights

Sign of Mars, Dreamless nights. Sunshine, continued cool. Go ahead, browse those voice personals and find that special someone. It's only $1.89 per minute. Tomorrow scattered showers in morning, cloudy the rest of the day. Things I intend to do in the not too distant future——study Braille, leave Chicago, read poetry, continue vocabulary study, talk to a dentist, wear a wig. I would be glad to "let my smile be my umbrella on a rainy day" but to date have not found a dentist with a realistic price. I need new scarves and paint. Should I or should I not enter Goldblatt's? They sold me bad paint a year ago. When I lived in Cleveland, a young woman told me that Baldwin Wallace College was doing experiments with rats. At times, I have an idea there is life from outer space and with free condoms advertised in the New City paper, some of them might be inside, adopting "human" form. I have no affection for this city. Must think of something neutral to control rage. Birth flower, May, lily of the valley, stemless convallariaceous herb, Convallaria majalis, with a raceme of drooping, bell-shaped fragrant white flowers. Think of something cheerful: a sweet pea. Draw a picture of it.

O fall, fall from that burning sky, white blossoms,
Come down! You insult our Gods, pale phantoms.
Holier is the saint who has known the abyss.

Gérard de Nerval, from the "Chimeras"

Passionflower

I still paint a picture of it every year: *Passiflora*, the passionflower. In Latin, *passio* is "suffering," *flos* means "flower" and the verb "to wander." *Passiflora*: flower of martyrs and paradise lost. Some say it can cure insomnia, melancholy, even madness. After the tragedies of 9/11, I painted one with crimson petals and sent it to my mother, who had been sleeping in baggage claim at the Cleveland airport before they kicked all the homeless people out. She wrote back: *Thank you for the package containing hosiery, warm gloves and the red flower. A ray of sunshine on a storm-ridden day.*

My mother made lists of plants and their medicinal properties in the journals we found at U-Haul. She stopped to draw plants on her walks and kept copious notes on how to make botanical tinctures for when she finally returned home. In her letters, she told me that if she discovered the right remedy, she could cure herself of hair loss, age spots, and the memory lapses she attributed to radioactive gas. She was particularly fond of the roses in the garden behind the house on West 148th Street, and in her diaries, she lamented her loss of the pink azaleas on the front lawn. *My greatest regret,* she said in one of her last letters to me, *was that I never learned how to put something in the ground. Maybe when we all move back to Grandma's house, you can teach me.*

Two months before I got the call from the hospital, my mother wrote from the women's shelter: *Most plants spend their lives rooted in one place and produce seeds to make new ones. Plant cells have tough, thick walls made of cellulose and contain a special substance called chlorophyll. Almost all plants belong to a group. Rachel has a birthday tomorrow. Where is the birthday girl? Where has everyone gone?*

In my palace, I leave Medusa and my mother behind and pass through a pillared hall of shadows. I enter another room. The ceiling is high and arched like the nave of a small church; the walls are a pale and lustrous gold. On the wall, a passionflower, glowing like an icon. The colors are shades of crimson, ocher, a deep Prussian blue. If you saw the flower from a distance, you might think it a portrait of a saint.

&

Carl Linnaeus, the Swedish botanist and grandfather of order and taxonomy, once invented a flower clock. He discovered, after careful observation, certain flowers opened and closed at specific times throughout the day. As a child, I search for sleeping flowers in my grandfather's garden. I know when they wake up each morning. My favorite looks like a tiny rose, its leaves juicy and small, its petals flashy neon pink: *Portulaca grandiflora*, the little moss rose. It closes when it's cloudy and goes to sleep at night.

I know when all the flowers go to bed, when the neighbors take their naps. When people are sick or sad I paint flowers for them. I make pictures for Mrs. Budd, the lady down the street, who drinks when her husband is away. I leave the pictures taped to her door when I know she is sleeping. I make pictures for my friend Patty's parents, Ruth and Army Armstrong, who live across the street from my grandparents and hide my sister and me when our grandfather is mean and drunk. When my mother is asleep, I place pictures by her bed so when she wakes up she'll find them. Maybe if I make enough pictures, pick enough flowers, she will stop talking to people who aren't there.

After Medusa arrived on Triskett Road she never left for good. I quickly grasped the order of things. If I heard strange sounds in the living room I never went in there, for who knew what I might find? I told no one about the invisible guests who came late at night uninvited or the ghosts who whispered to her through the walls. On days of agitated pacing and our mother's fierce conversations with herself, my sister and I stayed out of her way. We'd run to the back of our building, to the parking lot and small yard with the chain-link fence and rusty swing set, the overflowing trash cans, the lone pine. In the weeks leading up to these episodes, our mother would be nearly catatonic; she'd sit on the couch enveloped in blue tendrils of smoke, dismissing my sister and me with a wave of her cigarette if we said we were hungry. In our cupboard, these were our staples: pimiento-stuffed olives, moldy jars of cocktail sauce, TV dinners, stale melba toast.

"Grandma can feed you," she'd say. "Or go to a friend's."

Rachel would grab my hand and pull me out to the street, careful to look both ways. She kept an eye out for mean dogs and boys, and hurried me across Triskett Road. We walked the three blocks to our grandparents' house for the food that we knew would be there—corned beef on rye and *kashkaval*, the hard salty cheese from the West Side Market, honey-sweet halvah, warm pita with tomatoes and feta, peaches and pears from the yard.

After stuffing ourselves, we'd slip out the back barefoot and run as fast as we could to the field and woods behind the house. On summer days there was always the scent of rose and honeysuckle in the air. We came and went as we pleased as long as our grandfather wasn't raging at one of us for misplacing the butter dish, a pencil, or a spoon. "Hillbillies," kids called us, but I thought of us like sisters of Mowgli from *The Jungle Book*. If things got worse, Rachel and I could always live in a wolf den in the middle of the woods.

Sometimes we spent the night at our grandparents'. Rachel and I slept upstairs in our grandmother's room in two twin beds side by side. We covered ourselves with thin scratchy blankets while Grandma curled up on the love seat in the guest room. Our grandfather slept alone in the master bedroom, in his four-post king-sized bed. No one was to enter uninvited or they'd get the belt. "Good night," I'd say to him from the doorway, the sinister red rooster lamp glaring at me from his nightstand. "Good night, girlie," Grandpa would say from his bed, cigarette dangling from his lips, the air around him thick with smoke.

At breakfast, I'd tilt my head back so Grandpa could spoon orange-blossom honey into my mouth with his callused meaty hands. When I had a cold, he placed a string of garlic around my neck. Garlic and honey could cure anything; so could the raw eggs he tossed back in the morning with whiskey, or the yogurt he made in a vat, warm cultures growing beneath his brown leather coat. My grandfather told me what I should eat from his garden to make me strong and healthy—parsley for "the halitosis," plums for "the constipation," mint and apples to keep the doctors away.

Outside the house there was always something stirring in the deep ripe earth—green shoots poking up, rows of tomatoes and green beans, clusters of flowers and herbs. At our grandparents' there were three yards: the front lawn, tidy for show, with a silver ball on a white plaster pedestal; the middle one, with rose beds, dogwood and plum trees, and the birdbath Grandpa always forgot to fill; and the backyard, where the garden was, a shady magnolia, fruit trees, and a lush carpet of grass. The backyard was connected to the Bentes' and the Budds'; Rachel and I reigned over all three. Beyond the wall of trees that lined the yards was where the owls and the deer hid. At night I'd think about the quiet deer, and imagined wolves living in warm dark caves, waiting for my sister and me to come.

In the summer of 1965 I am six and Rachel is seven. Our mother sleeps all day and wakes right before dinner. She paces in the apartment or outside, where everyone can see her muttering under her breath. Will she have to go to the hospital? Who will call? Our grandma is ashamed to call but she's the only one who does. Grandma says, "What will the neighbors say now?" as the ambulance screeches into the driveway on Triskett Road and muscular strangers come bounding up the stairs. Where does she go? When our mother returns weeks later, she walks like a drifting boat. She says that the Nazis hooked her head up to machines at the hospital; they set her brain on fire.

"That mother of yours better straighten up her act," our grandmother tells us. And every few weeks, our mother seems to snap out of it. She dresses up, applies for a temp job as a medical secretary or stenographer, and for a few days or a week or two she is a working mom. "What a waste of those hands," our grandmother says. "She should be playing Severence Hall."

When she's feeling a little better, our mother takes my sister and me to the art museum or the zoo. Once in a while she ushers at Severence Hall so the three of us can get in for free. She doesn't talk about the music, but there is something unspoken between us—the way she squeezes my hand when George Szell lifts his baton before the symphony begins. We almost always leave before the concert is over, though, because something inexplicable has happened that makes her whisper obscenities in the aisle.

In the summer the three of us go to the Impett Park swimming pool, rub zinc oxide on our noses, and nap in the hot sun, our mother's little transistor radio always tuned to the classical music station. She places the radio right next to her ear, between her head and mine. Rachel and I do handstands in the water; we call out, "Look at me, Mommy! Look at *me!*" We swim, then play cards, the sound of someone else's tinny radio bleating nearby, more voices invading my mother's delicate brain—"Going to a Go-Go," "Can't You Hear My Heartbeat," Gary Lewis and the Playboys crooning "This Diamond Ring." Sometimes all that sound is just too much for her to bear. Within each song is the enemy's menacing threat. We want to stay but she gets up abruptly, stubs out her cigarette, lights another, and hurries us into the blazing afternoon.

One summer day, Rachel and I are on our hands and knees in the grass behind our grandparents' red brick house. We call out to our turtle, who is lost, "Henry, Henry, come back!" We search beneath stones, behind bushes. "Henry, please come home!" The phone inside is ringing. Grandpa shouts from the back door. Rachel and I snap to attention; we run as fast as we can to see what he wants. We can never run fast enough. "You, not *her*," he says to me. "Smarties spoil the party."

My grandfather and I climb into the shiny white new Chevy and drive east. I can smell the sun-warmed seats and my grandfather's Old Spice after-shave cologne.

"Where are we going?" I ask.

"Girls should be seen and not heard. Just do as you're told."

We stop at a package store to pick up a case of beer. The black guys hanging out in front joke around and slap him on the back. He is everyone's pal. He goes inside and is gone for a long time. It's hot and humid in the car. The windows are all rolled up but I sit, hands folded in my lap, and don't roll them down. When he returns, he totters back to the car, his face red and damp with sweat.

"Just look at those niggers doing nothin' all day," he says.

Grandpa lights up a big cigar, then starts the engine. "You want ice cream?" he asks. "Ice scream, you scream, we all scream for ice cream!" He tickles me hard in the gut until it hurts, singsonging, "Eenie meenie meiny mo, catch a nigger by the toe!" He buys a mint chocolate chip cone for me down the street, golden vanilla for himself.

"Who loves you most?" he asks.

"You do," I say, ever obedient.

Grandpa smiles and lays his clammy hand on my little knee. He keeps it there all the way to his sister's house.

When we arrive, Aunt Toda is slicing lemons. She makes lemonade just like Grandpa—lots of sugar, a squeeze of orange, and sprig of fresh mint. Toda is a wide woman in wide black skirts, with swollen feet and ankles; she keeps her coarse gray hair piled beneath a black net and a bright red babushka. My grandma says she's a backward but well-meaning quack. My mother says never trust anyone who believes in saints.

We sit in her stifling kitchen, windows shut, bundles of herbs hanging above our heads. Toda, like my grandfather, believes the wind carries disease and destruction. Does he think that was how our mother got so sick?

Grandpa pops opens a beer. He says something in Bulgarian and goes out back to take a look at her garden. Toda pours me a glass of lemonade and offers me *komat*, the same cheese pie made with feta and buttery filo dough my grandfather bakes on Sundays.

"Eat," she says, pushing the plate toward me. "You want a little yogurt? You like the yogurt? How 'bout a nice little peach?"

Toda's kitchen smells of Bulgarian rose, a distillation she makes from hundreds of petals, then stores in miniature glass vials. Each vial is encased in a slim wooden bottle painted with a red rose, the word BULGARIA burned into the side. The bottle tops look like the onion domes that crown my grandfather's Russian Orthodox church. His side of the family is not Jewish, a fact, I gather, he is proud of, since he sometimes calls my grandma a "fat-ass money-grubbing son-of-a-bitch kike."

Aunt Toda is talking to me but I can't understand. I find her a little scary, her coarse stubby hands and ruddy face, her dark skirts and mustache, the little white hairs poking out from her chin. She tells me in broken English that I have "the gift." She leads me to the back of the house, past icons lit by small red candles—the "Not-Made-by-Hands" bloody Christ, the "Tenderness Mother of God," and "St. Theodosius," patron saint of Grandpa's and her church. Toda smudges the hallway mirror with ash from her finger to ward off evil. She smudges every shiny surface she sees. We go to where she keeps her concoctions and herbal tinctures, her seedlings under glass, strange roots floating in oil; I breathe in essence of rose, the scent of oranges, cloves, and something from the dark center of the earth.

"You are old enough now," she says. "Sit."

Toda teaches me the ancient doctrine of signatures. How God made plants to cure men's ills. He gives us clues to guide us in selecting the right ones. Something in the way they look, an external "signature," suggests the inner virtue of the plant. Red clover heals the blood, walnuts heal the brain; kidney beans cure the kidneys. Is there a plant that could heal my mother? Toda pulls out dried herbs and roots from different drawers, tells me to crush them between my fingers and hold them up to smell. She opens a book and turns the pages to a picture of plants surrounding a human figure, lines drawn to each corresponding body part. What marked me from birth, made me special in the eyes of God? Is it the birth defect I have, the way my arms bend out from the elbow when they should fall straight? Or the bump I have on the side of each foot? Is it the moon-shaped scar above my knee? Did I possess a special sign that could make my mother happy and well?

Toda shows me how to lay hands on the infirmed, how to concentrate and summon all my inner power, let it flow into their sick and dying bodies, and into their souls.

After my lesson, Toda takes out jars of legumes and seeds, trays of herbs and roots, and sets them on the big oak table in the kitchen. I help her sort, bundle, and count. "Bad peas here, good peas in the pot." Grandpa returns from the garden with a basket of peppers and goes into the living room to take a nap. I can hear him hacking up phlegm.

"He's got the bad lung," says Toda. "I make him something to take home."

A lion roars on Grandpa's *Wild Kingdom* show; the sound mingles with his coughing while the narrator drones on about survival on the African savanna. I separate peas and beans for my great-aunt, just like I do for Grandpa at his house. Toda looks like Baba Yaga, the witch in the Russian fairy-tale book our father sent from far away. She has the same heavy skirts and red babushka. She makes me divide and sort, divide and sort, cut, separate, and soak; I do everything I'm told. But I have a glimmer of hope burning inside me now. I will find a miracle to save my mother. I would go into the dark forest to search for magic plants to save her, spin a room of golden thread in a single night, weave a thousand golden shirts, cross a bridge of fire.

Grandpa snores in the living room, Aunt Toda naps in a chair by the sink, while I dream and sort, dream and sort, a thousand petals simmering atop the stove.

If I'm not at school, no matter what I'm doing, if my grandfather gets the call, we jump in the car and drive to Aunt Toda's house. When my grandfather is drunk we swerve unsteadily along the roads while I hold on tight to my seat. Toda and I visit ailing pregnant women, sick old ladies, old men who smell like cabbage and pee. Once, we visit a little boy with no hair. "Poison blood," Toda says in my ear when we leave. "From the Evil Eye." I place my hands on all of them, close my eyes, and wait.

One day we go to visit a man named Mitchell, a relative on my grandfather's side who suffers from multiple sclerosis. He's in his forties but looks much older; the doctors say he is dying. Mitchell lies on a hospital bed in a dark room, his eyes fixed on the ceiling. A page from a newspaper is projected from a contraption someone has jerry-rigged so he can read what's going on in the world. The room smells of urine and rosewater. The curtains are drawn, the windows shut tight. Like everyone else on that side of the family, Mitchell's parents think that the wind carries evil and sickness into the home. Toda dribbles a foul-smelling tea down his throat, then motions for me to get started. I sit beside him like I sit beside the others Toda takes me to, and place my hands upon his arm. I close my eyes and imagine ivy springing from my fingertips, growing into Mitchell's body, his lifeless arms and legs. Aunt Toda says my hands are magic. She makes me believe they contain rivers and clouds, valleys and colorful birds, someone else's destiny. I sit in the silent room while Toda gossips and smokes in the kitchen with the family, drinks thick Turkish coffee from little gold cups. When we leave, Mitchell's father hands Toda a slab of bloody lamb wrapped in brown paper and a fat envelope stuffed with dollars.

Whenever we return to Mitchell's, it's the same routine. Toda forces tea down his throat, mutters a prayer, and leaves me alone in the room. Mitchell never looks at me, or talks, just stares at the *Cleveland Plain Dealer* illuminated above. Sometimes, after I'm done, Toda and I have baklava and sweet black tea in the kitchen with Mitchell's parents. Toda shows me how to read signs from tea leaves and Turkish coffee grounds. I drain my sugary tea, tip the cup over like her, and spin it three times. I turn it back up, stare into the bottom. The patterns of tiny clumps look like a dancing man, a greenish black heart, a furry monster, and a bird. She predicts I'll have five children, and a rich husband from the Old Country who won't beat me. She says nothing about our father coming back or if our mother will get better again.

———————

It's morning and my mother has been up all night pacing the floors. (When did the pacing start? Was it the day of Medusa? Was it the day I was born?) She gets ready for bed when the rest of the world is waking. Rachel is reading in our room, and I am in the bathroom watching my mother take a bubble bath. I've made a picture for her of a mother horse and its little brown colt. I hold on to it, a scroll rolled up and tied with ribbon, waiting for the right moment to give her the gift.

She lowers her languid body one limb at a time into the steaming tub, luxuriating beneath the lime-green foam. I sit on the damp floor and listen to her hum. The night before, I could hear her conversing angrily with some-one who wasn't there while *Aida* played on the stereo. (Or was it *La Bohème*, the scene when Mimi dies in Rodolfo's arms? For every memory about her there is a melody hidden inside my brain.) After her bath, the moment never quite comes to give her the picture, so I stick it in a drawer. Later, someone is reading to me from *Through the Looking Glass*. My mother? My sister? Alice is lost in a garden of talking flowers.

"O Tiger-lily," says Alice. "I wish you could talk!"

"We can talk," says the flower, "when there's anybody worth talking to."

The radio is on low while my mother naps in her bed. It's still summer vacation, so Rachel and I run over to our grandparents' to play in their yard. In the garden, my sister reads while I pretend I'm a bee. I sip nectar from honeysuckles and fly around the yard. I pluck little plums, split them open, scoop out the pits, and pop them in my mouth. When I'm outside I can hear singing. It's the wind but I hear music too—arias, the trembling of leaves, mourning doves and sparrows, melodies my mother plays on the piano. Everything else is background noise—the Vietnam War and race riots, all the sick people Aunt Toda wants me to heal, my mother's night voices, her despair. Lately a book called *In Cold Blood* distresses her. She says things like, "You never know who's going to try to kill you when you're asleep." Or, "There are men with guns who watch you at night," which she will continue to say for years to come. I block out her voice and listen to the mockingbird and chickadee, the goldfinch up above.

I spy a volunteer lily that has sprung up in the middle of the backyard. Light glows from the inside of the flower—maybe it's the way the sun falls on it, maybe it's magic, either way I am struck dumb by its radiance. Is there a fairy inside the bloom? Has it come to take me away, to leave another in my place? I tear the bloom apart to see where the light is coming from, to see what's inside—sepal, anther, stigma, stamen. The flower smells sickly sweet; a lush river of seeds, sticky and pungent, clings to my hands. I press the petals to my face and cover my nose with pollen, then squish what's left of the flower into my pocket.

When Rachel and I return home after dinner, I run into my mother's room to show her what I have found. She's lying on her side, her face to the wall. There are tiny drops of blood on the sheet; one of her arms is covered in gauze. I tap her back with my little hand. I am always afraid she will die.

"Mommy? *Mommy?*"

"Leave me alone," she says. "Let me sleep."

"Look, look what I found."

She slowly turns around, the color drained from her face. "What *is* it?"

I pull the wilted flower from my pocket and place it in her hand. She sighs and lets the petals, now stained red, fall to the floor. "It said 'hello' to me," I say. "The flower said hello."

☙

When school starts up in September I enter the first grade. One day our teacher, Mrs. Atzberger, announces we are going to have show-and-tell. Mrs. Atzberger is big and loud and not at all like my kindergarten teacher, Mrs. Bemis. She tells us to get out the special things we brought from home. Each child clutches a small treasure—a Barbie doll, a stuffed bear, a little red car, a portrait of Jesus, a Cleveland Indians baseball cap. I hold my prize in a brown paper bag. One by one the children talk about their things. When it's my turn I stand petrified in front of the class, bag in hand. Mrs. Atzberger tells me to show-and-tell what I have brought. I can't speak. I haven't brought a toy, a bear, or a blue-eyed Jesus. I have made a grave mistake. "Open it," the teacher barks. I slowly lift a small dead sparrow, decaying in its nest, and hold it out to show the class.

Mrs. Atzberger's face contorts in rage. "What is that?" she demands. "Throw it away!"

I want to say to her and the other children that it's a bird, and that it isn't dead, it's only sleeping, and that after I found it beneath a tree I put it on my windowsill by my bed so I could watch it change every day, and that the nest had soft green moss in it and little bits of colored string, and that the bird is magical, and how do they know that I can't raise something from the dead? Who says I can't save someone's life?

My mother is summoned to school to meet with my teacher but she never shows up. The event is forgotten. I'm a good student, quiet and dutiful, and when we have show-and-tell the next time I bring in one of my three toys, Pony, my beautiful plastic horse. My mother gets invitations to PTA meetings and open houses at school but never RSVPs. She is just the signature, sometimes neat, sometimes wobbly, at the bottom of my report cards from school. My mother is the mother no one sees—at least not yet.

Behind the house on West 148th, we each have our favorite things. Grandpa fusses over his tea roses, especially the red ones. He gently plucks Japanese beetles off their leaves each morning and drowns them in a jar of soapy water. He is proud of his fruit trees and has one of each: apple, plum, peach, and pear. Grandpa wears a sleeveless tee and baggy tan pants when he's working in the garden, his belt loose around his waist. He clenches a cigarette between his teeth as he bends over the bed with his clippers and trowel. I watch and learn. "Dead heads no good," he says, and shows me how to clip off brown leaves and dying blooms. How to pinch back the parsley, prune a rose's long thorny stems.

In spring I help Grandpa clean the beds and plant tiny seeds in rows. When shoots start pushing up through the soil, I weed the beds for hours. I am a good girl; Rachel doesn't like to weed, she is bad. It's as simple as that. In the summer, Grandpa takes us to pick yellow peppers on a farm somewhere in the hot sun. I like driving out of the city, the way the factories disappear and turn to rolling hills and fields of waving corn. I love the scent of earth when I'm pulling peppers off tough green stems. I stack the peppers in a basket and count them at the end of the day while Grandpa supervises, a can of Budweiser in one hand, cigarette in the other. He is waiting for my sister to make a mistake. I want him to think she is good. Things would be easier if he did. She planted a sunflower seed in the hard rocky yard out back of our apartment and it grew six feet tall but he doesn't care. He doesn't care that she teaches our new friend Stephanie, and Patty and me how to write poems in the basement at the house on West 148th. She writes one about seasons on a cracked blackboard on the wood-paneled wall: "Winter, Spring, Summer, Fall / These are seasons count them all / One, two, three, four." We recite the poem together, then write it down. Rachel checks for our mistakes. My grandfather yells down into the basement, "What you girls doing down there? Smarties spoil the party!"

Rachel starts a secret club and we meet each week under the magnolia tree, and even though she's the only one allowed to be president we don't care because none of us wants the job. Grandpa calls her a little cunt, bitch, whore, words we don't know the meaning of yet. But she gives us new words—poems and stories, and a phrase no one else can know except the members of our club: "Red snake over the green grass."

My sister and I make things in the garden—pictures, stories, garlands of flowers for our hair. We write secret comic books together, a series called *Grumps*. I draw pictures of our grandfather leaning over the table, slurping up food with his hands. I draw him belching, farting, guzzling whiskey and beer, throwing chairs at us with expletives shooting from his mouth. I feel bad about the comics, but they make my sister and grandmother laugh.

Grandma only loves the garden when our grandfather isn't there. She waters the lawn to get out of the house. She smokes Benson & Hedges beneath the magnolia tree after Grandpa whips her across the face with his belt for looking at him the wrong way. She smokes outside when he's inside doing shots while rolling out filo dough and making his thick Bulgarian yogurt. She'd love for him to disappear so she could sit among the flowers, quiet and alone, with a tall glass of lemonade, a cigarette, and a slice of pecan pie.

"Hey, did ya watch today? I can't believe she'd go marry that son-of-a-bitch," my grandma shouts across the bed of roses to Mrs. Bente. Grandma and Edna Bente love the soaps—*As the World Turns, General Hospital, Days of Our Lives.*

"You don't know what I have here," she tells Edna, shaking her head and sucking in smoke.

Mrs. Bente invites my grandma over when Grandpa is on the rampage. She invites me in too, offers me milk and cookies and tells me jokes in her living room beneath the portrait of her dead husband, Al, who used to swing me around by my arms before he died. Mrs. Bente grows neat little rows of marigolds, snapdragons, and petunias. Her door is always open when I need a place to hide.

When my mother comes with us to visit our grandparents for the occasional Sunday dinner, she likes to go to the garden to smoke. Sometimes she walks in circles, taking quick puffs from her cigarette, talking to herself. The sunlight illumines her face; she looks beatific beneath the trees. She wears a sexy dress and high heels in the garden, sometimes a little scarf for color, red lipstick, and a dab of Tabu. Of all the things in the yard, my mother loves the trees most of all. They are giant green umbrellas; she can spread a blanket beneath the old blue spruce, sit and close her eyes, smoke her cigarettes, and rest. The shadow of the tree is soothing; her dark brown curls blend into the bark, making her disappear into the tree. Years later, when she is homeless, she will make charts of trees from all over the world. She'll send me children's books about the little animals that live inside them: squirrels, sparrows, chipmunks, and bugs. *Even squirrels have a home to live in,* she wrote me once on a McDonald's bag from a Greyhound bus station. *Even birds have a place to sleep.*

Some Sundays, Grandpa takes me to Saint Theodosius, his green oniondomed church on Starkweather Avenue, not too far from the West Side Market where he buys his *kashkaval* and freshly butchered lamb. Inside the church, Saint Theodosius is luminous and foreboding in candlelight, walls covered with bloody saints and gold. My mother doesn't like that my grandfather takes me there. She says the priest would like to murder all the Jews.

My grandma can't stand Grandpa's church either, or any other. When she's not working in the credit office at Acorn Chemical Company, she shuffles around in pink floppy slippers, hand on hip, cigarette hanging from her pink, pouty lips. She carries a little notepad in the pocket of her housecoat that hangs below her knees. She is two inches shy of five feet and everything she wears looks too long. Grandma writes down phrases by Trotsky, Lenin, and Marx and pulls them out as needed. "Religion is the opiate of the people!" she says, squinting behind Coke-bottle glasses.

At the eastern end of Saint Theodosius is a wall of icons rising up to the ceiling, the iconostasis—the golden wall separating sanctuary from nave. In the center is the "Beautiful Gate" through which only the priest and clergy can pass. People cry in front of the pictures and pray. The wall is a door between this world and the next, between sinners and the Incarnate God, His Mother, the angels, and the saints. In the church, there are deep voices chanting, incense and candles, and glowing things in every dark mysterious corner. What is on the other side of the golden wall? What do the pictures mean? Can a painting save a person's life?

I'm at our grandparents', sitting on the couch with my mother, listening to the radio drone on about how many soldiers are dying. I learn the word *amputee* and hobble around, pretending I am wounded in the jungles of Vietnam. Everywhere I go I hear about kids who've lost their fathers in the war. It's on the radio and television, in the *Plain Dealer* and the *Life* magazine that gets delivered to the house. Is my father there too? My mother listens to the news while I stare at the pictures in *Life* of corpses in mass graves, hippies holding flowers out to soldiers in tanks. I've been Aunt Toda's apprentice for months now and haven't healed a single man, woman, or child and I've yet to see a miracle in the church with the big green dome. I pray in front of the golden wall every time my grandfather and I go, but nothing happens. Everyone I'm supposed to heal is still sick or dead. I'd rather watch *The Monkees* on TV or play Pioneer Days in the backyard with Rachel and Patty than sit beside people suffering from cancer, heart disease, arthritis, and stroke.

It's hot and my thighs stick to the thick plastic covering Grandma puts on all the furniture for protection. The furniture is old but she keeps the plastic on anyway. "Someday everything will be nice and new," she says, "just like in *House Beautiful*." My mother sits smoking, staring into space. "Catatonic," the doctors have recently decided. Every time she's admitted to the hospital, they give her shock treatment and a different diagnosis: Disassociative. Antisocial. Manic-depressive. Delusional. Psychotic. Paranoid schizophrenic. Hysterical. Mad. The kids in the neighborhood call her a drunk.

I take my mother's hand in mine. Her hands are cold, even in summer. Her latest obsession is the Jewish military leader, Moshe Dayan. She keeps a picture of him by her bed and takes it out from time to time to stare at it; she has conversations with him in her head. He wears a black patch over one eye just like I wore when I was five. I have no idea who he is but I think he's a Nazi because his smile looks evil. There's talk of my mother getting shock therapy yet again, of zapping the sick part right out of her head. She sits in silence, her ear tilted to news about massacres, jungles going up in flames. She smokes one cigarette after another. I picture my breath going into her body like a flowing river, a river of light, flowers, and vines.

My grandparents have only one plant in their house, a spindly pathos with heart-shaped leaves that hangs over the kitchen sink from a small brass pot that can barely contain its twenty-year roots. Grandma pours leftover coffee in it sometimes, old tea and juice. When my mother comes over, the place looks like a bar—there are three people smoking eight to nine packs of cigarettes a day between them. How does that plant keep on growing? Sometimes I picture it creeping from its pot, slinking along the floor across the living room to my mother, growing into her mouth, filling her heart and lungs with leaves, wrapping its tendrils around her bones.

"I have to tell you something important," she says.

"What?"

"Don't drink milk before going to bed."

"Why not?"

"Because rats like milk."

"What?"

"A rat will eat your face off if it smells milk. And Myra?"

"What?"

"You girls are my most precious possessions."

"I know."

"Promise me you'll never leave."

"I promise," I say.

Years later, in one of her diaries, she will write: *The same unhappy anxious dream as always: I am still young and have small children. The girls are ahead of me walking too fast. I don't want them to leave. I try to call out their names but no sound comes from me. I have fear of radiation and cannot talk. The girls disappear. They always disappear in my dreams.*

One autumn day, when Toda and I go to Mitchell's house, everyone is in a hurry. People rush around carrying things; someone wipes his forehead while a nurse hooks him up to a big white machine. Mitchell's eyes always look vacant but this time he stares right at me, like he finally knows who I am. There's the smell of incense and beeswax burning, the smell of cloves. Toda mutters prayers over his body, tells me to go away. Mitchell is dying—why should I go away now? People from the church arrive, short ladies in black babushkas who don't speak English, talking too loudly for the quiet dark room of a sick man. A woman blows her nose into a handkerchief at the foot of the bed.

"Go outside and play!" Toda insists, pushing me out of the room. There is no place to go, just a busy street with a tiny front yard. It's chilly outside and it's begun to snow. I kick stones down the driveway. I wish my sister were here. We could make games, or sing something from *The Monkees*, like "Another Pleasant Valley Sunday" or a song from a Broadway show. These people don't even have a tree. More cars pull into the driveway, men slam doors, women kiss each other's cheeks and give advice, cry and blow their noses, drink endless cups of thick black Turkish coffee. I sit on the stoop and wait.

At the funeral, the priest chants and glides toward Mitchell's casket; his white and gold robes form a great sparkling bell. The crowd parts to let him pass. He stands over Mitchell's long thin body and blesses him with holy water, then says a prayer as he swings the silver censer back and forth like a pendulum. The smell of burning spices makes me dizzy. I've never seen a dead body before. I had seen dead birds before and once saw three dead rabbits, but never a man lying face-up, like a mannequin in a box.

Toda leans over and kisses Mitchell's forehead. "Now you," she says.

"What?"

"You kiss him. Don't worry, I help you up."

"No!"

"Kiss him! People are waiting, now kiss!"

I start to back away but feel my body lifted off the ground. Toda's big leathery hands are around my waist and she has me pinned against the casket. She pushes my head down so my nose touches Mitchell's. Pee is trickling down my legs. I can feel everyone staring.

"Kiss him," says Toda. "Do as I say."

She hisses something in Bulgarian and pushes me down again. I squirm and kick. I can hear people whispering in the crowd. I'm afraid they will crush me or shove me into the coffin, slam the box shut, and that'll be that. The line of mourners goes on forever, winding around the corner into the sanctuary of the church. Finally, I slip out of Toda's sweaty grip and shove my way through the crowd to the door. I heave it open and run around to the back of the church. I pause beneath a crabapple tree and look for a place to hide. But here, in the world of the living, there is only the cold rainy street, the city beyond the hill, the impenetrable sky.

After Mitchell died that fall, our mother was sent to CPI, Cleveland Psychiatric Institute. She had stayed up several nights in a row, walking back and forth down the street in the rain, shouting about some man in California who she said raped her when she was nineteen. "I just want what's due me," she said. "That bastard has to pay up." When she made cuts all the way up her arms, my grandma finally called the police. "What will people think?" was my grandma's constant refrain.

I visit her in the psych ward with my grandma. At first we can't find her, but then we see her in a corner of the common room, dressed in a nightgown, smoking and talking to herself, a television game show blaring nearby. Grandma and I start to approach her, but are intercepted by a young woman with greasy long dark hair."Did you bring me something? What'd you bring?" the woman shouts. She looks right at me. I grab my grandma's hand."Who invited *you* to the party, bitch?"

An elderly white nurse is passing out tiny cups of pills and water. Another nurse, a hefty black woman, doles out cigarettes, one to a patient, then lights them. The nurse with the cigarettes is in earshot. She turns her head.

"Hey, you little slut," says the dark-haired woman."Where's my money?" The woman is coming straight toward me."Where's my fuckin' money?"

The black nurse puts the tray down and walks in long strides over to us. She places her hands on her hips and stands in front of the woman, blocking her path. The dark-haired woman backs off, cowering, and shuffles back to her chair.

Grandma and I go up to my mother and I hug her carefully, as if she were made of glass. She looks up, then quickly looks away, like she is looking for someone who didn't come.

"He says . . . he says . . . They tie you down here," she says. "They use microphones, camera tricks."

"I made you some pictures," I say.

"Where are my cigarettes? Where's Rachel? You've got to get me out of here."

I offer her a stack of drawings—bunnies, flowers, horses and dinosaurs, Snoopy and Charlie Brown. For years to come I will make pictures and bring them to the hospital, but her smile, when she sees them, will be ever so brief.

My mother ignores the pictures, takes a quick puff on her cigarette. She is trembling and cold. How can I stop her from shaking? I wish I had painted a tiny icon she could wear around her neck—a golden saint lifted up by birds or a Madonna with a wreath of flowers around her head.

"Where's your sister? You kids have got to get me out of here. They're poisoning my food. Did someone kidnap Rachel? They're killing me in this place."

I wish I had made a towering wall of luminous saints and flowers, a hundred vats of rosewater, a thousand pots of magic tea.

She tells me they're going to perform a lobotomy on her and take out her womb."It's common knowledge they sterilize the poor."

"Get ahold of yourself, Norma. You don't know what I have to contend with," my grandma tells her daughter, who is rocking back and forth. "It's hard enough with that bastard, and now I got the girls. If you know what's good for you, you'll behave."

"Give me a cigarette. I'm dying here," my mother says. "The cheapskates only give you three a day."

Later, I'm in the garden with Rachel. I don't want to tell her about the hospital, the zombies in pajamas, the nurses with their long trays of pills. All that suffocating smoke, the windows with bars, the crazy lady going after me. Instead, I open and close the mouth of a yellow snapdragon, pretending it can talk. We are putting on a play using snapdragons as characters. The cast is made of tiny lions; the cluster of colorful stones and violets by our feet is our stage. We are the Queens of the Flowers, rulers of earth and sky. My sister will make up stories with anything at hand. She can't help herself—a bunch of wilting daisies, a rotten apple, a caterpillar, or a rock. Outside we can do anything, be anything at all. When we finish our play we run fast holding hands across the three adjoining yards, our grandparents', the Bentes', and the Budds'. We run out behind the row of spruce and pine trees, out to the fields and woods to no-man's-land.

We would like to keep running and running away. She could write stories and I would paint pictures and explore the world. We could travel to France or maybe to the Amazon. We could live in the jungle or Paris or London or maybe someplace in Africa where people eat breadfruit and antelope meat. We don't want to be martyrs or priests, doctors or saints. We would like to be wolf pups or birds. We would like to be fast horses. We want to be all the flowers of the field. How far can we go in this stretch of tall grass and goldenrod? How far in this forest of fragrant trees?

Nobody Hears a Mute But I Hear Myself

Today when I came back to Friendly Towers, the Jesus Hotel, I sat down and tried to study one of Diego Rivera's "Day of the Dead" paintings from a book I got out from the library. Unusual for me these days as I am slowly going blind. But blindness doesn't mean muteness. Nobody hears a mute but I hear myself. In the picture I could make out white skeletons floating in the air and the color red, and faces like the masked people I see in the corners of my room. The picture was trying to tell me something. But as I stared at it, a radiologist in the clinic across the street or perhaps the drug pusher next door, or someone from my future who I haven't seen yet, projected gas into the room and I dozed off with the book in my lap. As they say, the days fly by whether you are in or out of love. Or in my case, a Baby of the War left without a pot to piss in. In regards to pain and sorrow, you might say it is the universal human condition. But I have learned to discipline myself and reserve my pain and sorrow only for sleep time. That said, sometimes in my dreams I am taken out of the city to a place where they monitor the hearts of Jews and other marginalized citizens. Recently, I discovered I was given a pacemaker without consent.

4

No se puede mirar. (One cannot look.)

Francisco de Goya y Lucientes, inscribed below a print from his series *Disasters of War*

The Eye of Goya

Once when she was homeless, my mother sent me a postcard from a Chagall exhibit with a letter written on the back of a Dunkin' Donuts bag:

Dear Daughter:

I am trying to adjust to life with a white cane. Many years ago, there was a man in Cleveland who made a point of rap-tap-tapping by my way but I am a little slow in the game of Simon Says. These days I keep a journal. There is always the continuous anxiety of blanking out again, and I need to be reminded of myself constantly. One can't always rely on who was there, but on oneself. Within your sphere of interest, the painting you made for me in the 80's called "Selective Forgetfulness" is missing, stolen or confiscated. I have some Complaints going as you can imagine. By the way, when you translate the message in the above dots, you will learn nine (9) letters of the Braille alphabet. Note to your artist—the color pencils you sent are being used by yours truly. I thank you. P.S. when I have something nice to write about I'll let you know.

Love, Mother

My mother sent me postcards from all the art exhibits she went to in Cleveland, Chicago, Los Angeles, and New York during her extended stays at shelters and motels. She went to museums on free days, or right before closing so she didn't have to pay. I wanted to send my mother postcards from shows but if I did she might find out where I lived or traveled to in the years we were apart. When she lived in Chicago the same time I did in the early nineties we even went to see the same exhibits. I'd always wear dark sunglasses and tuck my hair up in my hat just in case.

Each year for her birthday on November 17, I sent her a museum date book. I found most of them in her storage room at U-Haul. She had made notations each day about the weather and what she ate. She also copied the pictures with oil pastels or colored pencils and glued them onto large collages she called her "posters of intent." My mother told me about them in her letters, how she would put them up against windows in shelters and motels to block out radioactive gas and the projected thoughts of others.

When my mother sent me one of her drawings or collages, she added commentary on the back. Sometimes she threw away the picture and just sent the commentary: *I copied the Dubuffet for you then added a little color. Should have left as is. When I finished the picture I destroyed it. Afterwards, I typed all the M's in the dictionary, bathed, and contemplated my own labyrinth. Enough said. Mom.*

In one letter, ten years after she had been on the street, she enclosed a small drawing of goats. She wrote: *You asked about my eye problems. I've been legally blind but did not walk with cane until Chicago. Enclosed is a small picture for you of two mountain goats conversing in a field. Someone asked me the other day how a blind person can draw and I said there was a man who was deaf who composed music. His name was Ludwig. I am still not on his level. (But I am not dead yet.) Mother.*

My mother and I loved artists and famous people who suffered from horrible afflictions, like Beethoven, Joan of Arc, Frida Kahlo, Anne Frank. Burned at the stake or crippled at birth? We wanted to read about it. I don't remember talking about our shared obsession; it was just something unspoken. Perhaps she connected viscerally to their suffering, while I tried to understand hers. Beethoven was my mother's muse, for me it was the Spanish painter Francisco de Goya y Lucientes; both men became deaf late in life. My mother and I were equally fond of Vincent Van Gogh. When my mother had a particularly bad day, she'd write in her journal: *Another ear to chop off, Vincennes!* Sometimes she just wrote: *Another ear!*

When I received my first letter from her, two years after she became homeless, I noticed that my mother had written my sister's name in the corner of the envelope instead of her own. From that point on, she referred to herself from time to time as *Rachel N. Herr, the Helen Keller Annie Frank of Chicago—Deaf, Blind, Mute Baby of the War.*

At the hotel in Cleveland, while my sister lay sleeping, I searched for pictures in my mind. I was trying to find a particular one by Goya from the Cleveland Museum of Art, hoping it would lead me back to my mother, to a time long ago. I whispered his titles like incantations: *The Sleep of Reason Produces Monsters, Saturn Devouring His Son, Tantalus* . . . Martyred peasants appeared, tormented souls howled in corners of asylums, winged monsters emerged from clouds of bats. Goya's dark figures writhed on the black walls of La Quinta del Sordo, the House of the Deaf Man, where, in tortured silence, he conjured demons with cannibal teeth. But none of these pictures were what I was looking for.

I closed my eyes and entered the palace. Through the door, past Medusa and my mother's photograph, the passionflower glowing in its frame. I paused and turned right, then entered a sunlit room filled with paintings. Straight ahead was a portrait of a man sitting at a desk. The portrait was by Goya. It wasn't that remarkable—for Goya, that is. If I had seen it in a museum, I might have passed it by. But when I thought of it then, a memory bloomed from when I was nine: I was back in Cleveland in the spring of 1968 and my mother and I were boarding the eastbound Rapid Transit, heading to University Circle and the Cleveland Museum of Art.

As we pull away from the platform we pass the junkyard. I watch big yellow cranes lift rusty cars and another machine smash them flat, then stack them on a pile of metal. One machine looks like a monster with an evil grin; it's a dragon, and a princess is held captive beneath the mountain. Perseus arrives on his winged horse just in time as we travel far above the banks of the Cuyahoga. I hold my nose because the river smells like rotten eggs; a year later when I am ten, it will catch on fire. I'll remember the burning river, people running from shore, although I am almost certain I wasn't there. The fire will be quelled in twenty minutes and no one will be harmed, but I'll remember it like a painting by Hieronymus Bosch—a hellish river in flames, boiling and black, naked people drowning and crying out in terror. I'll remember how my mother saw signs before it even happened in the paintings we visited at the museum.

It's a good day and my mother is taking a nap. She's not talking to herself or gesturing to the window as if she's making a point to someone, saying, "Well, *he* says the CIA's involved" or "*He* says another plane's going to crash." She's not channeling Crazy Guggenheim or Pearl Bailey, strutting down the aisle, shouting out random punch lines from her act, or impersonating Sammy Davis, Jr., or whispering to my father's old Chicago pal, Saul Bellow; she's not swearing at Jesus or God.

When we arrive at the station on the east side of Cleveland, my mother and I make our way past condemned buildings and empty parking lots toward University Circle. Patty and Stephanie and the other kids from our neighborhood don't even come to this part of town. In 1968 there are shootings here, riots and gangs.

"There it is!" I say. "The lagoon!"

She smiles and reaches down to take my hand. We are almost there—I see the pond sparkling in the distance. It's a warm afternoon in spring; everywhere there are swans and waterbirds, a maze of trees and winding paths graced with irises and columbines. In front of the museum is a fountain with neoclassic statues and gushing water. It's warm and my mother and I take off our shoes to dip our toes. She lights up a cigarette while I circle the fountain wall, balancing one foot at a time. We could be any mother and daughter, out for a Sunday afternoon—an exotic beauty in a bright red dress and her shy dark-eyed daughter, knees stained green from sodden grass.

Before ascending the stairs, we pause in front of *The Thinker*. Rodin's muscular patinaed nude is hunched over, head in hand, oblivious to the world. My mother laughs softly, says something I can't make out. Is she talking to me? She suddenly charges ahead, eyes glued to the ground, and tosses her lit cigarette away.

"Come on, kiddo," she says, "Let's go inside."

Inside the museum, we stop at the old stone wishing well. I stand on tiptoes to reach the top and make the same wishes I always do, tossing three pennies in, one by one: *Please make my mother happy, make me a great artist, and please end the war in Vietnam.* My goal is to hit bottom, dead center. My mother casts her three coins at once. Her face is flat, without emotion. What is it she wishes for?

After the well, we enter the room of Madonnas and illuminated books. There are gilded paintings by Sienese and Florentine artists—stigmataed saints, stern unhappy angels, stiff Madonnas with their baby-men Christs suckling from apple-round breasts. I love the painted books most of all. I touch the glass with my finger, tracing the birds and flowers scrolled around the ancient text. There are Books of Hours painted on vellum, intricate hymnals, Psalters, antiphonals, breviaries, bestiaries, herbals, and luminous Bibles for monasteries and kings. There is even one with a tiny naked man urinating on a large initial letter, surrounded by putti and a pair of fornicating goats. The labels say the manuscripts were painted in egg tempera and illuminated with gold leaf. Where could they have plucked leaves of gold? And paint made from eggs—what kind of eggs? A swallow's? A hummingbird's?

After the Middle Ages, my mother and I head straight for Picasso. We stand in front of his Blue Period painting of emaciated circus performers. My mother bends down, brushes the hair out of my face.

"You're my little Picasso," she says. "Someday your paintings will hang on these walls."

"Why is Picasso so sad?" I ask.

"He wasn't so sad. He painted sad people."

When we come to the surrealists, we see a world upside down—a man with no hands and a bull's-eye for a face, a painting of pink pianos and monstrous things, a field of bizarre forms dissolving into a desolate sandy beach.

"There is something to be said for realism," says my mother. "Do you remember your dreams?"

"I draw them."

"Let me see."

I open my sketchbook that I take with me everywhere and show her pictures of my dreams. I tell her how I fly around the neighborhood just like the floating figures in paintings by Marc Chagall. I travel up the canopy of trees on West 148th Street, but it's hard to get off the ground so I have to wave my arms up and down really fast to get started. I point to the picture of a horse and explain how I become a different animal every night—a cat, a bird, a swift whitetail deer. I don't mention that in my dreams she is a predator and I am her prey. Or that sometimes she is a crocodile standing on two feet, trying to devour me whole. Instead I tell her about my other dreams, the ones where I'm a knight who saves her.

"There's a house and it's filling up with water and you're drowning."

"And you save me?"

"And then we're in the basement and there's an evil giant and he's swinging you around by your hair and you're screaming, but then—"

"You should have been a boy. Then you could be a knight or a prince."

"But in my dreams I have a sword. Joan of Arc had a sword."

"Joan of Arc was a nut. I need a cigarette," she says.

We wind our way through the bowels of the museum till we come to the place I call the Spanish Room, where my mother leaves me when she goes outside to smoke.

"Don't move an inch and don't talk to anyone," she says. "I'll be right back."

In the center of the room stands an equestrian statue. An armored man sits atop a dark horse cloaked in steel, alert and ready for battle. Surrounding the metal horse are solemn seventeenth and eighteenth century paintings: martyrs, saints, prophets, priests, and kings. There's a greenish gray Christ on a cross by El Greco, his face twisted in pain. I had seen this look before in Mitchell as he lay dying. Next to the El Greco, there's a portrait of an ancient prophet emerging from shadows. The ominous paintings and dark horse should make the room dismal but sun pours in from the skylight above and envelopes the place with light. In every corner there are flowers and voluminous ferns. It feels more Monet than El Greco or Zurbarán, a room meant to embrace Renoir, my mother's least favorite Impressionist. "What a faker," she says whenever we pass one of his pink-cheeked blond and busty French girls.

I sit on a bench in the shadow of the horse so I don't have to look into the eyes of the portrait across the room. I'm not sure why it bothers me. It's just a man, a portrait of someone named Juan Antonio Cuervo by Goya, but I think it is Goya because his name is on the label below. The stern-looking man, who I think is Goya so I'll call him Goya, wears a stiff black coat and holds a compass in his hand. An architect's plan is spread out before him on a desk. I imagine him watching me. I know he's not really watching me, but still, there he is. How did the painter learn to do that? I settle in to draw—a horse, a rider, a potted plant with red flowers and pointed white tongues.

The light shifts, clouds pass overhead. I've already sketched the horse and rider, the plants, Christ's tormented face. A case of spiked gauntlets, crossbows, and cranequins. A close-up of my left hand. How long have I been sitting there? Goya's eyes stare at me from across the room, as if to say, "Your mother's never going to come. Why don't you just go home?"

It's getting late and I want my mother to come back. But what if she never does? I could wait here an hour or a year, set up a bed in the museum. Seasons could change. The weather could get cold, it could snow and still she might never return.

I get up and walk across the floor to Goya. I have to look up and strain my neck to see the man in the picture. What else is there to do but to keep on drawing? I practice what I learned from the art book my mother bought for me—first break the figure down in simple shapes, an oval for the head, a triangle for the torso. I hold up my pencil and squint to judge the distance between his eyes and nose, his nose and mouth. An announcement comes over the loudspeaker, "The museum will be closing soon."

Somewhere, outside, my mother paces. Where is she? In the rose garden? It's too early for roses. By the fountain? I want her to come back and take me home and I want her to leave me there and let me finish my drawing, get the details in—the gold brocaded cuffs and collar, those eyes that keep on staring.

When she's late there's the dreaded feeling of being found out, that my mother is sick and they will capture her. Like the policemen did that time she cut herself up her arms, right after Mitchell, the sick man, died. Or the time she teetered on Grandma's balcony, shaking her fist at the sky. Men in white coats didn't come like they do in the movies, just two policemen with their flashing lights, their guns and clubs, talking to her like she was mentally retarded or a foreigner or a person who is deaf. I imagine her speaking softly to herself in the garden. Does she ever think of me when she wanders? Does she ever talk to me in her head?

They will hurt her; I am always worried about that—the authorities, men in uniforms. I can see a crowd gathering in my mind. I am always afraid of the crowd that gathers. Of the person who says, "Is that your mother?" "No, I don't know her, why? Does she look like me? Do I look like I'd have a mother like that?"

"The museum is closing in fifteen minutes," a voice booms from above. I hear the tap-tap of heels against hardwood but they're a man's shoes. I slip into the next room, then the next. Why am I running? Someone turns off the lights one by one.

I should return to the Spanish Room, to Goya and the green man on the cross, but instead I find myself in American Decorative Arts, lost in a sea of colonial furniture and pewter mugs. There's a black velvet rope separating me from an eighteenth century bed covered by a faded red canopy. I slip beneath the rope to the other side. I hear a noise, so I tuck in behind a tapestry hanging on the wall.

"The galleries are now closed," says the scratchy loudspeaker voice.

Did I mishear her? Maybe she said, *I'll meet you outside.* But where? The front? The back? Maybe she's in the Spanish Room right now and is with the guard, waiting. She's growling at the guard like an angry mother wolf: *I'm not going anywhere without my child!*

I travel from Colonial America to Ancient Egypt. I find an ancient stone sarcophagus, and wonder if I should climb inside to hide. Ancient Egypt is a dark hidden place with plenty of nooks and crannies to disappear. That is what I really want, to disappear. To sail up the Nile on a reed boat, searching for mummies in buried tombs. I want to eat figs, run around naked looking for dung beetles. I want to see a real sphinx, see a real live scorpion in the desert sand.

I walk in circles, sneak past Greek and Roman gods, black and red vases, animals carved from stone. I find myself back in the Spanish room with Goya. Light seeps in from the skylight and cuts across his arrogant face.

I can't stop looking at his eyes. How is it that they follow me wherever I go? Is this what it's like to be my mother? To feel like objects can read your mind? I get an idea, a strange notion that has to do with magic. I make up magic rules all the time. If I don't step on a crack, my mother will have a good day. If I cross my fingers when we board the train, she won't talk to people no one can see. I come up with a new rule: If I can touch one of Goya's eyes and count to ten, my mother will return.

I stand up on my tiptoes and reach. A bellowing voice behind me stops my hand in midair. "Don't touch the art!"

The guard leads me all the way to the front of the museum. I tell him that that's where my mother said to wait and he believes me. He lets me out and closes the heavy door behind him. It is that easy. The sun is setting. No one is there; I turn and run down the stairs. I get a hunch that she's in the back. That's where she usually goes to smoke. I run around the museum to the other side.

There is always this memory: A group of young men walking toward me in the parking lot. They move like one solid body, a single organism, a paramecium of men. I tense up like I do when the neighborhood boys approach me in the field behind my grandparents' house, or on the way to school when one of them makes fun of my shabby clothes and grabs my violin case and throws it in the mud. The men are getting closer. I say to myself, *I will not cry*, and form my hands into tight little balls. I imagine I have claws; I am the invisible cat. Then I hear a voice, the sound of wild, cruel laughter. There's a woman at the far end of the lot marching in my direction. The men look at her and laugh, then veer off toward the street. As she gets closer I can see the woman shaking her fist.

This could have happened: I run to my mother and she hugs me, says, *I'm so sorry, sweetheart*. She tells me she tried to go back to the Spanish Room but they had already closed up shop. She'll never leave me again. She says, "Let's go get some food, how about that cafeteria downtown? You can get a nice grilled cheese."

But memory is impossible to ensnare, even if you build a palace to contain it. This could have happened too: I run to her but she doesn't know I'm there. She's yelling at someone only she can see and he's going to be with her for a very long time, at least forty more years. He will be telling her what to do, what to think, when to write a letter to the police, when to put a knife inside her purse, when to hide a gun for when the Nazis come knocking. He will be there till the day she dies.

"Who were you talking to?" I say.

"No one."

"But I heard you," I say. "You were talking to someone."

"Who were those men?" she asks.

"*What?*"

"Those men. What did they want? What did they say to you?"

"I didn't talk to those men. Who were *you* talking to?"

"You're imagining things. It wasn't me."

"I heard you. Who is it you always talk to? Tell me."

"No one."

My mother will always say *no one.*

This could be the first day I pay close attention to how we get home so I can remember which streets to cross, which trains to take, and where to make our connections. This could be when I become a navigator in a turbulent city, a master of subway systems and bus routes, when I learn to carry coins in my coat, a hidden dollar in my shoe. Just in case. Later, when I'm ten, traveling by myself on the bus to the museum, I will watch two men smashing all the windows of a store. Another day I'll witness a man getting mugged in an alleyway; another time, a crowd of people with signs marching toward a police blockade. Cleveland is burning all around us in the sixties; the world is on fire—the river, the dying lake, my mother's beautiful brain.

And this could have happened—something more mundane: a misheard word said in passing, a misremembered place. A mother loses track of time. She waits on one side of a building while her daughter waits on the other. There is no group of men, no woman laughing, just two people, a mother and child, humming a tune to keep themselves from falling further in the dark.

Movies I Wish I Had Never Seen

Awoke hearing my curses, echo of a life under thieves. Dreamed that Myra tells me she works taking care of a boy. I tell her the "boy" is 56, a pedophile on the lam. I ask if the other daughter is in a whorehouse but she remains silent. Later, I walked to Fairview Hospital for dollar coffee; stopped at U-Haul for red thread. Spent night sleeping at the Rapid Transit station on hard bench. $3.70 supper, 50 cents tea. $3 for one pack of cigarettes! B is for Bastards! Think of all words beginning with B to control rage: Breezy, Bestial, Bewitched. The Bactrian camel has two humps. The Arabian dromedary has only one. Baron: In Britain, lowest grade of nobility; a cut of mutton or lamb, two loins and hind-legs, as in "a baron of beef." Baron: an air-cooled gas operated machine gun that uses 303 caliber ammo, fired from the shoulder. I can think of a few men I'd like to use that baby on. B is for Babies: where did my little girls go? Sometimes I watch movies to forget. Tonight, highlight of evening at the Manor Motel: Gloria Swanson and William Holden in Sunset Boulevard. Made me think of all the movies I wish I had never seen: Gone with the Wind, Wuthering Hts, Dr. Jekyll & Mr. Hyde, Kramer vs. Kramer, One Million Years B.C. and all Tennessee Williams plays put on screen.

5

But we little know until tried how much of the uncontrollable there is in us, urging us across glaciers and torrents, and up dangerous heights. . . .

John Muir, *The Mountains of California*

Triceratops

Cave Girl

In my mother's storage unit, I found a box of my favorite books from childhood: *The Call of the Wild, Robinson Crusoe, The Jungle Book.* She had kept all my adventure books and the ones about Arctic exploration, ancient civilizations, and prehistoric worlds. At the bottom was a tattered red book on dinosaurs that she had covered to protect against further decline. Inside, tucked between two pages, was a picture of piano keys, like the one I found inside the book of Russian fairy tales. How many had she made, and why? In another section of the book, marking a chapter on glyptodons, was a note torn from one of her diaries: *February 28th, 2001. Awake to usual Gauguin dawn. No need to read mysteries. Life is a mystery. I am still the stepchild of the universe. I miss Rachel very much. She lives on a ship and plans to return home in the spring. When I think of Myra, I think of Mozart and his early sonatas.*

Why did she choose that book and not another? Did she, like me, dream of exploring ancient lands? In her letters, she said that she time-traveled but often against her will. When she took me to the Museum of

Natural History in Cleveland a lifetime ago, did she stare at the dioramas and wish she could climb inside? I wanted to crawl through the glass and enter the timeless world of Inuit hunters searching for seals or creep beneath the shade of an African baobab tree. I longed to enter the den of stuffed wolves, curl up beside them, and sleep for a while.

I made my first diorama when I was ten. I built all of Africa in a day: tiny plastic babies arranged in a circle, snapdragons for lions, and small animals made from clay. I filled up shoe boxes with the Amazon, the Ice Age, and the Pyramids at Giza. Once I built the Mesozoic Era—180 million years in a box—moss, ferns, pebbles, and chicken bones for fossilized remains. A lifetime later I am building a world inside my head: I run down narrow staircases, dark halls and passageways, chased by the fear of forgetting. Inside a room is a diorama from deep time, when dinosaurs ruled the earth.

In 1969, the year our mother's younger cousin, Philip, shipped out for Vietnam, and our father stopped sending us child support, I turned ten years old. I wondered if we would ever see Philip or our father again, and if, when the astronauts finally landed on the moon, they would find dinosaur bones buried beneath the rocks. How fast does light travel? I wondered. Where does our father sleep? How far is the nearest star?

My sister Rachel thinks about the moon all the time. She'd fly to other galaxies if she could. She is eleven and a half going on twenty and wants to travel as far away from our mother as she can. She and her friends spray Lemon Go Lightly on their hair to make it look kissed by the sun, as if they've all just come back from Hawaii. They write secret messages to boys they like, nasty notes to ones they find distasteful and rude. They gather in small groups and discuss which boys are cute, which ones are ugly and dumb. Rachel, who doesn't have to try hard to be pretty, primps and preens, tying little bows in her thick auburn hair. She knows the words to all the new songs—"Sugar, Sugar" by the Archies, "Build Me up Buttercup" by the Foundations, "Time of the Season" by the Zombies. My favorite records are a 1959 Folkways recording of the Bulgarian Women's Choir and Prokofiev's *Peter and the Wolf*—but I keep that information to myself.

Inside our apartment on Triskett Road the air feels tropical. It's a cold morning in late February, but you'd never know it with the heat blasting from the radiators. My mother walks into my sister's and my bedroom wearing only a bra and panties, a wet washcloth stuck in her cleavage to cool her down. I am getting ready for school.

"We're going to a movie today, just you and me," she says. "You'll like it. It's about dinosaurs—*One Million Years B.C.* starring Raquel Welch. I called the school and told them you were sick. Happy birthday, Baby!"

The year before, on my ninth birthday, my grandfather took me to the pound to pick out a puppy. I chose a tan and white collie-terrier mutt and named her Ginger. Pets are forbidden in our apartment so whenever she barks I lecture her on the benefits of being silent and invisible.

I follow my mother into the living room, Ginger close at my heels. My mother flips on the record player and the sound of trumpets fills the air, music of glory and pronouncement. It's her favorite Spanish bullfight album. She is in her Latin phase. After the bullfight songs she will probably put on Herb Alpert and the Tijuana Brass, or some steamy Brazilian jazz.

"Maybe we should go on a day I don't have school."

"You sound just like Grandma. Now get ready and don't dress like a bum."

My mother sometimes takes me out of school to see James Bond films with sexy lady spies and masked men in speedboats shooting guns. There are signs embedded in the Bond films—symbols laden with meaning, clues that can unlock a code she'll decipher later on. Will she find messages in the dinosaur movie too?

My mother wants to take me to a beauty salon to get my first real haircut and manicure before the matinee. My grandfather usually cuts my hair. He makes me wash it with soap and icy cold water in the basement sink to save money. In the summer he sets up a chair on his front lawn, places a bowl on my head, and trims around it. Neighbors come out of their houses to watch the spectacle. After he cuts my hair I look like Moe from the Three Stooges. Patty from across the street runs over to console me; tells me it isn't so bad and offers me her half-eaten Fudgsicle.

In the fancy salon, the hairdresser sculpts my hair into a stylish flip with
a mini-rat's-nest teased up the back of my head. I poke the nest with my
finger; it feels like the wad of steel wool Grandma uses to clean her pots.
My mother gets her hair done too, reads a magazine while she sits under
a giant silver dome. Meanwhile, the manicurist dips my fingers into soapy
green water. She massages my palms, the tops of my hands, pushes back my
cuticles, and trims my dirty jagged nails. My mother, who has been on welfare since our father stopped sending money, pays the lady out of what's left
from her monthly check. Sometimes she spends all of it by the middle of
the month, buys a fancy fountain pen for herself, several pounds of frozen
shrimp, some T-bone steaks, or takes the three of us to see a play. When my
mother and I leave the salon, I hold my hands and arms in front of me, fingers fanned out so I don't smear my newly painted nails. I keep my head stiff
so my hairdo stays in place.

"Put your hands down," my mother says. "You look like a zombie. Did I
ever tell you how your grandpa rubbed bacon fat on my hair to make it shine
when I was your age? A pack of dogs used to follow me all the way to school."

We laugh; my mother takes my hand in hers and we walk like that, all the
way to the show. We arrive just before the rain. The theater is almost empty.
We sit down in front of a middle-aged bald man just as the lights dim and
the big red curtains part.

The narrator of the movie tells us that this is a story of a harsh and unfriendly
world, early in the morning of time. He says that there are creatures that sit
and wait, beasts who must kill to survive. Clouds swirl across the screen,
something explodes, and lava pours down a mountain into a river of fire. But
after the lava scene, a scruffy dark-haired caveman appears, wrestling with a
warthog. Another man, his father, pulls an animal horn from his loincloth
and hands it to the warthog-wrestling son. The son blows the horn, pounds
his fake fur-covered chest, then the shaggy tribe squats in a circle, rips the
warthog wide open with their hands and teeth, and begins to gorge. The
men remind me of my grandfather, how he shovels down a plate of greasy
lamb.

A giant iguana comes on the screen, then a fake brontosaurus and a live tarantula blown up as big as a ten-story building. Other creatures come and go, chomping off heads and knocking each other off cliffs and sand dunes. Suddenly, from the primordial mist, a nubile, bronzed Raquel Welch appears, scanning the horizon for mega beasts.

"Goyishe whore," my mother says. "She's a bigger slut than Liz Taylor."

We get a glimpse of silky thigh beneath the cave girl's animal-skin skirt and a bird's-eye view of Raquel's cleavage bursting out from her top. Her unblemished body and luxurious hair remind me of Barbie and the teen-age girls in my *Archie* comic books. "Having fun?" asks my mother, a bit too loudly. "Like the movie?"

I whisper yes in her ear, and ask her to lower her voice.

"Don't shush me, honey. I'm not speaking too loud. So do you want a milkshake or a pop? Aren't you thirsty? I sure am."

"Maybe later," I say.

On-screen, the story flips back to the dark tribe dining on warthog. The father steals his son's hunk of meat. A fight ensues and the son falls off a cliff. The son is alone, standing in a vast, barren desert. Giant taran-tulas appear, a brontosaurus, and smaller, but deadly, dinosaurs. The young hairy man escapes from death and stumbles beneath the terrible sun. He finally collapses. Nearby, at the shore of the sea, barely clad blond women giggle and spear fish for their dinner. The young women see the fallen man and run over to help. Lurking nearby is a mega-turtle. Luckily, Raquel is at the ready. I picture myself in her place, spear in hand. She tries single-handedly to battle the beast, even though it is a hundred times her size. Someone from her tribe blows on a conch shell and other smooth-skinned blondes arrive.

My mother says, "I'm going out to smoke."

After she leaves, the man behind me leans forward and whispers into my hair, "Hey, where'd your mom go? Want some popcorn, honey? Have a piece."

I pretend not to hear him and sink lower into my seat. The blond people look like they could be related to Debbie and Linda Kamps, the nice German-American family in our neighborhood who belong to various athletic and social clubs. My mother says their family breeds Hitler Youth because their daughters are in Girl Scouts and another club called the Rainbow Girls. *Those people are Nazis, just look at their hair and their little brown shirts!* The blond tribe on-screen could be from the tribe of the Brunners, the Bentes, the Budds, or the other families that are blond and whose last names begin with B on our grandparents' street. *Why do all their names begin with B?* My mother wants to know. *B, B, B, always B's! What does it mean?*

"Hey sweetheart. Your hair smells real nice."

Raquel and the hairy guy have fallen in love. I hope nobody kisses, especially with tongues. I sink down farther into my seat. Everything looks phony, and yet, even though I can see they're really lizards and turtles enlarged with cameras to look big and scary, they *are* scary in a way, the way the creatures come out of nowhere and stampede the tribe, just when everyone is having such a nice swim in the river. It's the way they devour a man, like he's just a little bug, that sends a shiver down my spine. I can feel the man's hot breath on the back of my neck again. Something about him reminds me of my grandfather but I can't put my finger on it. Maybe it's the acrid scent of beer and cigarettes, maybe something else.

"Where's your mom? She leave?"

I consider leaving. But what if my mother came back and I wasn't there because I was outside looking for her? Then she'd be alone with the man. He might do something to her, like touch her, or say dirty words. Or she'd think I disappeared and she'd call the police. What if she called the police and they thought she was crazy for taking me out of school for the day? Maybe they'd put her in jail.

"Hey, doll, come an' sit back here with me. I'll buy you a Coke."

I close my eyes and make myself so small I could be a tiny creature inside a shoe box filled with moss and lumps of clay. Better yet, I am hiding behind a rock on-screen while a massive horned beast rips off the head of a hissing raptor.

My mother returns; the man relaxes into his chair. She's distracted, rummages for something in her purse. Items fall to the floor: a lipstick, a hairbrush, a pack of Doublemint gum. The man picks up the lipstick that has rolled beneath his seat. When he passes it to her, he leans, half out of his chair, and hovers over her a bit too long. It reminds me of how the hairy dark men in the movie size a woman up with just one glance, then grab her by her hair and drag her to a corner of their cave. It reminds me of the way they eat the warthog.

My mother twists and turns in her seat. She can't get comfortable. The scene we're watching looks like it could turn romantic and I can't get comfortable either. I have to pee but I'm worried that if I leave, she'll leave again too. I whisper to her that I have to go to the bathroom.

"Do you want to come with me?" I ask.

"I just went. You go. I'll watch our coats."

"Don't leave," I say. "I'll be right back. Stay right here."

In the lobby, I can hear thunder and lightning from outside. We forgot to bring umbrellas. It's February and there should be snow. Will things always be like this—strange unpredictable weather, creepy men lurking about; our father, lost in a jungle; my mother, one foot in this world, the other in a dream?

When I return, my mother is gone again and so is the man.

My red dinosaur book tells me that the Eryops was the lord and tyrant of his day. His mouth was so wide and deep that he could have swallowed a man whole. My book about the North Pole tells me that if you are trapped in the sea ice and starving, you can always boil your boots in a pinch. But nothing, not one single book, can tell me how to find my mother in the rain.

The movie ends. Should I leave? I have money hidden in the bottom of my shoe; I know which bus to take back home. The way back is much shorter than taking the subway alone in the dark after a day at the museum. It's not too bad if you look at it that way. Then, outside, beneath the marquee, I see a woman with dark curly hair, pacing, smoking in the thrumming rain. She is alone and muttering to herself. Something about her reminds me of the old lady downtown who wears three coats and asks people on the street for a dime. I run to my mother, even though she could be that lady with the coats, the lady who has no teeth and who talks to her hands. When my mother sees me, she hugs me close.

"I was worried sick about you," she says. "Where the hell did you go?"

The walk to our apartment is just over a mile, but it seems far in the damp cold. I'm tired and want to take the bus, but my mother says that someone could commandeer the vehicle and take us out of the city to a place where they hook up the hearts of Jews to machines. Even if they didn't kidnap us on the bus, a man sitting across the aisle could take our picture with an X-ray-vision camera hidden in his shoe, just like on the TV show *Get Smart*, and that would just help the enemy along with their plan. At least when you're walking, you can run if you're being followed. If you have a knife in your pocket, like my mother does some days, even better.

By the time we get home, my feet are soaked; my hairdo has fallen flipless and limp. The nest on the back of my head is a damp tangled blob. I study my fingernails under the light to see if they got damaged from the storm. They are still pearly pink.

Later that evening, my sister and I are playing Sorry in our room. You don't have to think that much to play. Sorry is a game of chance, the only game Rachel doesn't always win. We scurry our blue and red pieces around the board, knocking each other's men out of their little colored squares. Our mother calls me to her room. "I'll be right back," I say to Rachel. "Don't cheat!" even though I know she never does.

In her bedroom, my mother lounges in a short beige slip among the disheveled sheets. The song "Lemon Tree" plays softly on the radio. She has the heat turned up high; the radiator by the window hisses and spits out steam. Was this what it was like in a primeval jungle, this clammy prison of a room? My mother's eyes are part wolf, part human: the suspicious eyes that dart from here to there, the red eyes of all-night rants, the prelude to another round of shock treatment.

"Do you like this song?" she asks.

"It's okay."

"It's not Beethoven," she says, "but I like it. So what do you want to be when you grow up?"

"You know. An artist."

The rain outside that turned to sleet has turned to snow. I can hear wind rattling the loose glass in the window frames. Everything needs fixing in our place—the windows, the stove, the toilet that clogs up.

"You'll always be my little Picasso. But don't you want to get married and have babies too?"

"I don't know. I guess."

My mother is staring at a stack of magazines at the foot of her bed. She points to them and says, "Pick that up—the one on top. I want to show you something."

She lights a cigarette and motions me to climb up beside her.

"I'm in the middle of a game."

My mother pats the bed. "Come on. I'm not going to bite you."

I clamber up over her legs gingerly, a vigilant cat, placing myself as far as I can from her sticky flesh.

"Come closer."

She reaches for the magazine I'm holding from the top of the pile.

"Look," she says.

My mother taps her finger hard on a picture that, at first glance, looks like a bunch of people playing Twister. Then I realize it's a large group of naked white people doing something else. Men and women are licking and thrusting and kissing every possible body part; it's hard to tell where one person begins and another ends.

"Do you know what they're doing?" she asks.

"No," I say. "Can I go back now?"

"Has a man ever done that to you?"

She points to a bearded blond guy entering a young Barbie-like model from behind. The woman looks a lot like Raquel Welch. Could it be the cave girl I just saw?

"You don't know this yet," she says, "but there are men who want to do that to you. They did it to me. I know they want to do it to your sister. She's asking for trouble."

It's the same thing my grandfather says only not in so many words. He always warns me, "Boys are rough-and-tumble. They take you down to the river and won't give you even a glass of water!" When he says that I wonder,

Why would I want to drink from a dirty river that caught on fire? What does he mean?

I don't want to look at the picture, or my mother, so I stare at the floor. There are plates of old food and stacks of *Playboy* and *Penthouse*, piles of books and newspapers everywhere, baskets of dirty laundry, my old green Mr. Magoo sippy cup overflowing with cigarette butts. There is a picture of flowers I made for her, crumbled and coffee-stained, sticking out from beneath the bed. I can hear Ginger whining and scratching at the bedroom door.

"Ginger has to go," I say. "She's crying."

My mother sighs; waves me off the bed.

"Oh, all right. Why don't you be a good girl and go buy your old lady a pack of Benson & Hedges? I'm all out."

I sneak out of the building, so no one can see I have a dog, and we walk down to the corner store. When a man honks his horn at another driver, I jump and Ginger trembles. I bend over to rub the soft white stripe down the front of her face. "It's okay, girl," I say, kissing her nose. "It's okay." Ginger is jumpy, like me—sensitive to sound and sudden movements. She wasn't that way at first but one day after we got her, Grandpa told me to stand still outside and hold her leash tight. Then he shot a gun off by our feet several times. "This is how girls learn to obey," he said. "How to be seen and not heard."

I'm nervous at the counter, afraid the clerk will think I'm buying cigarettes for myself. I search my pockets for my mother's five-dollar bill; there's money left over, so I get some cherry licorice for Rachel, malted milk balls for me. Ginger and I race home in the dark. It seems I can never finish anything: a game, a drawing, or a song on my violin. By the time I get back, my mother is dozing. The radio is blasting something Cuban, with lots of brass and drums. I put out my mother's cigarette resting precariously on the edge of an ashtray and shut her door. My sister is already in bed, reading, our board game scattered on the floor. The phone rings in the kitchen. I go to pick it up.

"Hello?" I say.

"Myra?"

The man's voice sounds uncertain, like he doesn't quite know who I am, but I know who he is. I know it's my father, even though I haven't talked to him since I was four. I barely remember him. He is the man who hid upstairs in his studio for hours and wouldn't let me up there to play. He is the electrical smell of a train leaving a station, a tall dark-haired man in a suit, photographed laughing at a bar. He is a serious face on the back of a serious-looking book my mother keeps on the nightstand by her bed. My father is a stern figure standing at the edge of a dune, looking out at a cold blue lake.

On the phone, he says he wants my sister and me to come live with him and says I have to decide right away. Where is he calling from? Is he going to save us? Should I tell him about the man at the movies who leaned forward and smelled my hair?

"I'll go get Mom," I say.

"*No*—just tell me yes or no."

"I can't."

"Why?"

"Who will take care of her?"

Does my father tell me that he lives in a strange and beautiful jungle where there are peacocks and tigers and all sorts of monkeys and birds, like the worlds I want to explore? And if I move there we can eat snake meat when we're hungry, grab breadfruit right off the trees? Does he tell me we can ride wild horses? Are there wolves where he lives? Are there bears?

"Decide now. I'm calling long-distance."

"I can't . . . I promised."

"All right. If that's what you want."

"Don't you want to say hi to Rachel? I'll go get her. Just a sec."

"I'm saying goodbye."

"Hello? Are you there? Hello?"

Always there is that memory of holding on to the heavy black phone, whispering, *Hello?* into a void. And the nothing at the other end, and the waiting for the nothing to become a voice, but it never does, and the creeping back down the hall to bed, the light still on in my mother's room, radio still blaring, my sister asleep in our room, open book upon her chest, the sound of her little-girl breath soft and steady. She is the only one I can count on in this changing world, to play a game, to race with across the street, to help me write a poem.

In 1969 I am filled with so many questions: When did the first birds appear? What exactly is a sauropod? When will my mother stop being crazy? Will our father ever return, now that I made him mad? We are entering a new era. I can feel it—something has shifted, is changing fast. When did she start buying those magazines? Why did all the dinosaurs die? How smooth is the surface of the moon? Will I ever reach the Serengeti or the Pole? When will the soldiers come home, Cousin Philip, who is somewhere in the jungles of Vietnam, all of our neighbors' sons? Who will come to save us now? Will Jesus? Or our father? Will Neil Armstrong and his crew?

Enchantment

My only thought yesterday was of the beguiling, deceptive charm of writing and music. One could write a tale of enchantment but I don't have the inertia. Truth is, my sense of ego when I was young was like the celestial above and I felt the "nothingness" and feeling of nothing extending on and on into the future. A more literate person would say—well, even in "nothing" there is composition. Then, last evening I was typing words from the "I" section of the Dictionary I wish to retain, some which have legal importance. I lay down to rest a few minutes and had a half-dream or kind of visual picture (not really out of the ordinary when you consider all the possible intrusions into a person's live-in shelter, i.e. mechanics, radio, photo, all illicit but used). I had a clear picture of myself standing in front of a large monolith with writing inscribed I could not make out, and I was weeping copiously and a kind of presence, a fast image wearing a blue and white checkered suit pulled me away. I went down for coffee, then thought: "The Child is Sleeping."

6

Above you in the still air floats the Pelican . . . If you endeavor to approach
these bird in their haunts, they betake themselves to flight.

John James Audubon

My Year with Audubon

In my memory palace, two pictures hang on the wall of an atrium: the first, a white pelican, looking out toward the sea. The other, a child sitting on the floor, pressed up against a piano, eyes shut tight to stop the room from spinning. Her mother is arched over the keys, fingers flying. She doesn't know the small child is there, an invisible form, a little dark-haired nothing. The room is a living and breathing machine, an engine of sound behind the walls, inside her bones. The child floats on a flimsy raft alone; it's like white rapids on a river, all that music crashing through her. This is the closest they will ever be, this shock wave of sound between them. *This is what love is.*

But by the time I turned eleven in 1970, our mother was too ill to work even the occasional temp job. We couldn't pay the bills with the pittance she received from welfare and we hadn't heard a word from our father in over a year, ever since his call on my birthday. There was no choice but to move from our apartment to our grandparents' house on West 148th. I don't remember packing, or much of anything else, only a vague feeling that something would eventually, most certainly, explode.

Rachel and I took over our grandmother's room and she moved into the little guest room with the love seat and balcony. At night, our mother tossed a blanket over herself and curled up on the lumpy green couch in the basement. Grandpa stayed where he was, in the master bedroom, alone.

I tried to be optimistic—we could still walk to Newton D. Baker Junior High, where I had just started seventh grade, my sister the eighth. My dog Ginger could run free in the yard and there was a garden full of flowers and trees. The park was closer to West 148th Street; so was the West Park train station, Patty's house, and Dairy Queen. But most importantly, at my grandparents' house, there was a piano.

When she felt stirred to play, my mother's fingers hovered above the keys for a moment, then flew across them with fury. She played Beethoven with such ferocity that at times I couldn't bear to be in the same room. But when she played Bach, a sense of calm filled the house, if only for the length of a prelude. I longed to master Bach like my mother, play the rise and fall of an arpeggio with the same precision, order, and grace.

In rare moments of lucidity, she taught me scales, chords, and intervals; introduced me pared-down Brahms and Béla Bartók's pieces for children, his *Mikrokosmos*. The Bartók melodies sounded like the old folk songs on my grandparents' records from Russia and Eastern Europe. When I played them, I pictured myself in a snowy field in Siberia, bundled up on a fast moving sled drawn by horses.

My mother's white hands fluttered over mine like birds, waiting for mine to make a mistake. She sat on the bench next to me and chain-smoked, ashes falling onto the keys and my small fingers. She tapped her foot like a metronome. *It's allegro, not adagio. Speed it up a bit.* Some days she'd start whispering something I couldn't hear and suddenly get up, slam the door, and bolt outside, heading toward Grapeland Avenue. "Crazy bitch!" my grandfather would shout after her. Where did she go when she ran out the door?

In one of her diaries from the seventeen years we spent apart, my mother wrote: *I am thinking of the song "Pale Hands I Loved Beside the Shalimar." Now, in retrospect, since I have been projected into the future, maybe I am thinking instead of the loss of my piano and my life. The other day I had forgotten the two words in music that mean one voice is stationary while the other is in motion: "Oblique motion." The closeness in French, obli: forgetfulness; oublier: to forget, influenced my slowness to remember. How many other things will they force me to forget? Was that the problem with my mother's brain—while one voice was stationary, another could never be at rest?*

One day, my mother told me she had run into her old piano teacher downtown. "Mr. Benjamin said he'd teach you girls for five bucks an hour. You want to take lessons? He's the best around."

Was it true? She told me once that Sammy Davis, Jr., was going to propose to her. "I still have my girlish figure," she said, explaining his desire for someone outside of show business. Aliens had begun to send my mother "penises from Mars" through the hot dogs Grandma brought back from Pick 'n Pay; she communicated with Moshe Dayan through photographs in *Life* magazine. She talked to Golda Meir. Did Mr. Benjamin really exist?

"You girls can start next Sunday," she said. "And don't dress like a shtetl waif. Put on a clean blouse and brush your hair."

It's a radiant fall Sunday in 1970, and the air smells like fallen apples after rain. As the train rumbles east from West Park to Cleveland's Terminal Tower, where we transfer to the bus for Shaker Heights, I watch houses change from small bungalows to stately mansions with manicured lawns. In the vast green yards are old stone fountains and big magestic trees. I wonder if this is what France looks like, or maybe a quaint old town near London.

My mother asks, "Why didn't your sister come today? I think she's on drugs."

"What?"

"She goes to rock concerts with bad girls."

"I go too, and so does Cathy."

"Cathy's a good girl. I'm not talking about her. You know what happened to the girls who fraternized with Charles Manson. They listened to rock music and took drugs. They killed an unborn baby."

"Rachel's not going to kill a baby," I say. "She just likes rock and roll."

It was gradual, my mother's transition from her neglect of us to unremitting intrusion. But when did it first occur? Was it when my sister started fussing with her hair, flirting with boys at school? Or was it my fault? Was I changing too?

"You wouldn't take drugs, would you?" she asks. "You wouldn't let a man see you without your clothes?"

Mr. Benjamin's wife greets us at the heavy oak door. She ushers us in, then leaves my mother in the living room to wait. I follow her through the house.

"I remember the way your mother played. There was no one like her. When she played Beethoven ... well, that was long ago. She told me you play violin and piano and that you're quite a little artist."

I nod, embarrassed.

"My husband loves art too. Would you like to see something beautiful?"

She leads me down a hall lined with giant pictures of birds, each one illumined by a tiny lamp that makes them glow like the icons in Aunt Toda's kitchen and my grandfather's church.

"John James Audubon," Mrs. Benjamin informs me. "These are original prints from his Elephant Portfolio—his *Birds of America* suite."

"Oh, yes, Audubon," I say, as if I know who he is. We pause at each bird on the wall. Mrs. Benjamin names them one by one.

"This is the painted bunting, that is the swallow-tailed hawk."

"Swallow-tailed hawk," I repeat. I say each name softly so I'll remember. "Arctic tern. Yellowshank tatler. Great cinereous owl."

Bird after bird, our walk down the hall is a largo, walk-*pause*, walk-*pause*, in front of each framed print. At the end of the hallway we stop to look at a large white bird. Mrs. Benjamin tells me its name in Latin: *Pelecanus erythrorhynchos*. The American white pelican. It's not really that beautiful; there is something about it that is rather cold and severe. But I am curious. What is it looking at? The sky? The sea?

Mrs. Benjamin confides in me that collecting Audubons is her husband's greatest passion, perhaps even more than music. "The harder one is to get, the more he wants it," she says. She tells me that sometimes her husband can't sleep the week before an auction. "Oh, look at the time. He's waiting," says Mrs. Benjamin. "Go on downstairs."

At the bottom of the basement steps is a small wooden table with a stained-glass Tiffany lamp and a Cleveland Indians bobble-head doll. The heating vent kicks on and makes the mascot's smiling head waggle. The bobble-head reminds me of President Nixon on TV when the sound is off and you can't hear him talking. To the left of the staircase is a sleek black Baldwin where Mr. Benjamin waits. Is this where he waited for my mother too, his beautiful young prodigy? The girl destined for Carnegie Hall? My new teacher wears an old-fashioned suit, a starched white shirt, and bow tie. He is a short man with a paunch and small freckled hands.

"Hello, hello! Come sit down," he says. "Let's begin."

Mr. Benjamin invites me to play a short waltz I have brought along. The piano has a warm tone and is delicate to the touch. My new teacher follows my every move.

"How old are you now?" he asks.

"Eleven and a half."

"Play the piece again."

He closes his eyes and listens. When I finish, he says, "Anyone can play piano. Not everyone can make *music*."

Does he mean that I can make music or I can't? A white cat rubs up against my leg and purrs as if to say, Yes, Mr. Benjamin thinks you are good. As if to say, You can stay here with us forever.

"Let's try the Bartók." Mr. Benjamin places some music on the piano. "Listen."

His fingers are not long and graceful like my mother's, but he plays with great tenderness and feeling. After he's done, I scan the music. I take in the page of notes, a gestalt of black birds on a wire. I try to play what I see.

"Your mother was a good sight reader too," says Mr. Benjamin. "What a quick study. She was going places. What talent … what …"

I look down at my feet. Mr. Benjamin clears his throat. "You like kugel?" he asks. He goes to the top of the stairs and shouts to his wife, "Bring some kugel down for the girl. The girl needs a little *kugeleh* and tea."

When we leave, I tell my mother about the birds.

"I've seen them. You can have those birds."

She tells me that the birds terrify her; to her they look like the ones she sees in her dreams. She says they remind her of Alfred Hitchcock's movie.

"The world is a dangerous place. Birds like that can peck your eyes out."

"Mrs. Benjamin says her husband wants to own all the Audubons in the world."

"He's a nice man but just remember, you can never trust the rich."

Mr. Benjamin covets other people's birds and I covet his. I covet his house, the smell of sandalwood and roses in the foyer, the Baldwin in the basement, the Steinway in his den. I covet his life, his little white cat, his quiet world of birds and music, and his dark wooden living room full of leather-bound books. And most of all, I covet his pelican, the universe of sea and sky swirling inside the eye of that terrifying and wondrous bird.

When my mother was twelve, she had already surpassed her first teacher, the one she had before Mr. Benjamin, or so my grandma had said. By fifteen she was preparing for the concert stage. In the few photographs from that time, something looks a little off, the way her eyes glance sideways, even though her mouth is turned up into a smile. When did the dark shape first form at the back of her brain, force her to sleep all day, spend her nights wrestling with demons? When did the voices first whisper to her through the radio, the clock, and the walls? What did they say that very first time? *The Germans are coming, the Germans are coming?* The voices told her not to say a word but my mother rebelled: *Nobody hears a mute but I hear myself. I will fight them to the end. No one will put me in an oven, not the Nazis, not the Golem, not my father or the CIA. Nobody hears a mute but I hear myself.*

In the beginning, my sister comes along to Shaker Heights. Sometimes we learn duets. I sit on her right, and then we switch places. She plays the right notes but holds something back, the soul of the music. Or is she just afraid to make mistakes? At the house on West 148th, we all have to be careful about every little thing. A misplaced cup could mean the belt or the back of his hand; one wrong note and who knows what our grandfather could do?

When I play Bach or Mozart, I see colors and dancing shapes inside my head. Something gets stuck in my throat when I listen to Rubinstein playing Rachmaninoff, Caruso singing arias on my mother's old 78s. Where does the soul of a song reside? In your body? In your hands? When my mother was in music conservatory, before her first breakdown at nineteen, did she see colors when she played? Did her heart swell like mine when she listened to Schumann, Fauré, and Ravel?

When we lived in our old apartment, I used to go alone on the train all the way to the art museum. My mother wouldn't know when I left, when or if I returned. But now, sometimes en route to our lessons in Shaker Heights, she shoots out strange new questions to my sister and me for everyone to hear: *Are you menstruating yet? Who are you sleeping with?* Rachel is almost thirteen and mortified. *Do you know how to use a sanitary napkin?* The people on the train turn to stare, so we try to shush her, slap our hands over her mouth, or get up and walk down the aisle, pretending she isn't our mother at all. *I'm your mother*, she shouts. *You can't run from me! Answer me! Is that sperm on your leg? Pull up your skirt and let me see.*

As winter approaches, Rachel begins to lose interest in the lessons. Why put herself through the unbearable train rides when she could be writing stories, studying at the library, or hanging out with her friends? She tries to find excuses to get out of our grandparents' house. Both of us do. We love school, even though you are supposed to hate junior high. We want to learn as much as we can, hide in between pages of books at the library, crawl inside our favorite paintings at the museum.

My sister has her life mapped out at thirteen. She will get straight A's, get into a good college, and get the hell out of Cleveland. Then she'll become a famous writer and English professor and live far away from home. She reminds me to do my homework, to not let my grades slip down. She knows this is the only ticket out, the only way we can leave. All I know is that someday I want my mother to see my pictures hanging in a museum. I want to play piano like her, and keep her safe from harm. But sometimes I dream that I live on the other side of the ocean, as far away as possible, so she can't ask me on the train if I have been raped or if I think my sister is a whore or if someone removed my uterus while I was asleep.

On those Sundays when Rachel is playing with her friends and my mother is too catatonic to get up, I travel to Mr. Benjamin's alone. My mother's old negligence kicks in and I am free to go. She doesn't ask questions. I am an invisible cat once again. "I am leaving now," I say, and kiss my mother's soft cool cheek. Grandpa is passed out on the living room couch and Grandma is watching her shows on TV, her head nodding like Mr. Benjamin's bobble-head doll, on her lap a big plate of banana cream pie. I tuck money in my boot, extra change in the pocket of my coat. Ginger whines and nips at my ankles to stop me from flying out the door.

On the train, I tap out Bach and melodies I invent. Alone, I can finally hear the music in my head, not my mother playing, or her ranting on about Nazis. The music I hear is like an Audubon print glowing under glass, or like sitting high in a tree peering into the nest of a bird. It's the feeling of lying face-up in a field alone, squinting at a cloud moving fast across the sky. Everything is entwined—the soaring birds, the Audubons, the paintings at the museum, the sound of a stream, sun breaking through a cloud, a cloud transforming into an elephant or swan, my fingers gliding across gleaming keys.

And then, sometimes, I feel something stick in my throat. It nags at me, this small sad pebble of guilt. I think of her, curled in a ball beneath her blanket, her radio blasting, the air thick with smoke. Should I turn back? Should I go home? Will she ever be okay?

At school, my seventh-grade science teacher introduces us to Linnaeus. We learn about his incredible trip to Lapland, and the strange plants and animals he saw and gave names to in the Far North. I fall in love with his lyrical taxonomy, his reassuring order of things: kingdom, class, order, genus, and

species. Linnaeus said there should be two names for everything in life, one
to identify each genus and one for each species. When I title my drawings,
I emulate his binomial nomenclature by making up my own secret code.
Below each drawing I compose a cryptogram, a hybrid of pig Latin, English,
and French, neatly labeling each picture in tiny calligraphic script: *Binroba-
tus rouge* for red-breasted robin, *Chicadeenus chapeaunoir* for the little black-
capped chickadee.

My mother tells me that Leonardo da Vinci did the same; he wrote in
secret code, backward and upside down. She says a lot of things in the world
have hidden meanings—movies, for instance, and advertisements on TV.
Years later, in her letters, she will remind me of this from time to time: *I read
a juvenile book about plants today and retained only one word: photosynthesis. What
is said or written is often in code and not what is meant. When I finished the book I fell
asleep. In my dream, a fair-haired girl who looked like Rachel was near a lake in darkness. The girl had no time for me and I felt terribly sad. Then a voice said, "I will give
you a girl whose sobbing will end with a gag-like sound in her throat." When I woke
up, it was raining in an open window and I have always, religiously, kept my windows
tightly shut. Once again: proof that my future was written long ago.*

After a particularly harsh winter, buds finally appeared on the magnolia tree
where sparrows had already begun to nest. In taller trees, crows were staking
their territory, sending out sentinels to guard their homes. My grandmother
had bought me a watercolor pad with special paper from France, and a paint-
brush made from sable. I traveled on my bike, far from West 148th Street,
to find birds to paint and draw. Sometimes I asked Cathy to come along.
We would sit in a field or beneath a tree, side by side in silence, and draw the
world as it unfolded—the shifting clouds and changing light, the rush of
some small creature up a tree. Afterward, I rarely invited Cathy back home; I
rarely invited anyone at all.

Once, after a lesson, in the spring of '71, Mr. Benjamin showed me a book
on John James Audubon. He said that when the artist was young, he skipped
school and roamed the fields all day in search of specimens, returning home

at dinnertime with a basket full of birds' eggs and nests, lichen, flowers, and stones. He said that when Audubon grew up, he wandered the world in search of birds, risking his life to track them down. I pictured myself as Audubon, traipsing through the wilderness in shaggy buckskin clothes, a box of paints upon my back. Could that be me someday? Could I really leave her so far behind?

Summer was unbearably hot that year; I remember the sky heavy with clouds, as if something ominous were about to happen. Hundreds of bodies were being sent home from Vietnam in black zippered bags; we watched it all on the television set downstairs—fuzzy black-and-white pictures of caskets draped with flags, Nixon looking concerned on cue, children in thatched huts running from bullets and fire. The war seemed to validate all of my mother's worst fears and prophesies. She became even more paranoid about Nazis and the CIA infiltrating our home. And there was some doctor in California she wrote obsessive letters to each week, some man she claimed had raped her when she was young. *It will happen to you if you don't watch out,* she warned us. *It's only a matter of time.*

One July afternoon a midwestern storm began with the sound of electricity crackling in the air. I watched the sky turn from cobalt-blue to yellow-gray in minutes. All the songbirds near my window suddenly scattered and torrential rains stampeded down. It rained for three days straight, trapping my sister and me in the red brick house. We tiptoed from room to room, careful not to say the wrong word to our grandfather, or put a glass on the shelf where a cup should be, or shut the bathroom door all the way when we had to pee or take a bath, because closed doors were simply not allowed. When I awoke on the fourth day I saw a little black dog clinging to a tire, floating down West 148th Street, which was now a rushing river. The current pulled the dog under, right before he reached the end of our street, and I buried my face in Ginger's soft warm neck, grateful that she was safe inside. That was the only Sunday I missed my piano lesson, because of the flood, all that water seeping into our homes and dreams, and even then I would have waded in sewer water to the station if the Rapid Transit hadn't been shut down for the day.

After the flood, throughout my summer vacation I practiced whenever I could. By the time I started eighth grade in the fall, I knew four pieces by heart. Meanwhile, the leaves on Grandpa's apple tree had begun to turn vermilion-red. Some birds moved on, but others were still around to draw.

One day in science class, I hear someone outside, calling my name. The teacher opens a window to see what's going on. The voice from outside becomes louder and a couple kids go to the window to look. "Someone's calling you," the boy next to me says. "Is that your mother?" asks another. Everyone wants to know: "Who is that? Who's the lady on the bike?" I say nothing; I am invisible, after all—a small form pressed up against a piano, a little dark-haired nothing. The bell rings to save my life and I pretend to look for something lost inside my desk. Her voice drifts up into the classroom: "Where are my children? Someone has kidnapped my children!" After everyone leaves, I go to the window. There she is—two stories down, circling the school on her rusty red three-speed, coatless in the cold autumn rain. It's pouring down upon her head, but she keeps calling out my sister's and my name till her voice becomes too hoarse to shout. She rides around and around in circles, ringing her persistent tinkling bell. For many long years, she will ring her little silver bell inside my ear, over and over, until I wake up at night, sweating, hands formed into fists in front of my face.

Shortly after that day she showed up at school, our mother is admitted to the hospital. Maybe my sister calls this time; or maybe I do. Maybe this is when the two of us begin to take over our grandma's job of reluctant mother, triage nurse, watch-keeper of the night. When our mother returns from the psych ward, Rachel starts chopping up medicine into her food: first Thorazine, which doesn't work, then Haldol. When she's medicated, our mother is dazed and can barely speak without slurring her words. Her throat is dry, her tongue always swollen, her hands trembling and cold. If she sits at the piano, she only stays a moment and stares at the keys, then lights a cigarette and wanders, somnambulant, out the door.

Despite my mother's setback, I begin preparing for my first piano recital, to take place late February, on the week I turn thirteen. I am going to perform the pieces I have been working on over the past year: a short rondeau by Couperin, a Mozart fantasia, one of Bach's *Two-Part Inventions*, and a movement from a Beethoven sonata my mother had played long ago. The Bach comes easily, but as always I wrestle with Beethoven, my mother's muse. A couple weeks before school lets out for Christmas, Mr. Benjamin tells me that there is something new he is going to give me to learn over the holidays, a complicated piece by an Armenian composer.

"It's a hard one," he warns. "Not for sissies. I hope you are ready."

After the lesson that day, he pulls my mother aside. "I need to talk to you, Norma," he says, ushering her into the den. I stand outside the door to listen.

"At least two hours a day she must practice. Are you listening to me, Norma?"

"Yes."

"Don't worry about money. She can come for free."

"If you say so." My mother's voice is completely flat.

"Soon we start the Khachaturian. Norma, you're not listening. Look at me, not out the window. She's almost ready. You need to make sure she sticks with this. She's starting late. Now go, take care of yourself. Get a permanent, find a nice man. Are you taking care of yourself? Are you seeing a good doctor? Did you hear anything I said?"

The next Sunday morning I go downstairs to practice. It's the weekend before Christmas and in the corner of the living room is Grandpa's sad aluminum tree he has hauled down from the attic. Over the fake fireplace Grandpa has nailed up a pair of Grandma's nylon stockings. Inside each one he has tossed a few coins, our one holiday gift. Grandma does nothing to celebrate Chanukah, nor does our mother. None of us even knows what a menorah is. "Let the old man have his fun," my grandma tells me. "Or we'll pay for it later." When I was little, I would sit in bed and pray for Santa and his reindeer to save me and take me with them to the North Pole, while my grandfather staggered drunk around the tree in a Santa hat, shouting "Ho, ho, ho!" This year will be no different. There will be an excess of eggnog, turkey, and booze, and I will have to play "Jingle Bells" for him over and over again, his whiskey-hoarse voice bumbling along to the tune, meaty palms pressed down upon my shoulders.

"Today," I say to myself, "I will receive the Khachaturian."

We eat an early afternoon meal together—my grandfather and grandmother, my mother, my sister and I—chunks of greasy lamb on rice, fried okra, feta cheese, and tomatoes drenched in oil. My grandfather drinks a few beers and a couple shots of Jack Daniel's to wash it all down. He's been cooking and drinking since morning. He sits hunched over his plate in his dirty tee, swearing under his breath, just like I draw him in cartoons. No one says a thing; Rachel and I exchange looks as Grandpa noisily sucks the marrow from a bone. Beneath the table, we press our chunks of meat between napkins to squeeze out the grease. Ginger sits at my feet, tail thumping, waiting for something to drop.

"Whatchu lookin' at?" My grandfather snarls at my mother.

Our mother is staring off into space. She has barely touched her meal. "Eat the lamb," he says to her. "Finish your goddamn plate."

"Not this again," says my grandma.

"I cook all day for you whores. Now eat!"

"I'm not hungry," my mother says in her small flat voice.

"You eat what's on your goddamn plate."

"Bastard," says my grandma under her breath.

"What did you say, you son-of-a-bitch?"

"Ignoramus," says my grandma softly. She starts to laugh her nervous laugh, then says, "Third-grade education. Can't get a job. Can't even write a sentence."

"I'll teach you a lesson you won't forget, you motherfucking bitches," says Grandpa. "Misery loves company."

She laughs hard until her voice chokes with tears. Grandpa pushes his chair back from the table and stomps downstairs. When he comes back up from the basement, he is holding something shiny in his hand; his face the color of beef.

Grandpa points a gun at my mother's head and says, "Nobody leaves this room until you eat that lamb."

I nudge her plate toward her to stop the sound of all of us holding our breath, but she doesn't want it, doesn't want the lamb at all. Her plate is full of greasy meat and bones, and smells of garlic and something I can't quite remember from the world downstairs where Grandfather keeps his dark and urgent life, his good cigars.

"Eat the goddamn lamb," he says again, and takes another step toward the table.

Later, we are all still alive. When my grandfather falls asleep, I slip down into the basement. Below the stairs there's a cellar room where Grandfather comes and goes. Above the cellar door, a broken clock and a Mason's oath of honor. Beside the door a faded print of the Lord's Prayer: "Our Father Who Art in Heaven Hallowed Be Thy Name." For once I find the room unlocked and go inside. There are rows of canned tomatoes, hot yellow peppers, twenty years' worth of toilet paper and insulation, a hunting knife and a gun. There's a rifle, ammunition, an arsenal of war in case the Russians bomb us, the Communists, the hippies, or the Cubans and we are left to die here all alone.

I sit in the cool dank room until my eyes adjust to darkness. It's quiet here, calm. I sit for twenty minutes or an hour or so or more. No one comes. It's peaceful among the peppers and the guns. All those jars in rows, such order, such silence. I hear someone walking above my head. I shut the door behind me and go into the other part of the basement where the television is, where my grandma keeps her books, the big ones: Dostoyevsky, Tolstoy, Dickens, and James. I reach behind them till I find what's hidden, shiny and smooth, Grandma's stack of *True Crime* magazines. I hear a door open and Grandfather's heavy feet at the top of the stairs; he singsongs my name into the basement to see where I have gone. "I'm down here, Grandpa," I say. "No need to worry." I place the magazine I'd taken inside an oversized book, *Beowulf* or maybe *Westward Ho*. I put it there so I can hide it fast.

Everyone is napping or pretending to nap, and Ginger creeps downstairs with her tail between her legs to sit beside me and gnaw her bone. I turn on the record player. The needle falls onto the worn-down vinyl groove. It's Maria Callas singing Verdi. I tilt my head to listen. Her voice reminds me of my mother when she sits at the piano but cannot play, her hands suspended above the keys. The song is the ache I feel when I look at Renaissance paintings at the museum—not the angels or the saints, the bloody Christs or prim Madonnas, but what is in the distance: the cypress trees on the horizon, pink clouds tinged with gold, birds disappearing into blue mountains. Callas sings the beckoning world I see inside the white pelican's eye. Her voice fills me up like a bottomless well and I open the window so she can sing into all the tidy darkening yards and secret lives, into the windows of the red brick houses and the trees where the owls live, where in my dreams I travel and build a home of sticks and feathers and leaves. I sit back down and turn the pages of the latest *True Crime*. I read about nice old men who lure children into their homes, feed them peppermint candy, soda, and chocolate cake, then kill them, put them in a pot to boil. Callas's voice soars, drowning out the waking voices above my head, the shifting of feet on creaking floors, windows slammed shut next door. I feel sorry for these old men I read about, how hungry they are for innocence, for someone else's life—a beating heart, a tiny hand, a delicate and beautiful ear.

When it's time to leave for my lesson, I tiptoe past Grandpa, who is passed out on the couch. "Come on," I whisper to my mother, still planted in the kitchen chair in front of her plate of cold congealing meat. "It's time to go."

She stares ahead at nothing, fork in one hand, in her other a burning cigarette. "Let's go," I say. "It's getting late."

I want stay a little longer today, even though it means coming home in the dark; maybe copy of one of the Audubon prints. Maybe today I will start to sketch the pelican. My mother says nothing; I sit down next to her at the table.

"We should call and tell him we're going to be late," I say. "Should I wait for you? Should I see if Rachel wants to go?"

The clock ticks three o'clock, four o'clock, five. I hold her hand; it is soft and cool. Her fingers are long and slender, and can reach far beyond one octave on the piano. They possess a kind of music I could never play in a million years.

We are frozen at the table in the kitchen, with its white lace curtains stained yellow from smoke and the spindly pathos plant hanging in the win-

dow above the sink. I can hear the sound of a sitcom from the downstairs
TV and my grandma's nervous cackling. Suddenly my mother turns to me,
as if she just noticed I am there. Her voice is devoid of feeling.

"We can't go there anymore."

She has no explanation. I think, could it be just a fleeting fear, one among
many? Maybe she's afraid I'll get kidnapped. Or a cyclone could hit on our
way home. Hadn't she predicted the flood in July? All those fallen trees, the
waters rushing into the streets like the end of the world? My mother warns
me all the time now, about what is coming down the road: *A tree could fall
on your head. A man could rape you. A hurricane could sweep you away.* Should
Rachel chop up more pills in her food? Would that do the trick? But there
are so many Sundays; I'll get the Khachaturian next week or the week after
that. My mother stares right through my face as if I am a ghost and says,
"There are those who wish us dead."

When school starts up after Christmas, my mother announces one day
that a man has been following her. "He's planning to kidnap and rape us. Do
unmentionable things. It's been planned for months now. Don't you know
that the Gestapo is everywhere? Outside the window, beneath your bed?"

She keeps the man's letters in the same drawer where she stores copies of ones she writes to some doctor in Los Angeles. She says he was
her psychiatrist when she first became ill and that he raped her at every
appointment. "This bastard is targeting all three of us," she says. "It's only a
matter of time."

At first I think the letters from my mother's stalker are real, and I'm
frightened. They are full of sexual references to her body and to her "sexy
little girls." But when I examine them more closely, I'm not so sure. They
have my mother's loopy, trembling *m*, her messy sprawl of words when she is
on a downward spiral, the way she signs our report cards right before a trip
to the psych ward. The *t*'s are crossed and the *i*'s are dotted so hard that there
are holes right through the onionskin paper.

"Go to your room; pull the shades down. Stay away from the window.
Someone is watching us. I don't want you to go to school today."

Is that when our mother begins to come into our room late at night when we are deep in our watery dreams? In our grandfather's house, where closed doors are taboo except for his? Where all the locks have been removed, all the keys thrown away? It's so easy to just barge in, flip on a light, and interrogate a small, startled child. *Has a man ever touched you there? Is that sperm on your leg? Are you having sex for money? Why won't you tell me the truth?* Did Rachel and I heave the dresser against the door then, or did that come later, the next year or the next? We huddle beneath thin blue covers as the door creaks open and the light from the hallway pours in. *I am your mother! I have a right to know!*

At night, Rachel climbs into my little bed; we hold hands and tremble. I try to think of all the Audubon birds I know and list them in my head: Painted bunting, swallow-tailed hawk, great cinereous owl, whip-poor-will, the hemlock warbler ... When our mother finally returns to her bed in the basement, I lie awake thinking about Audubon, trekking across America, seeking all those elusive birds. I consider what Mr. Benjamin told me once, how Audubon killed up to a hundred birds at a time to create a perfect picture. When I think of my mother beating her cold white fists against our flimsy door, and how I can't go to my lessons anymore, I don't know whether to kill her or to take her in my arms and sing her to sleep.

Each wintry Sunday leading up to my recital in February, I still got dressed and ready to go. My mother could always change her mind. I tried to practice as much as I could, like Mr. Benjamin had suggested, just in case. He had once told me how difficult it was for Audubon to rally support for his *Birds of North America*. Few believed in him, and most thought he was crazy, his goal out of reach. I envisioned Audubon in the Louisiana bayou with nothing but a shotgun and his paints, surrounded by a labyrinth of brackish waters, interlocked and never-ending. At home, a dark and interminable swamp surrounded us all—my mother's moments of faint lucidity had disappeared, and Grandpa's rages became the norm. The days when our mother seemed to not know whether my sister or I came or went were few and far between. Now she had eyes at the back of her head. And yet, when I sat at the piano or when I drew, I felt a glimpse of something boundless and divine, something Audubon must have found in the forest, at the edge of a bog, on the shore of a vast and shimmering sea.

The day of my recital I woke to the songs of birds—chickadees, juncos, and sparrows, the ones that stay behind, even in winter. I was up before everyone except Ginger, who, like every morning, came running to me to lick my face. Outside my window, the lapis sky was tinged with pink. I packed a sandwich, suited up, and headed out the door. It had rained the day before, but during the night the temperature had dropped. By morning the ground had turned to ice. I plodded slowly across the slippery yard, walked past the tree-lined border separating our yard and the world beyond, and made my way to the woods.

After a couple tries, I found a tree I could climb. I perched on a low sturdy branch glazed with ice. I leaned against the trunk and waited. I don't remember if I thought about my recital that day, but I remember what I drew: a little black-capped chickadee, *Poecile atricapillus*, clinging to the underbelly of a branch. More chickadees arrived and I worked quickly to capture their busy little bodies, their black crowns and throats, their puffy white faces and rusty flanks. They didn't seem to be afraid of me at all. I could have picked one up and held it in my hand if I wanted, but was content to listen to their song: two single notes, low-pitched and slow. I drew until they vanished in one swift sweep up toward the sky.

That February 1972 I turned thirteen, started my period, and kissed a black-haired boy who smelled of wintergreen. I let my hair grow long and kept it wild. On Sundays I shoveled manure at the horse stables in the park in exchange for free rides, and one day I lost my virginity on a fast brown mare while racing through a bumpy field without a saddle. I thought about this secretly in English class, while reading William Blake's *Songs of Innocence*, and drew birds and tigers around the margins of the text. I thought of that liquid feeling of losing time and self while sailing through a meadow; how birds rise up from the grasses with one single *whoosh*; how no one can reach you when you have four strong legs and are galloping toward the horizon. No one can catch you when you are in a tree, minute as a hummingbird beneath a leaf, or on the ice spinning circles around a pond.

I never returned to Mr. Benjamin's. Instead, I bought the Khachaturian at a music store and learned the piece on my own. I would play it my way, right or wrong. And maybe someday, in the distant future, I would walk up to my teacher's big oak door once again.

These were the things I drew after my year with Audubon: red tanagers eating berries on a branch, the great blue heron, the cormorant and quail. I sketched the common birds around me—sparrow, robin, mourning dove, and chickadee—until, after weeks and months of keen observation, they ceased to be common, but rather things of infinite wonder. I drew what surrounded me, and what lay deep in my wildest dreams—a firebird like one from our Russian fairy-tale book, a bird that sings to the lonely and forsaken deep in the heart of the woods. I thought of the firebird when I played the Khachaturian for the recital that never came, and when our mother burst into our rooms late at night. And one night, in a dream, I followed the white pelican. I grew wings and flew from my grandparents' roof over the small square yards of red brick houses and rows of sycamore, buckeye, and pine. I flew back to Mr. Benjamin's quiet house, with its plush carpet of red, his gleaming pianos, his steadfast and magnificent birds. And I kept going—high over Severence Hall, the Art Museum, and lagoon of golden koi and swans, over Terminal Tower and the seedy Flats, the winnowing Cuyahoga, bubbling with petrochemical debris. I kept flying far above the clouds, beyond the dying, smoke-filled city.

Flood

Flooding in streets, awoke to more rain. Went for coffee and toast then out again at four a.m. for the obligatory pie. Fell asleep at motel, thinking I wouldn't mind sitting in on a séance to see if I can plummet something or someone in my subconscious I have never known and should have known, someone from my family perhaps? Then I thought, I wonder how those white birds can fly so far from the lake, and yet are in this area when it rains? These days, one must carry an umbrella wherever one goes.

Woke up today with strong desire to be "home." Memory of three figures sitting on the piano bench—two obscured, one a smiling corpse. If I ever have anything close to a normal life, I might feel like killing myself. I have not found my little Atlas since the flood. I think it was stolen. Why? Why the persistent harassment? Wasn't there something that was going to be done for me? My American College Dictionary was stolen too. I feel toward it as a child feels toward a teddy bear. My reading has been, since the womb, a hodge-podge of letters in a foreign script I have not yet learned. Dream again, this time of Myra who won't obey me and is trying to run away. There are spectators who leave in cars down a rain-drenched street. The White Goddess says: do not go into that part of the forest but I am always in that part of the forest so what can I do? I wish I had a better biography of myself. Will have better memory when I do more drawings. At our first apartment in Cleveland, the girls made drawings for the walls. I remember sitting there alone, not seeing the pictures even though they were in every room. Memory is tricky. Was I projected into the future? I am feeling distance from the old me. You might say I am wrong but I have evidence: shoes with heels I have not worn in years, my music in storage, this endless, pulsing rain.

7

Wing back down the round sleep of waters
. . . tell them it never ends.
Give me peace.

Michael Donaghy, from "Envoi"

The Vigilance of Dolphins

In my palace is a chamber that is hard to find; inside, an endless sea. To enter you must possess the vigilance of dolphins, which sleep with half their brain awake. You must be swift as a fish; possess the heart of a determined young girl. I stand at the threshold of the room and see them just below the surface of a dream—a pair of sleek white dolphins, arcing through deep waters. It's my sister and I, transformed by the hand of some benevolent god, escaping into waves.

There are fleeting pictures in twisted hallways of my palace, improbable stairs, like an Escher print, leading to doors that do not open, rooms too dark to see. This is how the memory of trauma works, how we glimpse forgotten years trapped inside the amygdala, that almond-shaped center of fear in our brain. Years are erased or condensed into hazy snapshots: The three of us moving out of our grandparents' house into a place called the Stuart House on Triskett Road in 1972. The name resonates with Old English aristocracy, but our two-room basement apartment is really a dump. Barely any furniture: cheap plaid couch made of foam where my mother will sleep, smoke, and interrogate us, plastic card table to eat upon, dirty yellow shades, low ceilings, dark walk-in kitchen. In the room where my sister and I sleep in our single bed, there's just room enough to turn around. A torn Degas print pinned to the wall, a child's cheap plastic turntable, a ficus straining toward the sun. An enigmatic self-portrait I will find years later in my mother's storage unit. The only view out the window is the bottom half of people walking back and forth, or cats meowing to get in, or dogs depositing their business behind a bush. And then this picture: My mother shooting a gun off behind the building. Birds scatter, squirrels, chipmunks, a neighbor's dog. Doesn't anyone hear her? Why don't they call the police? Another image flashes by: My mother showing up at a football game looking for my sister and me, calling out our names on the PA at halftime: *Myra, Rachel, come home at once!* My sister, on the field, a pom-pom girl in distress, forcing a smile to cheer her team on while sinking deeper into despair, and me slipping into shadows beneath the bleachers, an invisible cat. Then another picture, repeated many times like a Muybridge print: two girls in perpetual motion, heaving a heavy dresser against their bedroom door to keep their mother out. We have been up all night, vigilant, holding down the fort. *Let me in, let me in! I'm your mother! I have a right to know!* our mother cries, pounding on the door, but what is it she really wants to know? That we have been raped? That we have sex with men for money? She questions us over and over again, the same old thing, it doesn't matter what we say. This could be an interrogation room in some gray cell in East Berlin circa 1955. There is no right answer for someone so ill; there is nothing to make her stop.

※

The year I turned fifteen my mother bought a gun. I had been sifting through her drawers for something, more disturbing letters to that doctor in California, or some other rambling missives to strangers. I'd look for these things and destroy them, as if by ripping them up or setting them on fire on the top of the stove I could delete them forever from my mother's brain. I found the gun in her underwear drawer. Or did my sister find it? Did we find it together? We always worked best as a team.

Our mother said she needed the gun for protection. Protection from whom? I asked. Kidnappers, of course. How could I be so naïve? Patty Hearst, the newspaper baron's daughter, was kidnapped by the Symbionese Liberation Army. They threw her in the trunk of a car. Now they're holding her at gunpoint until their demands are met. What's to stop them from coming here?

I demanded that my mother tell me where she got the gun and why. How could anyone sell a woman so obviously ill a loaded weapon? She finally confessed that she needed it to kill my sister's best friend John. *He's a Nazi. You can tell by his name. John Heilman. Heil Mann,* my mother said. *See? A man who salutes Hitler. It's right in front of your eyes.* My mother could break the secret code for just about anything. *We have to arm ourselves against him,* she said. *Against them all. If I don't protect you girls, who else is going to?*

"Have you shot the gun at anything?" I asked, trying to remain calm.

"Just for target practice."

"What target?" I said. "Where?"

"Outside in back. I shot at a garbage can but missed."

"You could have killed someone—a child, the neighbors, a dog!"

"I know what's what," she said. "You're so naïve. We're Jews. There are those who wish us dead."

My sister became frantic when she found out my mother's plans. What was to stop her from killing all of her friends? What was to stop her from killing us? We took the revolver away from our mother and gave it to our grandma, who took the gun back to the store. She yelled at the owner for selling a firearm to someone who was mentally ill. He gave back our mother's money and apologized. "Sorry isn't good enough," my grandma told him, always more forthright outside the confines of home. "My daughter is a sick person. Anyone can see that. She was going to kill a boy! Who knows what could have happened? You should be ashamed."

After the gun, my mother is hospitalized once again, although she isn't kept in as long as usual. She returns from her two- or three-week incarcerations trembling, inarticulate, and drugged. Which is worse? To lock her up in a place where she is left to sit all day in pajamas, or for us to be locked up in our basement hell, the phone torn from the wall, our mother trying to break into our bedroom late into the night?

When we are forced to commit her, each stay in the psych ward at CPI—Cleveland Psychiatric Institute—seems to be shorter than the last. This is 1974, and for the last ten years, asylums have been releasing more and more patients out into the streets. This had been President Kennedy's revolutionary plan for reforming the nation's shameful treatment of the mentally ill. We would replace our backward state hospital system with newer and better neuroleptic drugs and free comprehensive community care. But for my mother, in 1974, not much has changed. The doctors still pump her with drugs that make her mute, incontinent, and unable to move. They strap her down in restraints and zap her with what she thinks is radiation. She imagines Nazis torturing her. *I will fight until the end,* she thinks. *I will save my girls. There's a reason for everything. A reason poltergeists set fire to my chair. Everything is a sign.* The only change is that they release her before my sister and I have had a chance to catch our breath. The miracle drugs the doctors give her at CPI, first Thorazine, then Haldol, don't seem to help her at all. As for the comprehensive community care, we are still waiting for it to arrive.

When I begin my senior year the fall of '75, my sister leaves for Northwestern University in Evanston, Illinois. The year before, our mother had ripped up all her college acceptance letters but my sister swiftly cleared up that nearly devastating snafu. She is fiercely determined to succeed. What will life be like without her? I am dreadfully sad she is leaving. What if she just disappears; gets tired of all this trouble at home? What if she leaves me too? How heavy is a dresser when you're the only one pushing it against the door? I feel truly on my own. If there is an emergency, it will be up to me to figure things out. My grandmother doesn't want the job anymore. She has enough on her plate these days without having to deal with her daughter Norma who is out of control, now that she's got cataracts, a husband she hates who is sick with cancer, one girl in college, a dog to take care of, a big unruly yard. Since she retired she spends most of her time sitting in front of the TV watching soap operas, sitcoms, detective shows, anything to transport her away. "I'm too tired to deal with this crap," she informs me. "She's your responsibility now."

There is a picture from that time, after my sister leaves home. It lurks in some subaqueous place in my brain: My mother grabbing my arm and squeezing hard, trying to pull me away from the front door. I push her back; she falls against the red plaid couch littered with ashtrays and plates of old food. Everything falls to the dirty shag-carpeted floor. She comes at me, fists flying; I push her back again.

I remember the catalyst: me wanting to go out that night with a boy named Jerry from my school. Jerry wants to be a minister or a gospel singer or an artist. He comes from hardship too, but what kind I don't really know. Something sad from when he and his parents lived down South, before they all found Jesus. When I'm at his house, we make out in his room but never get far. We are both saving ourselves for marriage, and besides, we can hear Milly, his mother, in the kitchen cooking and singing gospel songs and hymns. Jerry's mom, perfect hair and smile, always baking or sewing clothes, arranging flowers in a vase. His chain-smoking dad, Roy, stout and good-natured, loves to talk about how Jesus, once crucified, rose gloriously from the dead. All three believe in miracles.

My mother is enraged that I want to date a boy, especially a born-again Christian. She says I am only sixteen and calls me *jailbait*. "You aren't going anywhere with that Jesus freak. You're staying right here. We have a lot to discuss."

For the last couple weeks I have been staying with her every evening after school and on weekends because she doesn't want to be alone, now that it's just the two of us. I've had to take off work from Higbee's Department Store and call in sick at the Cleveland Play House dinner theater where I work weekend nights. If I don't get out of our apartment I will explode.

My mother rises up off the couch and narrows her eyes. "Now sit down and answer my questions."

"I am leaving whether you like it or not," I say.

She lights a cigarette and takes a quick puff. "Over my dead body."

"You can't stop me."

"I'm your mother! You must obey!"

In our stifling living room, I have no miracles up my sleeve and little faith in salvation. I make a move to put on my coat. My mother reaches out to grab my hair.

I run to the walk-through kitchen. On the stove is a pan of burnt chicken legs, black little things, inedible and shriveled up. The air smells like sour milk and trash; the sink is black with cigarette ashes.

"I'm calling the police," I say, and sneak a small carving knife from a drawer into the back pocket of my jeans.

"I'll tear the phone out if you do. You stay put or else."

"I need to get out of this place or I'll go nuts."

"What are you planning?" she asks. "Who are you really going to see?"

"I told you a hundred times. I'm going to see Jerry."

"Who are his associates? I want you to sit down right now and make a list, names and numbers, addresses too."

"I'm warning you," I say. "Leave me alone or else."

"Don't tell me what to do!" she shouts. "I'm your mother!"

I walk to the door but my mother beats me to it. She locks the deadbolt and stands arms crossed, blocking my way. There is no moving her. "All right," I say, pretending to comply. "Let's sit down and talk."

My mother glares at me, then finally returns to the couch. She lights up another cigarette. "Let's start with that boy. That Jerry, if that *is* his real name. No more boys from faith-healing families. It's going to be a whole new ball game around here."

"I thought you liked Jerry."

"Don't question my authority. Just do as I say."

She starts in again; she can't help herself: *Did a man ever touch you down there, is your sister a whore, are you menstruating, has someone stolen your womb?* I am always trying to be calm, to be passive and invisible, but this time something snaps a little inside. I need to get out of there, even if it's only an hour or two. I rise from my chair and pull out the knife I had slipped in my pocket. I would never harm her; I just want to scare her off until I can back out of the door. She throws herself on me; suddenly she wants the knife. She is pure

adrenaline and fire; so am I. Her lit cigarette drops onto the carpet; we could
both go up in smoke, this place, the street, but I don't care anymore, I just
want a little bit of peace. I grab her wrist that reaches for the knife.

"Stop, you're hurting me," she pleads.

I tell her that I will kill myself if she doesn't let me leave. I tell her that's
why I got the knife. I'm not serious, for I have never been suicidal, but I want
to scare her into stopping. Her response startles me. She picks up the phone
and dials the hospital, while I run to the bedroom. She tells the intake nurse
at CPI to prepare a bed for her daughter, who is mentally ill and wants to
take her own life. I use the old dresser trick once again, blocking the door. In
this moment, it seems fortuitous that we live in a basement, with a window
opening right onto the street.

My mother is still on the phone when I open the window and screen,
climb out, and run down Triskett Road. She doesn't even know that I am
gone. I don't have time to bring a thing—a jacket, a purse, my books for
school. I run down the road in the chill autumn air till I come to a gas station
and call Jerry with a dime I always keep in the pocket of my pants. There is
always a dollar in my shoe.

The next day, Roy, Jerry's father, is talking to my mother on the phone. "No,
Norma, we won't let her come back until you get help. Your daughter is fine.
She can stay here as long as she likes." He is kind to her, not condescending.
But he is stubborn, unwilling to take me home if she is still there. He tells
her that if she shows up at their house, he will call the police.

For some reason, she backs down. Maybe she is afraid that I'll never
come back. I don't want to go home. Why would I? Milly, Jerry's mom, is
making me a new set of clothes: a ruffled gray skirt that falls to the floor,
a frilly gray-and-white-striped blouse. I look like a Victorian mission-
ary in my new clothes, feminine and prim. Jerry's mom helps me to make
French braids; puts fancy clips in my hair. She cooks sit-down meals of fried
chicken, mashed potatoes, and peas. At Jerry's house there is always milk,
and cereal in the cupboard, and in the bathroom there are fresh clean towels.
The three of them pray before supper, "Thank you, Jesus, for your great and

wonderful gifts," while we hold hands and smile, then tuck in to our meal. After supper Jerry takes me up to his room and we listen to music: bluegrass, gospel, and Christian rock. His attic bedroom is huge, the ceiling pointing up like a steeple. On his knotty pine walls are his paintings, portraits of homeless men, old women standing alone in sad, rainy streets. People he wants to help someday. How long do I stay there? Days? Weeks? I won't go back until my mother checks herself into the hospital. It's the only deal I'll cut with her. She tells me on the phone that I am like Patty Hearst, who fell in love with her captors.

∾

I don't remember how my mother ends up back at the hospital. Maybe she agrees to check herself in or maybe my grandmother reluctantly commits her. My grandma hates to make the call. What if the neighbors hear about it? After all these years, she's still afraid what people will think. While my mother is gone, I live in the apartment by myself. I pay the rent with money I make at Higbee's and the theater, and my grandmother helps out too. I cook for myself, clean the place up; even have friends over a few times. My friends from school think it's cool that I have my own apartment. They look longingly at the pool with the cheap concrete patio out back, the tiny kitchenette inside our claustrophobic flat, the coin-operated washers and dryers down the hall with little boxes of powdered soap in machines, the ultramodern avocado-colored everything. "I wish we didn't have to live in a stupid old house," one friend says. "Some people have all the luck."

When my mother is gone I get busy. I work on my portfolio and fill out college applications for the following year. I work extra hours at Higbee's so I can save as much money as I can. Rachel reminds me on the phone that when the time comes, I *will* get out. I'll have my own place, far away, just like her.

One warm spring weekend while my mother is still at CPI, Jerry picks me up and tells me he has a surprise. He says we are going on a picnic but he won't tell me where. After we head out of the city, he stops the car and ties a red bandanna around my eyes. "You can't look until we get there," he says. Jerry has packed a basket of food, a blanket to spread on the grass somewhere, and I know once we get there he will sing, and when Jerry sings it's the most beautiful sound in the world.

His car has a sunroof, so I stick my head out to feel the wind. It's like when I was five and wore the black patch over my eye, pretending to be blind, only this time I feel safe and happy with Jerry by my side, my mother far away. It feels like I'm in a boat on the sea, all that wind in my face and hair. I promise myself that someday I will see the ocean. I will sail out so far that I won't even be able to see any land and then I will jump right in. Below me will be fish and dolphins and whales, and above, the clearest blue sky. If my mother saw me with that bandanna she would think I had been kidnapped, but she isn't here and I try not to think of her. Jerry takes me down winding roads; opens up all the windows. We are laughing, exuberant, and free. Suddenly the road gets bumpy; we are driving on dirt. "Okay," he says, "we are almost there. Hold on." He slows down; the tires roll onto grass, then stop. "You can look now."

We are in the biggest meadow I have ever seen. Surrounding us are wildflowers and hills, houses in the distance, a herd of grazing cows. Above is a vast azure sky. "Where are we?" I ask. "Amish country," says Jerry. No, I think. This isn't any country; this is heaven. Heaven is a sea of grass, the longest day in the world, and no one to answer to; it is guilt lifted for an afternoon, it is a boy singing, and a girl closing her eyes to listen for a while, to breathe and to rest.

Later, back at the apartment, my grandma calls to tell me that my mother is coming home. When she arrives she is shaken to her bones—slurred speech, trembling hands, eyes glazed, full of sleep and fear. I know it is only a matter of time before the cycle begins again. But this time, something feels different. The system is changing; I am changing, and in a year I will be leaving home for good. This time, my mother's return is the beginning of a new kind of knowledge, different from when Medusa first emerged. I feel in my bones that my mother will always be sick. She might have a week or two of some semblance of normalcy. Maybe even a month. But she will forever be spinning in some dangerous orbit, knife in hand, and if I'm not careful, I will forever be that small child frozen behind the wall. At sixteen, I vow to hold on to beauty, no matter what—to sitting in a rich carpet of grass, a concert hall, a museum full of art—in a place that has nothing to do with the unbearable glare of grief.

In my palace, in a chamber below, I glance back to see my mother across the room pacing, waiting for me to swim back and save her. I can barely make her out, but she is there, a she-wolf moving toward me in sleep, over water, over shore, pulling me into her den. She wanders without love or shelter, ever hungry, waiting for my return. And I am forever a dolphin in blue sleepless waves, swimming toward a distant fathomless light.

Something is Missing

Now, after everything else, something is missing. Apparently, someone comes into my storage room every day to make my life miserable. Recently I had to glue Myra's little horse together. Someone had broken its leg. I am trying hard to come out of their "spell" but they even bid on stolen dreams. It may well have been planned when I was of the age of infancy although I never was an infant any more than I was a child. Do they really die, or do they just metal horse into another costume? The question really is: are they of this planet? There may be those in their world who also suffered wrongdoing, I would not deny that, but I am and will continue to be concerned only with Norma, that is Baby Norma, as I am a baby who has known its bones at birth and a baby who thinks ahead of her time and hopes to be allotted the time of biology and its accompanying changes. They have no knowledge of appearance as they are hideously ugly and an attractive, healthy appearance is only a commodity to them so they can kidnap you and exchange you for someone else. I know how fast they can move when motivated. Do not curse them while walking, even in thought. Be a good girl, Norma. Rest. Study. Stay calm. Keep hate and rage below. Think of all your nursey rhymes. Stay alert. Remember to replace stolen cane, stolen thoughts. Dress warm. I am my own mother.

8

Come away, O human child! To the woods and waters wild.

W. B. Yeats, "The Stolen Child"

Changelings

"Mother, when were you the happiest?"

"When you girls were babies."

"Why was that?"

"Because you were all mine."

"And what was I like as a baby?"

"You were very, very good."

"How was I good?"

"You never cried once."

There's a room inside my palace you need to break a spell to enter. In the middle of the room is a small wooden table. Perched on the table is a white dove; beside it is the head of a porcelain doll. The doll's head is a prop from a short film I made years ago. In it, a madwoman believes her infant has been stolen and a changeling has been left in its place.

It is 1980, and after two years of college in Michigan, I am living in Chicago, going to art school. My mother lives with my grandparents in the old house on 148th Street; my sister is out of school and working in Seattle. I live in a huge loft with my roommate Amy and six pet doves in an old converted warehouse called the Paulina Building. Our neighborhood in Wicker Park, just northwest of downtown, is a mix of Polish bakeries, Mexican apothecaries, and dilapidated brownstones with men who sit on stoops and sing as I pass by: *Que bonito culo! Tienes tetas bonitas!* At night, our bleak and gritty corner of Milwaukee and Paulina pulses just below the surface. You can hear the *thumpety-thump* from boom boxes and cars below, gunshots and screeching tires, sirens, breaking glass, and sometimes, late at night, a foreboding silence.

Amy and I are both twenty-one and go to the School of the Art Institute of Chicago. We work part-time at Matsumoto's, a Japanese art repair studio downtown, where we paint mended antiques. I also help a quadriplegic artist some evenings to put myself through school. Amy and I split next to nothing to live on the Paulina Building's top floor, with easy access to the roof. To have so much studio space is worth the gangs and muggings in the neighborhood, the two-shower bathroom that all eight floors have to share, the rickety elevator that rarely works, the neighborhood fires, the cockroaches and occasional rats, the break-ins, and the fact that we are renting a nearly condemned building from slumlords. Everyone covets our place.

It's late February, the week of Carnival and my twenty-first birthday, and a costume party is just getting started. Amy is dressed as the Virgin Mary, auburn hair flowing down below the waist of her bright blue gown she has covered with tiny plastic babies and glittering stars. I wonder what my old Catholic and born-again neighbors in Cleveland would think if they came to our party—the Virgin Mary in one corner, the devil in another, everyone else dancing, getting drunk, and making out.

Amy stands close to the wall so she can plug herself in; her halo and dress draped with Christmas lights twinkle on and off in time to the music. The year before, for Halloween, Amy had been a galaxy, before that the Arc de Triomphe. Next year she wants to be the Eiffel Tower lit up at night. Her costumes always involve large pieces of cardboard, movable parts, and electricity. Her bearded date, Saint Francis of Assisi, has also plugged himself into the wall so his tape recorder, hidden below his burlap robe, can play Gregorian chants all night long. I am a cross between Audrey Hepburn in *Breakfast at Tiffany's* and G.I. Joe—broad-brimmed hat tipped over one eye, a little black dress, and combat boots with steel-enforced toes. Perched on my shoulder, a nervous white dove.

In the center of the room, part of which Amy uses as her studio, is an old claw-foot bathtub filled with ice and beer. Shortly after we moved in, I had pulled a dead rat out of the drain. When I told my mother about it on the phone, she warned me: *I told you rats eat your face off at night. You better move right away.* When the phone rings I always jump to answer it. I leap at the slightest sound, thinking it's an emergency and I'm the only one who can perform triage. I'm not really afraid of her hurting me but of her harming herself. Who knows when the voices might tell her to go to the window, open her arms to the world, and fly?

Since I left Cleveland four years before, my life still revolves around her roller-coaster cycles. There are days when I don't hear from her. But things always escalate over three or four weeks until the calls starting coming ten to twenty times a day. When the phone rings in the middle of the night I'm sure everyone in the building can hear it. The walls are paper-thin, and someone is always up. The building buzzes with people making art or movies or installations. On the first floor is a painter; on two is a sculptor; above him is a performance artist who choreographs dances inside canoes. There are the animators on six, painters, photographers, filmmakers on four, five, and seven. Can any of them hear my mother talking to me? Can they hear her ask me if I have sperm on my legs, aliens in my bed, a surgically removed womb?

Ever since I left home in '76 and she moved back in with my grandparents, my mother has been getting steadily worse. Even though she goes to the occasional "recovery meeting" at the community mental health center they finally built in the neighborhood. She learns little phrases she says to herself to keep her head above water: *Pat yourself on the back. Do something constructive every day. Take baby steps and soon you'll walk a mile.* It does help, especially the cooking classes she takes now and then, and the arts-and-crafts workshop where she learns how to make wallets and small things out of clay. She sees a social worker there, and a doctor for free who gives her prescriptions she rarely ever fills. But how much does it help? There's talk of shutting the center down anyway, now that Reagan is in power. The last time my mother had a setback it was very bad. She took the bus to Chicago and barged into the plant store I was working at over the summer to tell me that a friend of mine was planning to choke me to death with a rope. She started screaming in front of customers and I got fired on the spot. How long before she shows up at the art repair studio where I work, at school, or at the house of one of my friends? When she asks for phone numbers and addresses, I give them to her right away. I am hardwired to tell the truth and obey.

Our flat is swiftly filling up with monsters, furry beasts, and devils, vampires, and fantastical birds. I watch a couple in orange jump suits and gorilla masks climb up the ladder to a cubbyhole in the wall and disappear. I can't tell who they are or their sexes, but they seem to be in a hurry. Nearby, in front of a tall window, are steps leading up to a platform with two love seats. Bill, the shy sweet graduate student I've been dating, is drinking a beer with a friend. I feel ambivalent about Bill; his Catholic upbringing makes him feel guilty about sex and he is always afraid I will get pregnant. Surprisingly, my mother likes him even though he's not a Jew, and believes he is going to be famous someday. She wants us to get married and sends us little domestic hints: a set of sheets, dish towels, a frying pan, a clock. *When are you going to make me a grandmother?* she asks. *I hope your womb wasn't taken out when you were sleep.*

I shout hello across the room to Bill. His shoulders are slumped, his shirt buttoned right up to his chin, even though our place is hot from all the dancing bodies. Bill reminds me of the boys from St. Mel's, the Catholic school on Triskett; always that look of shame in his eyes, like he's just done something wrong. I wonder if I have the same guilty look too, from choosing not to stay home to take care of my mother.

I need a break from the people and the noise, so I head to my studio, a large high-ceilinged room off a long narrow hall. In the doorway, a giant male fairy with butterfly wings is lighting the cigarette of a waiflike girl dressed in black. She looks like a French gamine, a little on the elfish side. Pixie hairdo, tiny turned-up nose.

"You guys all set for beer?" I ask.

"Yeah," says the gamine. "We're cool."

"Great. See you later."

"Wait a second," she says. "There's some belly dancer looking for a baby. You might want to check it out. She says the baby is sick."

"A baby? Sure. I'll check it out."

"See you later," the male fairy and gamine say in unison then walk out into the hall to mingle.

I sit down at my drafting table. What's this business about a baby? I don't know anyone with children. What kind of person brings a baby to a party like this? Suddenly the phone rings. I lurch across the table to grab it. I know that it's her, or it could be my grandma, calling me to say my grandpa is dead. His cancer has ravaged his body after four years. He is so frail that he sleeps most of the time, and never raises his voice. He doesn't even complain when my mother makes long-distance calls throughout the day to check up on her girls.

It's my mother and she's frantic. "Stop whatever you are doing *right now*," she says. "This is a matter of life and death."

"What's wrong?"

"I just got off the phone with your sister in Seattle," my mother says. "She told me you are going out there in the spring to go on some camping trip. She said you bought ... *a backpack*."

"I know. You gave me the money for it for my birthday."

"Listen. Do as I say. Very carefully, now, I want you to go to your room. Slowly place the backpack in its original box. No—wait. Better yet, is Bill there?"

"No, he's not."

"All right. Don't panic. This is what you do. Call Bill and ask him to put the backpack in the box and close it up tight. Then he is to take it back to the store where you purchased it and return it right away. That contraption is dangerous."

"What's dangerous?"

"The backpack. The straps could strangle you. You could get killed on a deserted road. There's no telling what could happen, wearing a thing like that."

"You've got to be kidding."

"This is no joking matter. Is Bill there now? Put him on the phone."

"No, Mother, I told you he's not."

"What's all that noise in the background? Are there men over there? Who are your associates? What the hell is going on?"

"I'm watching a show on TV. It's late. Can we talk about this some other time?"

"You better take care of this first thing in the morning. Promise me you won't touch the pack. You'll keep it in the box. Have Bill take it back. He's a man. He'll know what to do."

"Okay," I say. "I promise."

"And honey?"

"Yes?"

"I love you."

"I know you do. I love you too."

I hang up and feel drained. For every hundred calls from her, there are only one or two that possess some semblance of normalcy, but a detached normalcy, as if she is acting a part in a play. When she isn't interrogating me, she sounds small and very far away. And then there are rare moments when the wit and genius she was born with shine through, when she makes a brilliant remark about a piece of music or a book, or she tells me some dark and clever joke. It's then that I forget she is terribly ill. I romanticize her illness; she is my Zelda Fitzgerald, my eccentric and capricious mother, my tormented, talented muse.

What new terrors will she have tomorrow, and the next day, and the day after that? The year before she bought me a heating pad, then made me send it back for fear I would burn to death in my sleep. Now she thinks a backpack will strangle me. I imagine an animated movie of a backpack coming alive, growing in size, and terrorizing a city. I remember what my grandmother always says, "You have to laugh to keep from crying." I can't wait to tell my sister about the Killer Backpack. She will most likely turn it into a funny scene in a play.

———

At the party, a chubby guy in a pink ball gown and tiara comes into the room and asks in a loud slurred voice, "Hey, you got a baby in there? There's some chick in a bikini looking for a baby," then stumbles back out into the hall. Most of the people at the party are drunk or on the way to being there; I barely drink and don't take drugs. Tonight I will sip one beer all night long and nothing more. You never know what can happen when you lose control—you might have to rescue someone in the middle of the night or, worse, Medusa might show up at your door.

I should go look for that baby, but sometimes I get tired of being Florence Nightingale or Joan of Arc on a swift white horse. Let someone else save the day for once. What kind of mother loses a baby in someone else's home, anyway? I wish everyone would leave so I could draw. It seems that every time I throw a party, halfway through I just want to disappear.

On my wall behind my drafting table are sketches from my drawing class and a storyboard for a short film I am making at school. I love being in art school, love the freedom of working late at night in the editing room after most students have gone home. There's no phone in the room; no one knows I'm even there.

My film is a surreal tale about a woman locked up in an attic who believes she is at the North Pole. She imagines that her child has been kidnapped and a broken doll left in its place. For one of the scenes, I filled a room with shattered safety glass and hundreds of tiny white lights to make it look like glimmering ice. Everything in the film radiates—the actors have lights strapped to their bodies beneath gossamer robes; there are lights hidden inside flowers, furniture, and the corners of rooms. I am trying to capture the radiance of the lily I remember from childhood, and my grandfather's church lit by candlelight at midnight mass.

Across the wall from the storyboard hangs a painted scroll, a profile of a young girl. The signature at the bottom reads, *Lee Godie, French Impressionist.* I bought the canvas scroll a few months before from a homeless woman I met across the street from the art museum. The woman approached me and asked, "You want to buy a painting? I'm better than Cézanne." It was warm outside, but she was wearing a big scruffy coat.

She opened up her coat like a watch thief, revealing two pictures attached with safety pins: a woman with a rose between her teeth, and a man with a pencil-thin mustache. She held a bundle of paintings in the crook of her arm. I noticed that the woman had two big orange circles painted on each cheek, thick blue eye shadow, and very few teeth; above her real eyebrows she had painted two jet-black fake ones. "I'm Renoir's daughter," she said. "I'm sure you've heard of me—Lee Godie, French Impressionist, a friend to Cézanne."

This woman could be my mother in the future—she could even be me if I didn't watch out. What would it take for that to happen, to transform into a woman with layers of coats? The loss of friends, my job? Dropping out of school to take care of my mother? Somewhere, long ago, this woman might have had a mother who sang her to sleep, a father who lifted her into the air.

The woman set her bundle down and unrolled one of the paintings she had been holding, a portrait of a woman and a bird. "Here's one for you," she said. "She's a beauty queen, a Gibson Girl. Fifteen dollars. I call her *The Queen of the Night.*"

The party outside my room is getting louder. Someone has put on a Talking Heads tape and turned up the volume. I'm about to go dance when the phone rings yet again.

"Myra, is that you?"

"Mother—it's too late to call."

"What are you doing up?"

"I'm trying to sleep."

"What's all that commotion? Is that really the TV or do you have men over there? Have you talked to Bill about the situation?"

"What situation?"

"The backpack. I dozed off and had a dream that you were strangled to death by the straps. You have to do something about this right away. It can't wait till tomorrow."

"Please let me go to sleep."

"Promise you'll take care of it right away."

"I promise. I'll get Bill to return the pack, just let me sleep."

"Don't touch anything. He'll know what to do."

"Good night, Mother. I'm hanging up now."

"Wait a minute. Don't brush me off. We need to talk."

"We'll talk in the morning. Good night."

"I have to come see you. We need to discuss some things. I don't want to talk about them over the phone. It could be tapped."

"I really need to sleep now."

"What are you hiding from me?"

"Nothing. Please. We'll talk first thing in the morning."

"Maybe I should come there now. I could take the night bus and be there in the morning. We could go to IHOP and get pancakes and eggs."

"I have school on Monday. We'll talk in the morning. We'll figure out a time for you to come."

"I need to know one thing. Are you and Bill having sex?"

"Mother!"

"Do you know about birth control? Have you ever seen a condom?"

"I'm hanging up right now."

"I'm your mother. I have a right to know."

"Good night."

"Honey, please don't be mad. We just have things to discuss. I'll call you tomorrow. Promise you'll tell Bill about the pack."

"I promise. Now good night."

After I hang up the phone, a shroud of dread slips over me. Is she heading downhill again? Today it's a strangling backpack and a disappearing womb—what will tomorrow bring?

Years later, my mother will carry a backpack of her own. On a park bench, somewhere in the city, she will wake up at dawn, pull her dirty blue blanket over her shoulders, and take out her journal to write:

Happy Mother's Day. Wish I were home, or other. Early a.m. lapse of memory for Baby Norma, sleeping on hard bench. More heavy rain. Need to find a better place to snooze. I am feeling very calm today, despite my des-

peration. My enemies must have sprayed me with something. In the future,
I'd like to obtain a bacteria resistant Batman type mask to prevent further
infection. Last night in my dream I saw another person I identified as from
another planet. They were trying to replace me with someone else. At times
like this, I think it would be a good thing to learn, memorize and draw all
of the state birds of North America.

In my studio, I contemplate whether or not to unplug the phone. There's always the chance of my mother calling the local police if I do. She's done it before. She could tell them that I was being raped. I decide to leave it plugged in. I get up to join the party and notice the gamine, standing near the door.

"Some guy just let all your birds out of the cage. I thought you should know."

"Oh, crap," I say. "I better go get them."

"Have you found that lost baby yet?"

"I'm not really looking that hard," I say. "I think someone made the story up."

"Well, good luck. With your birds, I mean. And the baby."

I'd like to have a baby someday, maybe even two, but after my art career is doing well. The last time we talked on the phone my sister said she wanted to get her tubes tied. She's afraid if she has a child it will become schizophrenic. I suppose I should be worried too, but for some reason I'm not. I know some families can be happy. The Armstrongs across the street from my grandparents were. Cathy's family was. Jerry's too, or so it seemed. But then, there is always my mother. How safe would that be, to have a child whose grandma hears voices and carries a knife?

A baby, I think. Lost. Here in our strange cavernous loft. There must be some mistake. And all those birds flying around, hiding in the corners of rooms, ready to swoop down on unsuspecting guests, and the monsters, the fairies, the gorillas in jumpsuits, that would terrify anyone, especially a child.

In the kitchen, I search for the lost birds. I spy one of them perched on top of our red refrigerator. I reach up slowly to grab it, my hands formed into a cup.

Behind me, someone says, "Has anyone seen my baby?" The woman pronounces the word *baby* like *beh-BAY*. "My ba-*bay*," she says again. "I'm looking for my ba-*bay*. Have you seen it, *oui* or *non*?"

The woman is beautiful, but looks as if she is sleepwalking. She wears a shimmering bikini top, a G-string, red stilettos, and a skirt of translucent scarves. It's a Moroccan friend of a friend of Amy's who I heard was coming. The belly dancer is extremely high.

"Where did you leave it?" I ask.

"If I knew that, I'd know where my ba-*bay* was, wouldn't I?"

The woman and her scarves float out of the room. So it was true. A baby has gone missing, or maybe it was stolen, like the old Celtic stories about changelings. How could someone leave a baby and not remember where she put it? Someone taps my shoulder. I turn around. It's the gamine again.

"So I've been thinking about that baby," she says. "You should check the room with the coats. I thought I heard something in there, like a little cry."

Amy's bed is stacked high with coats, hats, and scarves, all sorts of winter things. I start tossing stuff off the bed: jackets, purses, backpacks, portfolios, sketchbooks, socks and shoes. My mother left me at the museum, at the grocery store, at the movies. I could have easily been taken and lost forever. But at least my mother had an excuse—she was sick. What's wrong with this belly-dancing fool?

From somewhere on the bed, I hear a small muffled sound. I claw wildly at the coats. Where is she? *She.* How do I know it's a girl? I just do. And then I see her little face, deep down in the pile, peacefully wedged between two leather coats. She yawns and opens her eyes, smiles up at me, and says—*ga.* Somehow, miraculously, no one had tossed a coat over her head, or a heavy bag. There is just a light wool scarf across her soft sleeping body. I lift her up and hold her to my chest. Her tiny fingers grasp a strand of my hair. She spits goo onto my Holly Golightly dress. The baby gurgles with delight.

"Hello," I say. "Welcome back."

I walk through the crowd of masked dancers in search of her mother, my fugitive birds forgotten, the small infant warm against my chest.

"I found her," I announce to anyone within earshot. "I found the baby."

A couple friends from school give me a thumbs-up.

Amy and St. Francis are dancing to James Brown, their electric cords dangling behind them like black monkey tails. The gamine is French-kissing an unmasked female gorilla on the love seat. Bill has gone home without saying goodbye. I hold the infant close, her sleepy face nestled against my beating heart. She seems a little feverish but doesn't cry.

"The baby was buried under a pile of coats," I explain to Darth Vader and a couple vampires smoking in the hallway. "I'm looking for her mother. Have you seen her? I think she was going this way."

I Am Still Waiting

I once had a little brick house. Inside was a piano and my mother's collection: Royal Doulton figurines, white porcelain ladies without faces, a blue boy and pink girl kissing beneath an umbrella, a rabbit with a broken ear. All those teacups from China. Where are they now? Must make an inventory of what I have lost. I'm now staying in a shelter run by Jesus People. There are crucifixes in every room but there is nothing expected of you otherwise. They did ask me recently if I believed in Jesus Christ and I said no, I have a goal instead. To end the persecution I've had to restore my home. On the bright side, Myra sent me a letter with a museum calendar of Matisse. The calendar is full of red houses, blue flowers and green ladies. If I had had another life as the person I was supposed to become, I'd go to France and sit at a red table and look out the window at blue and green waves. Someone who wasn't in hiding would serve me cheese Danishes and coffee without arsenic. About what happened in 1990, my daughter writes to say that I was diagnosed with schizophrenia and that I sold the house myself. I then projected a thought to her that went something like this: "There was someone in the family who was diagnosed schizophrenic, but it was a mistake. This was mother's nephew and I believe that the diagnosis was to cover up the fact that he was interned in a prisoner of war camp as a young man." I also projected a thought about my leg embolism and the persistent problem of vision loss, and that I wanted her to come home. I am still waiting.

9

Every collection is a theater of memories, a dramatization and a mise-en-scéne of personal and collective pasts, of a remembered childhood and of remembrance after death.

Philipp Blom, *To Have and to Hold: An Intimate History of Collectors and Collecting*

The Museum of Indelible Things

Up a set of stairs and down a dark hall, I hurry to a small locked room. I turn the key; the door swings opens. In the corner of the room sits an old oak cabinet, shelves lined with fossils, minerals, and stones. The cabinet is the illusion of order, the capture of pandemonium and time: drawers of bird bones and speckled eggs, a shaman's mask, the jawbone of an ancient horse, each neatly placed and labeled. In the bottom drawer is a symmetrical arrangement of specimens—red coral and butterflies, insects, seashells, and snakes. In the center, among the dead things, my grandmother's most treasured antique: a delicate pink teacup from China, a crack running down its thin gold rim.

After our grandfather died in 1980, Grandma loaded up the white Chevy with all of his guns, drove to Lake Erie, and tossed them all in. Then she drove to the carpet store. She bought wall-to-wall white shag carpeting, like the pictures she envied in *House Beautiful*, and had it installed right up to the toilet on the second-floor bathroom. For chairs, several colonial knockoffs followed, then a big garish couch and color TV. Why not add to her little porcelain collection too? An antique plate or two, a turn-of-the-century teacup, a slender white deer. It's been years since she's bought a thing for herself. "Someday, I'll give these all to you," she says. My mother says: *You are my most precious possession*. Neither of them told my sister or me about our grandfather's death, or the death of my old dog, Ginger, that swiftly followed, until two weeks after the fact. They never explained why we weren't invited to the funeral at Saint Theodosius, or his memorial steak lunch at Ponderosa that Grandpa, in his will, insisted should happen in his honor. I was heartbroken when they told me about Ginger, but as for my grandfather, I felt relieved. He had made everyone miserable for so many years, and now that he wasn't around, Rachel and I could finally talk to our grandma about what to do with our mother. Should we try to get her into a group home? We'd have to get her on a waiting list, since there were so few around. Since Reagan's massive cuts to social services, many mental health programs had closed down. Rumor had it that my mother's recovery center was next. Where, then, was my mother supposed to go?

In 1986 my mother begins the year by waving a butcher knife around at Boston's Logan Airport. The story makes national news: "Woman with Knife Threatens Travelers." Later, she tells me she was on her way to California to kill the doctor whom she said had raped her, but her ticket was bound for Boston, where my sister is living at the time, not L.A. My sister is convinced that our mother was on her way to kill her. I tell her that our mother must have believed she was protecting her from some imaginary harm; my sister isn't convinced. Hadn't our mother shown up at her apartment in Seattle the year before? Didn't she try to choke her on the street? Hire a private investigator to track her every move? And how did she get the money to do that? Is she stealing from our grandma now? What is going on in the house on West 148th?

Our grandmother, at eighty, is now our mother's reluctant and resentful watchdog. In the six years since Grandpa's death, we still have not had a reasonable conversation with her about our mother's tenuous future. And each year, our mother's condition gets worse. Whenever Rachel and I broach the subject, our grandma becomes irate: "You girls just want my money." She hates to be interrupted when she's sitting in her comfy chair, a bowl of chocolate ice cream on her lap, her new border collie, Lassie, sleeping at her feet: "*Marcus Welby's* on," she snarls. "Can't you see I'm watching my show?"

We tell Grandma that if she got sick or died, our mother, who has no savings or trust fund, no legal guardian sanctioned by the court to help her, could become homeless. Neither of us wants the job, and besides, Rachel and I both live out of state. But why should our grandma listen? Hasn't she had enough disappointment, enough drama and grief? "Leave me in peace," she says. "Who the hell are you to tell me what is what? You girls barely come home anymore."

When my grandmother does feel like talking about our mother, it's clear she just needs someone to lend an ear. "What a life," she says, sighing heavily into the phone. "You girls don't know what I have here." I listen as she tells me what it's like to live with a person who smokes all day in bed, sets chairs on fire, and who believes her heart is being monitored by Nazis. "We can do something," I say. "What a life," she says again. "Can't a person have a little peace?"

When I talk to my mother about her future, she insists that I move back home. "You're the only one around here who can fix things," she says. I change the subject and remind her to keep her doctor's appointments, maybe try a new medication he might suggest. "All he does is hand out prescriptions for cyanide," she says, "and besides, why should I listen to a guy who weighs five hundred pounds? You call me crazy? I can still fit into a size eight."

છ

On the surface, my life in Chicago in 1986 is a sharp contrast to the chaos in the red brick house on West 148th Street. I share a spacious three-bedroom apartment on a quiet tree-lined street in Irving Park with two women who are out of the country for most of the year. A gallery in New York is interested in representing me, I have art shows on the horizon, a wide circle of friends, and a handsome Italian boyfriend whom I adore. But underneath there is a growing sense of disorder and decay. A couple of my friends are tremendously needy and suffer from clinical depression and intense mood swings. Another should be in AA. I can't seem to stop myself from getting overly involved, ending up in the middle of someone else's melodrama, just like I did as a child. My relationship with Agostino is also wrought with strife, with me fervently pressing him for a future promise he just can't provide.

My sense of stability comes from making art and working in museums. I cobble together several part-time jobs but my salvation and sanctuary is the Field Museum of Natural History. I teach about the Arctic, ancient Egypt, and other lands I dreamed of traveling to when I was small. I also do odd jobs for the Department of Education, like order supplies for classes: owl pellets, ladybugs, feathers, preserved invertebrates, and seeds. I don't have an office, so I share a lab with other freelance educators and naturalists. The lab is quiet and ordered, with shelves lined with stuffed birds and mammals, drawers of insects and butterflies, bird skulls, microscopes, and specimens in jars.

On my breaks at work, I roam the upstairs halls. Behind the public displays and dioramas, the Field is a labyrinth of wonders: in the Division of Birds, I peruse long flat drawers of bird bones and little stuffed bodies carefully classified and tagged. The Division of Mammals contains a sea of cabinets filled with skulls and small furry corpses; in Botany, hundreds of fragile plant specimens, labeled in faded ox gall. Who knew the world could possess so many types of beetles and snakes, butterflies, barnacles, and shells?

Carl Linnaeus introduced a system of classification upon which all natural history was built. He divided the universe of living things into seven categories: kingdom, phylum, class, order, family, genus, and species. I remember the sequence by repeating a mnemonic device I learned when I was twelve: *K*-ing *P*-hilip *C*-ame *O*-ver *F*-or *G*-randma's *S*-oup. At the Field, I am happy and content, living inside Linnaeus's methodical, beating heart. When my mother's phone calls get too much for me to bear, I remind myself of his new world order, I chant my lists of birds, my growing vocabulary of plants.

Years later, my mother will write to tell me how she keeps lists in order to stay calm. She suggests I do what she does to keep sane: carry an almanac, encyclopedia, and dictionary, and thesaurus with me wherever I go. *When making a proper list, it is important to find the right word, she writes. For this, you need a thesaurus. Thesaurus, from the Ancient Greek: thesauros, meaning storehouse or treasury. Today I learned that topaz is a mineral, the fluosilicate of aluminum, usually occurring in prismatic orthorhombic crystals of various colors. It is most often used as a gem. By the way, I have seen a girl in Cleveland who looks like Rachel and a girl who looks like you. I need someone with me. Please come home.*

After work I draw and paint long into the evening. I grind pigments using a mortar and pestle the way painters used to ground lapis lazuli, burnt sienna, and cerulean blue centuries ago. I make my own egg tempera paint, the same kind monks used on the illuminated manuscripts I loved from the Cleveland Museum of Art, and on the icons in my grandfather's church. I crack eggs, and roll the yolk back and forth gently between my palms to separate it from the membrane. Then I pierce the sac and let the viscous yellow goo drip into a little glass cup. I mix the egg with water and pure pigment until the color is luminous and the texture smooth. On wooden panels, I paint with tiny meticulous strokes and try hard to ignore the persistent ringing of the phone.

One evening, my mother calls while I am in the middle of a painting.

"How's that *bad* Agostino? Is he in the Mafia?" She has been suspicious of my boyfriend ever since I brought him home to meet her two years before. "When is that guy going to produce a ring?"

"Can we talk about something else?"

"I called because I have some important news. A lawyer wrote me to say that your father is dead."

Was she telling the truth? "What?" I ask. "When did he die, and where?"

"Six years ago, the same year as Grandpa. Your father died in New Orleans."

My mother reads me the letter on the phone. It is so full of legalese and specific facts about my father's death that it has to be true. The estate lawyer wrote that my mother was the third and last person to be married to Paul Herr and, having been married to him the longest, she was entitled to his entire estate, $1,500, minus the lawyer's 30 percent fee. What a strange relief to get news about something real—a set of facts, a list of events. The lawyer said that on December 18, 1980, our father, at age sixty, died of a heart attack on the front porch of a boardinghouse in New Orleans at 9:40 in the morning. His death certificate said he was buried by the state in Kenner, Louisiana, at St. Rosalie Cemetery, just outside the city. Marital status: Unknown. Family: No next of kin. It took the bank six years to find out our father did indeed have a family.

I feel oddly satisfied, not sad. Will sadness follow? Regret?

"I'll send you a check for three hundred dollars as soon as I get the money," my mother informs me. "I hope you use it on a dentist. A woman's smile is her umbrella on a rainy day."

෴

Not long after I got the news that spring, my mother calls me from a budget motel on the east side of Cleveland and tells me that living with Grandma had gotten to be too much. Did I know that Grandma was losing her memory? That she might have Alzheimer's? That sometimes she wets the bed?

While we're talking, my mother sounds like she is getting short of breath. "Are you okay?" I ask. She tells me that she swallowed a bunch of pills a few minutes before to help her sleep. "Where are you? What's the name of the motel?" I ask. "Help me," she says. "I think something is wrong. Can you come right away?" She says she is having heart palpitations, sweaty palms, and can't catch her breath. "Have I been a bad mother to you?" she asks. "Do you still love me? Why won't your sister call?" My mother finally gives me the name of the motel and tells me what pills she took: an overdose of Navane, her new antipsychotic medication, and Cogentin, to help the flow of blood to her heart, neither of which is for sleeping. I get off the phone and call Ruth Armstrong, who, besides being such a loyal friend and neighbor, is a registered nurse. Ruth takes my mother straight to the ER. How long can I rely on the kindness of neighbors because I am too far away?

I assume the hospital will transfer my mother to the psych ward and keep her for a while, but they only keep her overnight, releasing her early the next day without cab fare or notifying her next of kin. In the fifties and sixties, they kept her for weeks at a time, medicated, electroshocked, and restrained, always with the looming threat that they might perform a lobotomy. Now, in the mid-eighties, they let her out after one day.

A week after the incident, my mother leaves the house again without a note, her bed stained with blood. I get yet another call from a motel, this time late at night. *Your grandma is a bitch,* she says, shouting into the phone. I am standing in the dark, twirling the black phone cord between my fingers, cold bare feet on the kitchen floor, wondering if I should hop on a plane and save her. I have a full week of work ahead of me, and a deadline for a show. *Why don't you come home?* she says. *I need you here. We have things to discuss. Now be a good daughter and come home.*

My mother returns to the house on West 148th Street after a couple of days. I cancel my museum workshops for the week, which means I don't get paid, and take a train back to Cleveland. Ruth and her husband pick me up, like they always do. What would I do without them? When my mother is sleeping during the day, I meet with her social worker, Colleen, a fervent young Catholic with four children. I strongly suspect that she thinks my sister and I should move back home. "Families should try to stay together, no matter what," she tells me when she picks me up at the house. She prides herself on keeping homes intact, even when sexual or physical abuse has been an issue. But Colleen promises that she will help us look into voluntary treatment and housing options for our mother, even involuntary ones, if need be. "What does that mean?" I ask. "You'll have to take your mother to court," she says. "Let's hope it doesn't come to that."

Six months later I am standing with a group of children in front of a case of Eskimo shaman masks at the Field Museum. I tell the children how the Eskimo spirit's pierced palms represent a magic hole in a place called the Sky World, where all animals pass through to repopulate the earth. A calm spreads over me while I'm talking. Even though the night before my mother had called me twenty-five times to tell me that her enemies keep setting her chair on fire. The Field is the one place where I feel safe: it is sanctuary, order; it is mythic time.

"The spirit's name is Tunghak," I say to the children. "Some say he lives on the moon."

"Where's the Sky World?" a girl asks. "Is that where the aliens live?"

"I don't know much about aliens," I say, "but I'll tell you a story instead."

I tell them the Inuit myth about Sedna, a woman who lives at the bottom of the sea, and how, when she was trying to escape her angry seabird-husband, his flapping wings conjured a terrible storm. Her parents threw her overboard to save their own lives. Sedna tried to cling to the boat but her father cut off her hands and she slipped away. She sank to the bottom of the sea, where her fingers grew back as fish, whales, walruses, and seals. The creatures made a home in her hair. Without hands she couldn't comb her long tresses tangled with sea-beasts and fish. All she could do was sit on the sea floor and watch her hair grow longer each day. I tell the children how some people believe that the *angakoks*, the shamans, swim down to the depths of the ocean to comb Sedna's hair for her. In gratitude, she sends hunters all the creatures of the sea.

"Is she beautiful?" asks another girl.

"I think so," I say. "But I'm not sure. I've never seen her."

Out of the corner of my eye, I see one of the museum's docents, an elderly woman with a cane, walking toward me. She pulls me aside. "I'm sorry to interrupt, but there's a lady in Education waiting to see you. She says it's an emergency. I'd hurry, if I were you."

The docent offers to stay and show the children the rest of the show. I tell her to take them down to the art room afterward so they can draw until I return—*if* I return, I add. "She seemed quite upset," the woman says. "She says she's your mother, but I wasn't sure if that was true."

I hurry past the display of Northwest Coast Native American art—cases of transformation masks—birds turning into men, men into bears, bears into otters, otters into whales. What is she doing here, in my refuge, my labyrinth of secret rooms, my cabinet of wonders? How dare she come here? This is my *home*. I have to run through the large central hall of the museum to get to the staircase on the other side leading down the stairs to Education. The two giant bull elephants, whose solid presence always comforted me in the past, look like monsters now. I break into a run.

What if someone lets her speak on the PA system, like when I was in high school and she showed up at the football game, calling my name for everyone to hear? Or when she circled Newton D. Baker Junior High on her rusty red bike. She is the relentless silver bell in my ear, even here, where I thought I was safe. *Myra, Rachel, where are you? It's your mother, come home!*

I run to where the docent said my mother was waiting, outside the Education office, but she isn't there. I search the halls. Not a trace. Then panic grips me. Someone might have told her I was in the Arctic Hall. She could be upstairs. She could be talking to the children if they haven't already left, interrogating them. *Where's your teacher? Which way did she go?* But why should I be afraid? She'd never hurt a child. Or would she? If they aren't in the art room by now, there will be twenty little children standing in front of a case of sacred hoop masks, waiting to make magic faces from paper plates, feathers, and sticks. I don't want my mother to scare them.

My mother is nowhere to be found in any of the rooms in the basement corridor, so I run back to where I began, upstairs by Tunghak and the other Eskimo masks. The children are gone. I look around the exhibit for my mother, but she isn't there. I head downstairs once again. As I hurry to the Education office I see a woman pacing in the hall, puffing on a cigarette beneath the no smoking sign. She looks up and rushes over to me.

"I've been searching for you everywhere," she says. "We have to leave right now."

My mother is wearing white rubber boots without socks, and her favorite winter coat, the blue one with the brown fake fur trim. Her hair looks like it hasn't been brushed in days. She is Sedna waiting for someone to comb the beasts from her hair.

"Why are you here?" I say. "I am working. *You have to go.*"

"Something is wrong with Grandma. You have to come home right now. I'll pay for the bus. This place is full of cameras. It's all been prescripted. We have to find somewhere safe where they can't see."

"You can't just get on a bus and interrupt my life."

"I'm starving," she says, grinding her cigarette into the floor with her boot. "I want a corned beef sandwich and a cup of hot coffee. Let's get out of here. Everywhere I look they have a gun pointed at my head."

I take my mother to a little Greek place called the Artist's Café on Michigan Avenue and watch her devour her food. She acts like she hasn't eaten in days. She has mustard all over her mouth and doesn't bother to wipe it off. Her voice is too loud and I feel sick to my stomach about what she could blurt out in public. It could be anything—Nazis, aliens, rape, murder, the forced removal of my womb. I am ten years old again, head hung low; slouching in my seat, hoping no one looks our way.

"Please keep your voice down," I say.

My mother takes a huge gulp of coffee and lights up a cigarette. "If you loved your mother you would come home."

"If you loved me you would leave."

"Sit up straight or your spine will grow crooked. When's the last time you had your hair done? It looks awful. You should get a perm."

"You have to take the bus home."

"Only if you come too."

"I can't. I'll come visit soon, I promise."

"I dropped one of Grandma's cups and she went crazy. You don't know how she can get. She blames me for everything. Can you fix the cup? You used to do that kind of thing. If you come home you can have your own room."

I don't know how, but I convince my mother to go back to Cleveland. I beg her, I cajole; I make promises I'll never keep. She has traveled over three hundred miles to see me but I put her right back on the bus after we eat. I feel profoundly sad for her, and hopeless. I promise that I will come home the following week and help her figure out what is wrong with Grandma. I promise to replace her typewriter ribbon, help her hang a picture on the wall, fix a million broken things.

"I know what has to be done," says my mother, as I lead her to the bus. "You have to come home and take charge. Your sister won't do it. She lives in a fantasy world."

"We'll talk about that when I come," I say.

"You're kicking out your own flesh and blood," she says, as I help her to her seat. "You don't love me anymore."

"I love you but I'm really mad. You must never, *ever* do this again. *Ever*. I could lose my job. Just don't do this anymore. I'll see you in a week."

I turn and walk away, without kissing her goodbye.

❧

At the end of December, my sister comes from Massachusetts to visit. Even though my mother has been calling me for weeks, threatening to kill herself if I don't come home, I decide to throw the New Year's Eve party I had planned anyway. I am setting out food before the guests arrive when someone rings the doorbell and doesn't stop. I press the intercom.

"Who is it?"

"Your mother, now open up!"

There is no question about what to do. When the police come, we meet them downstairs and the party goes on without us. Rachel and I spend most of the night at the hospital; our mother stays there a month. I am surprised they keep her so long. When she is released I send her home by herself on the train, heavily sedated and depressed. When I call my grandma to explain what happened, she doesn't quite understand. Something is definitely wrong with her, whether it is Alzheimer's or elderly dementia, but regardless, she is too old and tired to take care of our mother. Rachel and I decide that, if we have to, we will take legal action to get our mother a court-appointed guardian to make her medical and financial decisions. She just can't show up on our doorsteps anymore.

I imagine my life if nothing is done to change things—I see a pale green hospital waiting room at midnight, a television blaring soap opera reruns, and a vending machine dispensing endless cups of burnt coffee and tea. I see myself eternally waiting, unemployed and alone. This will be my purgatory: the knock at the door at midnight, my mother, hair wild as snakes, the sound of sirens and doors slamming shut, the violent rush of arms and hands, my mother placed in restraints and handed over to strangers. And me, sitting in a green room beneath cold fluorescent lights, tapping my foot to a song I played long ago.

A quote by the Italian philosopher Antonio Gramsci that I write down in my journal a month after my mother returns home: *The old world is dying away, and the new world struggles to come forth: now is the time of monsters.* If I don't do something different, who will become the monster, my mother or me?

The Year of the Horse

The horse is a large, strong animal with four legs, solid hoofs, flowing mane and tail. Domesticated in pre-historic times, it has long served mankind for drawing and carrying loads and riders. Specifically a full-grown male is called a gelding or stallion, the female is a mare. The horse is of the family Equidae that includes the ass, zebra, etc. It has a long breeding time. A single foal is born after conception in about eleven months. Size ranges from the smallest (falabella, height under 2½ feet) to the largest (shire, height over six feet). Today they are mostly ridden for pleasure and sport. In Chinese astrology, this is the Year of the Horse: a year for self-reliance, independence and travel. As for me, when I don't have fits of blanking out, which are numerous in this city, I try to be productive. I am working now on covering an old quilt with an abstract sheet. I had sent one to my cousin and would send one to my oldest daughter if I knew where she lived. I decided I needed one for myself to keep warm. They are called "comforters." From now on, I look after Number One.

10

Thou shall fly without wings, and conquer without any sword. Oh, horse . . .

Bedouin

Death, the Rider

In my memory palace, there is a painting from the Cleveland Museum of Art. The painting has two titles, *The Racetrack* and *Death on a Pale Horse*, but I always misremember it as *Death, the Rider*. Albert Pinkham Ryder, an American artist and favorite of my mother's and mine, painted it in the late 1800s. The story behind the painting goes like this: Ryder had a friend, a waiter, and, like Ryder, he was very poor. One day, the waiter mortgaged his house and bet his entire life savings on a horse. He told Ryder that if he lost, he would kill himself. The day of the race came and his horse didn't win. Ryder mourned the loss of his friend and made the painting shortly after he died. In the picture, Death brandishes a scythe, galloping on horseback the wrong way around a track. Sometimes Ryder referred to the painting as *The Reverse*. In the background is a dead tree. A snake observes Death from below; above hovers an armlike cloud reaching out to pluck the rider from his seat.

Ryder had an odd way of painting; he brushed on thick coats of varnish in between layers of wet paint. Consequently, none of his paintings survived very well. The surfaces are cracked and the colors have changed dramatically from their original state. Several years ago, my mother wrote me from a motel to say that she was protecting her "posters of intent" by putting a coat of varnish on them. *But now they're turning yellow,* she explained. *They are starting to look like Ryder's painting of Death. What should I do? I wish you were here to teach me. Please advise, Mother.*

The painting of Death and his horse invokes another picture in my mind, a white stallion leaping across an indigo sky. I made the large drawing for my mother when I graduated from art school in 1981. "I hope this cheers you up," I said when I gave it to her. "I dreamed I was a horse and came to your rescue. You were being carried away, up into the sky."

"It reminds me of Chagall," she said. "What's it called?"

"*Help Is on the Way.* Whenever you're scared, just look at it and think of me."

One of the first signs that my grandmother was suffering from Alzheimer's was when she began to believe the blue background in the horse picture could move. She stood in front of it one day and pointed.

"See that water?" she said. "It's moving. Like a river. Will it spill?"

She made a small gesture with her fingers, to show how the water was rushing down. "Oh, for Christ's sake, Steve's not going to like this one bit," she said. You better hide that whatchamacallit right now."

"Grandma," I said. "Grandpa is dead."

"I knew that. I was . . . I was . . . when did he die?"

By 1988, my grandma had begun to forget who people were. I was "The Baby," my mother was her mother. Lassie was Ginger and other dogs from her past. My mother did her best to help. She cooked the couple meals she had learned how to make in her recovery classes, before the community mental health program shut down. She tried to clean and keep up with the laundry. She straightened up the attic and painted a room in the house. "I am trying," she told me wearily into the phone. "But life with Grandma makes me tired. It is hard to distinguish between my dreams and the movie version of my life." How could she keep things in order when the voices in her head instructed her to do otherwise? They sent messages through the walls and windows, through paintings at the museum where she went to escape. Who should she listen to when she couldn't trust anyone to tell the truth?

My sister and I set up Meals on Wheels for her and my grandma, and asked an organization for the elderly, called Adult Protective Services (APS), to check up on them at home. Our old neighbor Ruth Armstrong had called to say that APS suspected our mother forgot to feed our grandma sometimes, and that maybe she was pushing her around. They had spotted Grandma wandering in the cold without a coat a few times, her arms covered with bruises. Had she fallen down, or was something else going on? "You're sending in spies," my mother said to me on the phone late at night. "Who are these professional manipulators you've sent in to check up on me? Who are they really working for?"

As my grandma's Alzheimer's worsened, my mother's surprise visits to my sister and me increased, as did her disappearances to shelters and cheap motels. It was as if she were in training to be homeless. She'd leave our grandma home alone and disappear for a couple days or call me from the Cleveland airport or bus station, saying that she had gone there to spend the night. Adult Protective Services tried to keep watch over what was going on in the house on West 148th Street, if and when our mother let them in. My mother started sending me angry letters in the mail: *Those bitches pose as do-gooders but they're imposters. If you were a good daughter, you'd move home and help me out.*

In 1988 I moved into a little apartment on Erie Street, a couple miles from my old neighborhood in Wicker Park. It had become too difficult to live with roommates or a boyfriend. Who wants to live with someone when the phone rings twenty-four hours a day or when your mother could show up at any time in a cloud of cigarette smoke, a knife in her hand, pulling her belongings behind her in a cart? My mother tried hard to keep the voices at bay but it was impossible to rein them in—there were so many of them, with so many terrible things to say.

One winter night, right before Christmas, Ruth Armstrong phoned me at my apartment on Erie. "I'm sorry I didn't call you earlier but everything happened at once," she said. "Your mother was on a window ledge and I couldn't get her down. She stabbed your grandma six times in the back—

there was blood everywhere. I had to call the police. But don't worry, honey. Your grandma's going to be fine."

They kept my mother in the psych ward for observation. Meanwhile, after treating my grandma in the ER for knife wounds, they sent her home in a cab, even though her chart said she had Alzheimer's. A neighbor out walking her dog found her, incoherent and wandering in the snow, wearing a bloodstained nightgown and socks. I knew that, statistically, schizophrenics were less likely to commit violent crimes than the rest of the population, but who knew what our mother's voices would command her to do next? Rachel and I had to legally separate her from our grandma, and find our grandma a safe new home.

I don't remember how it was that, in the winter of '89, I ended up going to the Cleveland courthouse alone. Why didn't my sister come? Why hadn't I asked Agostino to drive me there, to offer moral support? It seemed the older I got, the harder it was for me to involve even my closest friends.

In the courthouse, I spotted my mother across the room. She had dyed her hair and gotten a perm. She even dressed up for the occasion and wore a bright pink and blue scarf around her neck. If you observed her more closely, though, you could see something was wrong. She couldn't stop twitching and rocking back and forth; her tongue darted in and out involuntarily, signs of tardive dyskinesia, the long-term effect of antipsychotic medications. She glared at me as I listed the reasons she was too sick to take care of her own mother.

"She's starving her to death," I said, after recounting a Cliffs Notes version of my sister's and my childhood. "My grandmother hasn't had a bath in weeks. There are bruises all over her arms. My mother needs care herself. She refuses to take her medication and leaves our grandmother home alone for days. She tried to kill her with a knife. What other proof do you need?"

My mother lurched forward in her seat. "Traitor!" she yelled, shaking her fist at me. "Turncoat! Liar! Bitch!"

"You are completely out of order!" said the judge. He turned to my mother's lawyer. "You need to get control over your client!"

I wanted the lawyers and the judge to know that this was not my mother deep inside; she was a genius who could make music of infinite beauty. She would give her last dollar to someone in need; she'd put herself in harm's way to save my life. This was my mother too. The core personality of a schizophrenic always remains, even if it is buried deep inside. In the courtroom, I longed to be a small silent form, pressed against my mother's piano while she played. *This is what love is.* Not this public display of drama and betrayal. But instead, I was a loud voice telling the world that my mother had stabbed my grandma in the back.

When the judge finally announced the verdict in my favor, I glanced at my mother across the room. Her face was contorted in rage and I thought that maybe, just maybe, she could kill me if I gave her half the chance. I hurried down the courthouse steps to catch a cab to the Greyhound station. My mother ran after me, shouting, "Traitor! You are no daughter of mine."

Social services removed my grandma from the house, along with Lassie and a few belongings. They moved her to a private elder-care facility on the east side of Cleveland, run by a woman named Gloria, an African-American nurse who took care of a handful of Alzheimer's patients in her large, comfy home. My mother wasn't allowed to know where her mother lived and could only see her if she contacted the guardianship lawyer. A third party had to be present at all times. *Judas,* I can hear my mother hissing into my ear, even now, twenty years later. *You took my mother away.* To take her mother away also meant to remove her financial security; she would no longer be able to write checks from Grandma's account. How would she get by now with what she called her "once-a-month garbage" from disability?

"I like it here," my grandma said, when I came to visit after she moved in.

"Why's that, Grandma?"

"I like to be around my own kind."

"What kind is that?"

"Black folk," she said. "I'm black and I'm proud." Gloria and I cracked up. Then my grandma looked at me and said, "You're a nice lady. Does your family live around here? What's their name? Maybe I know them."

Gloria told me not to get upset if my grandma forgot my name or if she reacted a bit strange to certain things.

"What kinds of things?" I asked.

"You can't give her anything red to wear," said Gloria. "She thinks it's blood and that someone's going to hurt her. She does something else too."

"What?"

"Every day about ten to five she starts getting agitated. Her hand goes up to her mouth like she's got a cigarette in it. Annie seems to calm herself by pulling out an old checkbook she hides under her chair. She sits there and flips through it. She does that business for about ten minutes, then she's fine."

"A little before five?" I asked. "That's the time my grandfather picked her up from work. I guess the body remembers, even when we forget."

༄

My mother was alone now, for the first time, with no one to watch over her. There was always the same urgent message on my answering machine when I got home to my place on Erie: "Pick up the phone! It's your mother! This is an emergency!" If I was talking to someone else, she'd have the operator interrupt my call. "I'm letting another party come through," the operator would say. "She says it's a matter of life or death."

My mother would get on the phone. "Thank God you're there. Your sister died."

"What?"

"You have to come home right away. Tell that sister of yours to come too."

"You just said she was dead."

"I meant Grandma. They're sending poisonous gas in the house where she lives. Something must be done. You're the only one who knows how to fix things."

Sometimes she'd call to tell me not to get on the subway: "Stay home! Someone could push you onto the tracks!" One day she left more than thirty messages saying the same thing: *Someone is going to try to murder you today. You have to call the police!* When I finally talked to her she said, "A tree is going to fall on you tomorrow. I just know it. Don't go outside."

I said, "It's the city, Mother. We don't have trees."

If I took the phone off the hook, it was business as usual—she'd call the police to come over to see what was wrong. One day a policeman from the local precinct stopped by. He hung his head, embarrassed. After a lot of throat-clearing, he finally asked if there was any way I could stop my mother from calling their station because it was taking time away from real emergencies. He suggested getting a restraining order or changing my number. "I don't know how you can stand it," he said. "It would drive me insane."

What the policeman had said gnawed at me. What would happen if I stopped her from calling me all day long? She'd still show up at my door, but what if I lied and told her I moved? Gave her a post office box to write me at? What if I set down some rules, an impenetrable fence or two? What if things were on my terms for once? Would she survive?

Later that fall, I sent a letter to my mother. I lied and said I had moved and gave her a post office box number in another neighborhood. I changed my phone number; my sister did the same. We instructed all our friends and the places where we worked that they were not to give our information out to anyone, even if the person said it was a matter of life or death. Even if the person said she was our mother. It was hard to believe that it took me this long to learn that my mother must never, under any circumstances, know the names and phone numbers of any of my friends or colleagues. My mother wrote me immediately to say that if I didn't reveal where I lived, she would have to come to Chicago to track me down and save me from my kidnappers. She said she might have to buy a gun.

I was still working at the Field Museum and two other museums in town. On the side, I did proofreading for *Encyclopedia Britannica*. While Eastern Europe was reassembling itself at the end of the 1980s, I was proofreading the history of East and West Germany and the Balkan states. Every few weeks and then, increasingly, every few days, I'd get a call from my boss. "Stop production!" she'd say. "The Berlin Wall just fell!" or "Hold off on Czechoslovakia. I think they're next." It was hard to find order even in the book series that created it.

As for order at home in Cleveland, what little had existed in the house on West 148th Street had completely disintegrated. When I called Ruth to see if she had been to see my mother recently, she said that she and other neighbors were afraid to go near the place. Adult Protective Services no longer stopped by, since my grandma was safe and sound. Colleen hadn't been able to enter the house in weeks.

Everything around me—my mother's safety and future, the geography of the world—was changing at an alarming rate, but my own life felt in limbo. Death was always circling the track—my mother sent me twenty-page letters at my post office box, threatening suicide if I didn't come home, rambling on about conspiracy theories and how the three of us were on a hit list to be killed. And nothing was moving forward with my mother's situation. I felt held hostage by her illness and by the backward mental health system that once again was incapable of helping our family in crisis. I longed to be far away, in a place where no one knew me, a place impossible to find.

When I called my mother on Christmas Day, she told me that she had sold the house the week before. She had been threatening to sell it for weeks but I hadn't taken her seriously. The new owner was moving in in February.

"You sold the house?" I said. "How? It's in Grandma's name."

"Not anymore," she said.

Apparently, when my grandmother's memory had begun to slip, my mother had forged her signature on the deed and had gotten a real estate agent to help her put the house on the market. She told me on the phone that she had already signed the papers and now it was a done deal. She had sold the house and was going to move to a transient women's residence in Detroit where she had lived for a while after she dropped out of music conservatory. I didn't know at the time that it was the place where she had had one of her first psychotic breakdowns in 1945, not too long after America dropped the bomb.

The day after my mother told me her plans, Romania's dictator was executed in public. With the fall of communism in the East, Tianenman Square, the Iran-Contra Affair, *Exxon Valdez*, Ted Bundy's long-awaited electrocution, people dying of AIDS—much happened in 1989 to make my mother paranoid and disturbed, not to mention the fact that she no longer could reach either of her children by phone. But of all the events that happened that year, what stuck in my head was the discovery in Utah of a 150-million-year-old fossilized dinosaur egg, still inside the mother's sac. A CAT scan revealed the oldest dinosaur embryo ever discovered. At the end of the excessive and turbulent eighties, I found solace in the little egg, in the knowledge that, even amid all the turmoil, familial and in the world, something so fragile could withstand the test of time.

Rachel and I decided that we had to get our mother to agree to live in a supervised group home or some kind of treatment facility, and if she wouldn't agree, we would take her to court and try to declare her incompetent, thus forcing the situation to change. It was the only way we could imagine her being taken care of, staying on medication, and cultivating the life skills she never had the chance to learn. We were afraid that if she didn't live somewhere safe, she would become homeless.

My sister couldn't bear the thought of speaking out against our mother in court, nor could I, so our lawyer read our statements in front of the judge. We didn't want to ask Ruth or any of our other neighbors to speak at the trial either, when we couldn't handle going ourselves. Hadn't they done enough already?

After two separate hearings and two appeals, the court refused to hear us out anymore. She could buy her own cigarettes, manage a checking account, and cash her disability checks at the bank. According to the judge, those three acts proved she was competent. We were done; we lost the case. This time we were on our own. There was only one thing for us to do. We had to go back to Cleveland and somehow convince our mother to sign the guardianship papers without the help of the court.

Shortly before we left for Cleveland, I received a letter from my mother informing me that she'd changed her mind about moving to the women's residence in Michigan. Instead, the three of us would move back into the

Stuart House apartments on Triskett Road, where we lived together when
Rachel and I were in high school. My sister could drop out of graduate
school and I would have to leave Chicago and come home. We'd get another
collie because Grandma took her away. *We'll get a puppy just like Lassie. You can
go on welfare,* she wrote. *You'll paint at home and take care of me, just like when you
were young. You need to talk to your sister. She's probably worried about chores. We
can take turns cooking or go to Gene's for a nice T-bone steak if you don't want to cook.
Get your affairs in order and come home straight away.*

Cleveland is bitterly cold when Rachel and I arrive with Agostino and my
sister's boyfriend Michael in late January 1990. Agostino and I had broken
up the year before but were still good friends. I had recently started seeing
someone else, a Polish medical student named Robert, but the relationship
was too new and I didn't want him involved.

My sister's boyfriend and Agostino can't be more different from one
another—blue-eyed Michael, sweet and blond and clean-cut, and Agostino,
intimidating with his long dark hair, black leather jacket, brooding dark eyes.
The men can play good cop, bad cop, if we need them to.

Outside the house on West 148th the bushes have grown wild. What
had been my beloved garden is now a wilderness of brambles and frozen
weeds. The ivy my grandfather planted more than fifty years before coils
thickly around the house like an icy dark-green shroud.

When the four of us pull into the driveway, our mother runs out to meet
us barefoot, wearing a thin dirty nightgown covered with cigarette burns.
There's a flurry of fat wet snowflakes in the chill air but she shows no sign of
feeling cold. She's not wearing her dentures and her face is pinched into the
face of someone much older than sixty-four. She bobs back and forth, her
tongue darting in and out like it did that day in the courtroom. I feel a stab in
my chest. This is my mother, this wild creature before me.

"Who the hell is *that?*" she says, pointing at Michael, whom she has never
met.

"His name is Jim," Rachel lies. "He's from Chicago."

My mother turns to Agostino. "What's *he* doing here?"

"Hello, Norma," says Agostino. "Nice to see you too."

Agostino flashes his warm Abruzzese smile but it doesn't work any magic; it never has on my mother anyway. She looks like she wants to shoot him. "Go back to Chicago," she says. "Boys are not welcome here. You two get out!"

Rachel and I had talked this through beforehand and were prepared. We decided that our mother might trust us more at first if we were alone with her.

"That's fine," I say. "They can go out for a while."

We send Michael and Agostino out to shop for food and cleaning supplies. Rachel whispers, "Call us in an hour," and they leave.

Inside the house, the smell of shit, cigarettes, and rotten meat hovers in the air. It is obvious that she has been living in total squalor for months. She has been drinking coffee from a filthy pot, eating spoiled food. Her hair is unwashed and it looks like she hasn't clipped her toenails in months. They look like brittle yellow claws.

As soon as they are out of sight, our mother rips the kitchen phone from the wall. It's an old-fashioned rotary-dial phone and heavy. Rachel and I back away, not knowing if she's going to throw it at us. But our mother grabs a bottle instead, smashes it against the table, and comes after me, chasing me into the living room. Rachel follows behind, in hysterics. Ever since she was a teenager, and my mother came after her with a hot iron to stop her from going out with friends, my sister falls apart when our mother explodes.

I wrestle my mother to the ground; she lunges toward my face with the bottle. "I'll kill you," she says. "I'll kill you if you try to leave." I grab on to her arms; she is holding the jagged edge an inch from my neck, while my sister screams for her to stop.

I shout to Rachel to find a pay phone or a neighbor and call someone, or flag down a police car from the road. She runs out the door for help. I pin my mother to the floor, my hands clenched around her wrists, the weight of my body holding her down.

"I'm not an animal," she hisses. "Let me go!"

I squeeze her wrist hard so she'll loosen her grip on the bottle.

"I'm your mother! Let me go!"

"I'll let you go when the police come."

"They're full of shit."

"Let go," I say.

"They're all in on it together—the police, those bad men you brought, the faith healers, the Christian fascists, the Nazis. I don't ask for much. I just want you girls home where you belong!"

"We can talk when you let go of the bottle."

Across from me is an empty space where the piano used to be. She had sold it to a stranger a month before. What will happen to this house, these pictures on the wall? Behind me is the horse drawing I'd made for her, *Help Is on the Way*, without a frame, nailed crookedly to the wall.

"If you don't move home I'll kill myself," she screams.

I wonder if help is really on the way. When and if it comes, it will most likely be in the form of two gruff policemen, not well trained for this kind of thing, and they will use handcuffs on her like they had in the past. Why do they always tie her down? Yet here I am, pinning her to the ground. What makes me any different than the nurses and aides in lockdown? If I had a rope, I would tie her hands to stop her from doing something that I know now she could do. Albert Pinkham Ryder's pale horse flashes in my mind, Death, the rider, going around and around beneath an ominous sky.

I relax my arms for just a moment and it's enough for her to break my grip and push the bottle up to my neck. The jagged edge slices into the front of my neck, right below my Adam's apple, drawing blood. I push her back down again, harder.

Fifteen minutes or so pass and Rachel comes back to the house, sobbing. She had flagged down a police car on Triskett Road and pleaded with him to help her, but he told her, "That's a family matter, not police business. Go home and settle it yourself."

My mother's grip on the bottle finally loosens and I wrench it from her hand. I help her to her feet. She is even more enraged than before. She lights a cigarette and starts screaming about what she'll do if we don't obey her. A couple minutes later, Agostino and Michael drive up. I shout to them from the door to get back in the car and the four of us take off together, my mother chasing us down the road, barefoot in the snow, yelling, "Come back here! I'm your mother! Come back!"

The next day we run from police station to social services office to courthouse, then social services office again and file for our mother to be temporarily committed so we can buy time and figure out what to do next.

After our meeting with a judge, in which we explain how our mother tried to attack me with the bottle, Rachel says, "You know, she really could have killed you."

"I don't think so," I say. "I don't think she could."

"What makes you so sure?"

We get all our papers notarized, and then make arrangements at the police station for two officers to come at a specific time the following day to pick up our mother and take her to the hospital. The four of us go back to where we are staying—Rachel and Michael return to their hotel, and Agostino and I drive to his aunt's house. I fall asleep trying to remember that famous quote from F. Scott Fitzgerald's *Tender Is the Night*: about the brilliance and versatility of madness, how it is like water seeping through, over, and around a dike. And how it requires the united front of so many people to fight against it. How many people will it take to stop my mother's illness from devouring us all? It could take an army.

The police arrive at the appointed time the following day. They show up, sirens wailing, doors slamming, and lights flashing onto the faint dusting of snow. I had hoped for a more subtle entrance. The four of us park down the street so she doesn't know we are there too. Our plan is to sneak up after she is safely inside the police car. We want her to think that a neighbor had called the police to report her for disturbing the peace. We hide around the side of the house next door. I can hear my mother shouting at the policemen, "This is a family dispute! My daughters just want my money. You have no business here." She is wearing torn polyester pants and a dirty blouse. It's cold outside. Where is her sweater? I don't even know if she owns one. Where have I been all these years? I run from my hiding place to the front lawn.

"We don't have all day," the first policeman says to my mother. "Be a good girl and get in the car."

My mother is clinging to the front door and won't let go. The men pry her away; they each take one of her arms and pull her toward their car. Then she sees me. I am standing on the snowy lawn, unsure of what to do. She shouts at me, *Traitor! Gestapo!* as the men drag her, howling, to the car. The first officer puts his hand on top of her head and guides her into the backseat just like they do on Grandma's cop shows on TV. The other man gets into the driver's seat. My mother glares at me through the window. The lights from the squad car spin and flash on the snow as she presses her pale face against the window and mouths the words, *Save me.* She has no coat, no hat, no purse.

I run up to the car. "Stop!" I yell. "Wait! Let me get her a coat!"

One of the men nods, holds up his wrist and taps his watch; I better hurry and not waste his time. I run inside and bound up the stairs to my grandfather's room, where my mother has slept since he died. I need to find a sweater, something warm. I yank open drawers, the closet door. I can't find a single sweater, just her old blue coat with the fake fur trim—the one she will repair over and over again for the next twelve years or so, the one she will lose somewhere in a run-down motel in New York, or a bus station bathroom in LA, or on a subway seat en route to sleep at the airport. She'll write about the tragic loss of the coat in her diaries. She'll declare it stolen, and file a claim against the city and the motel and anyplace she might have seen it last, asking why did they steal the one and only coat from a woman who has lost her memory, her house, and her children, the only two people she has ever truly loved? I grab the soft blue coat and run back outside, but the officers have already pulled into the street.

I shout to them, "Wait, please, she needs a coat!" but they turn left on West 148th toward Triskett, taking her in winter like a thief.

———

In her letters, my mother always told me what Chinese zodiac sign ruled each year and what each animal sign stood for. A few weeks before the four of us came to Cleveland, my mother had sent me a card at my Chicago post office box: *Last year was the Chinese Year of the Snake, the year of deception. 1990 is the Year of the Horse. The Year of the "Metal" Horse, to be exact. Metal Horse people are unyielding, strong and determined. Not bad qualities if you live in a world of shysters, criminals and underhanded spies.* In the Year of the Horse, on a cold night in January, after my mother is taken away and the four of us have eaten a much-needed meal, we finally reenter the red brick house shrouded in frozen ivy. On the wall above the fireplace is my Chagall-esque landscape. There are horses floating in the dark blue sky, a red path leading from a house to a human heart. At the center of the picture is the big white horse my mother liked so much, the words "Help is on the way" hovering just above. What kind of help is this, setting her up behind her back, having the police take her by force, their sirens screeching all the way to the psych ward? I stand there, looking at my drawing, while somewhere on the other side of the city doctors are strapping my mother to a bed. She'll be given an injection to calm her down and make her go to sleep. The next day she'll feel like a zombie. And then what? Where will she go?

Once inside, we look around and assess what to do. It will take days to clean this place, or more like weeks. There is garbage all over and a layer of dirt on the countertops and on the floors. How could my mother live here like this? How did I let this happen?

My sister and I start digging for things while the men clean. We've brought packing tape and boxes, garbage bags galore. I turn on the radio; a quiet piano sonata plays in the background. The music calms me. I am glad I didn't bring Robert or even think twice about it. I wouldn't want him to see all this sadness and filth. I make a promise to myself: in my new life, there will be none of this.

"I can't believe we got through today," I say. "Great job, everyone."

Rachel asks, "How long do you think they'll keep her?"

"After all that stuff we said, about her trying to attack me, about her attempted suicides, don't you think they've got to keep her at least a couple weeks?"

"God, I hope it's longer than that."

As the men scrub, my sister and I rummage through boxes and draw-ers, searching for things to take back. We are partisans on the move during World War II, ready to spring at the slightest sound. Every time the heater kicks on, Rachel and I jump.

"It feels good to have a plan," I say. "With a little work, this house could look pretty nice."

"What's the next step?" asks Michael.

"We have to get her to sign."

"Do you think she will?"

"I don't know," I say. "Maybe, if she was on medication. But she's not. I just can't think about it now."

I start sifting through my grandmother's bureau in the dining room. The first drawer I pull out is stuffed with carbon copies of letters my mother wrote to the psychiatrist in California. I wonder if he ever read them. I always thought he was one of her delusions, but a year before our grand-mother started showing signs of Alzheimer's, she told me that the story was indeed true, that the doctor had really raped our mother, even sodomized her. He had threatened to perform a lobotomy on her if she told anyone that he had forced her to have sex with him every week. My grandma said that after our mother married our father, the doctor wrote a letter admit-ting to some of the things he had done. I asked if she'd pressed charges since she'd finally had proof. My grandmother said that she took the letter and destroyed it before my mother had a chance. She told me, "I couldn't let her do that. People would talk."

I open the drawer below. There are dozens of photographs scattered at the bottom of the drawer, and others stuffed in two round cookie tins. There's a stiff 1950s portrait of my grandfather in his red fez hat he wore to secret meetings at the Masononic lodge and a buoyant photo of my mother at sixteen, leaning out of a window, smiling. I find an old newspaper clipping of her in a French school play, at age fourteen. She is Joan of Arc, kneeling before the king. And another photo, and another. Where to begin? A sudden rapping on the back door makes me catch my breath.

My mother is at the door pounding. "Let me in," she shouts. "I forgot my key." How did they let her out? It's freezing and she has no coat, no hat or gloves.

"Let me in!" my mother screams. "This is still my house!"

I call out to the other three, "She's back! What do we do?"

My sister shouts, "Don't open the door!"

My sister remembers this differently, remembers the door being open, not locked, and my mother letting herself in. She remembers yelling at me to hold the door against our mother to block her entry. But I remember opening the locked door. What else could I do? My mother is cold and has no coat. If I let her in, I betray my sister; if I don't, my mother might freeze to death.

Our mother is a tornado. The hospital never even medicated her; they just sent her back out into the streets three hours after she arrived. After all the heartbreak and drama and running around to social services, the courthouse, and the police station, my mother just walks in the door and picks up where she left off.

"You aren't going anywhere," she says, pointing a lit cigarette at my face. "We've got business to attend to." She turns to the men. "You bastards get out!"

Our mother tells us that she will not, under any circumstances, let us leave. She reiterates the fact that she will kill herself if she has to in order to prove her point. We are to move back to Cleveland into our old apartment on Triskett Road and we will live together again, safe from the outside world. She has it all planned out. She is as determined as a Metal Horse. "I put a deposit down on the place," she says. "So we can be together again."

My sister and I try to reason with her. After all these years of living with this, we are still ignorant about her debilitating disease. I once asked a schizophrenic guy I knew in Chicago what it was like to be him. He said, "It's like your head is plugged into every electric socket in every house on every street." I had gone to therapy, read books, went to support group meetings and conventions on mental illness, and still had no idea how to talk to my mother about getting help.

"Please sign it. It's for your own good," says Rachel. She's holding the voluntary guardianship document in front of our mother's face. "Sign it. *You've got to.*"

"Cut the crap. Tell those boys to leave. They're not wanted here."

"If you don't sign that paper," I threaten her, "you will never see us again."

In the house on West 148th Street, pandemonium breaks out. Everyone is shouting and waving their arms.

"Stop," my sister screams. "I can't take it anymore." Michael tries to comfort her, while Agostino shouts at our mother in both English and Italian.

My mother is enraged. "Who's controlling you girls? Who are these men?"

"You have to sign this," I say, holding out the papers. "Otherwise this is it. You'll see. We'll disappear."

"You've been brainwashed. You'll do as I say."

My mother lunges toward me; I push her away. Rachel and Michael are shouting at her to calm down.

I run upstairs to use the bathroom, hoping it isn't clogged like the one by the kitchen. On my way back down I pause by the little nightstand at the top of the stairs. I pull out what's hidden in the bottom drawer—an old piece of violin rosin I left years ago. I can smell it through the chamois cloth; I slip the rosin into my pocket. Is this the only treasure I will take from my childhood home? Halfway down the stairs, I stop to survey the scene in the living room from above, detached. Agostino is pulling my horse drawing down from the wall. I am disappearing into the stairs; I'm just a shadow, an invisible cat.

"You don't deserve this, Norma," he tells her, yanking it off the nails. "I took care of your daughter better than you ever did."

"That's mine!" she screams.

"Not anymore."

I want to tell him, "Please stop, she is so sick. You're breaking what's left of my heart." I try to call out to him but something catches in my throat. I take short, shallow breaths.

"You bastard," says my mother. "You never even gave her a ring."

They both grab on to the picture and pull. I can't breathe—what if we can't get out? What if we have to stay here forever, locked in this house with her? I feel myself fading away and tumble down the stairs. I see the same scene I always see when I faint—I'm at the bottom of a laundry chute, looking up at piles of dirty clothes raining down upon my face.

"See what you do to her?" cries Rachel, as she helps me to my feet. "You make her sick."

I can hear my drawing starting to tear, but the paper is tough and maybe will withstand their fight. Agostino and my mother give it one more tug, shouting back and forth, while I sneak into the dining room. I am not a cat anymore but a horse, ready to run out of the gate. I can't be in this place another minute. As chaos explodes all around me, I slip into the dining room and open the bureau drawer again. I pull out a handful of photographs and shove them in a bag.

I shout to the others to get their things. "Let's get out of here—NOW."

The four of us run to the door, my mother close on our heels, letting the big white horse floating in blue fall to the floor.

"Come back here! You come back right now!"

As we pull away in our cars, I turn to watch my mother chase after us, her arms flailing around her as snow clouds gather in the sky. She looks like she is trying to lift off the ground, but just can't do it. I am worried about my big white horse, trampled on the living room floor. Who will repair it now? Where will my mother go? We get to the corner of 148th and Grapeland and she is a small spot in the middle of the road. We turn the corner and she is out of sight. Later, when I open the bag to see what photos I have rescued, I find I have scooped up pictures of people I don't even know.

Part II

The New World

Of course I am a wanderer, a pilgrim on this earth.
But can you say that you are anything more?

Goethe, *The Sorrows of Young Werther*

What Not to Buy in Travel

What not to buy in travel if you want to save the planet: Do not purchase reptile skins and leathers, commonly used in watchbands, handbags, belts and shoes. No birds and feathers. Never buy ivory souvenirs. Furs from jaguar, leopard, snow leopard, tiger, ocelot, margay and tiger cat. Other cats as well as furs of marine mammals like seals and polar bears. These cannot enter the U.S. legally. Coral is also prohibited. Plants prohibited from import include many cycads, orchids and cacti. Note to self: I never buy or have bought the above <u>anyway</u>. I am homeless.

11

As for the world, when you emerge, what will it have become?

Arthur Rimbaud, *The Illuminations*

Forgeries and Illuminations

It's the moment when I notice a woman opening a window in a small house on a bridge above the Arno that I think of my mother, somewhere across the wide Atlantic. The woman shakes a rug out, dust floats down like flecks of mica, the window slams shut, the light shifts, the river darkens. *Where is she? Is she dead?* In a letter my mother wrote me not long after our ill-fated visit that January 1990, she said that she had moved to our old Stuart House apartment building on Triskett Road and was waiting for my sister and me to come. I wrote back to say that I was moving overseas. My mother promptly sent a reply to my Chicago post office box: *I taped a map of the world to the wall in my room with a note: Ask no questions. They'll tell you no lies.* She added: *Where are your belongings—your books, pictures, and bicycle? With all the sales here in Cleveland, I'll spend some money on you when you return. For myself, I don't need much, just a small radio, some books, and a lamp.*

Right before I left for Florence that August, I sent one more letter to her. I said that I had a one-person show coming up in Europe that fall, which was true, but didn't say that the exhibit was in Italy. I told her I had no intention of returning anytime soon from the "European country" I was moving to. My letter came back with "Addressee Unknown" stamped across it. I tried sending another to her after I arrived in Florence. I described where I lived as a vague, imaginary place so as not to reveal my true location. "It's so sunny here," I wrote. "There are birds of many colors and the trees are russet and gold." Once again, my letter came back. If she wasn't there, where in the world was she?

The late September light shifts again outside the window at the Uffizi, and the green river sparkles below. I think of the woman in the window on the bridge, how she could be me living another person's life—a Florentine housewife with a couple of kids, a small white dog, and paunchy husband who sells jewelry in one of the shops below on Ponte Vecchio. My name could be Carlotta or Maria or I could take the name Agostino's grandparents gave his mother when she was born, Orienta, after a ship they saw pass by the port of Napoli. I could give myself the name of a ship, a vessel bound for the scalloped edge of someone else's country.

I turn and walk down the corridor to find Botticelli's *Annunciation*. The picture is like a scene from a movie: An angel enters a room, walks between two pillars to where Mary sits. She holds her hand out in a gesture of refusal. Gabriel offers her the job but she doesn't want it, won't take the lily from his hand. She is reluctant to be selfless and holy. But it's the background I've come to see, not Mary—the distant hazy purple horizon, the exaggerated perspective to make something look real when it's really not; the painting's verisimilitude—truth, besotted with lies.

I leave Botticcelli to find the round blue room of Mannerists. My favorite is Bronzino's portrait of Lucrezia, a stoic woman in a scarlet dress. I make a quick sketch of her pale, elongated neck, her chaste, enigmatic stare. Could I steel myself against the world like her? Her unwavering gaze follows me like Goya's did years ago. Engraved on her gold necklace are the words *Amour dure sans fin.* Love lasts eternally. Was she a happy wife and mother? Or was she hiding something, holding back tears?

In another room I find Caravaggio's painted shield. Medusa's eyes glare at me; her serpentine curls hiss: *How could you leave me? I sleep on benches, on bridges, on cardboard and leaves.* Will I ever let down this burden of guilt?

I return to the window. The woman is gone, but the river is still bathed in light. I look out at Ponte Vecchio, the one bridge left standing after World War II. Iraq had invaded Kuwait the week before I left for Italy. Saddam Hussein had declared, "The mother of all battles has begun." Are we about to enter World War III? Shouldn't I be back in the States, trying to find my mother? But here, it's hard to imagine war: from the window I can see bridge beyond bridge—Santa Trinita, Ponte alla Carraia, Vespucci, and Ponte della Vittoria in the distance. Is this what it means to wander? Gold, capricious light on water, arches unfurling, all the way to the sea? Is it a heart splitting open? Is it loss? Or is it the seductive verisimilitude of beauty, waving and singing a stranger's land?

In my memory palace, there is a long corridor lined with marble statues. The ceilings are decorated with Italian *grotteschi*: sylvan landscapes of centaurs, nymphs, gargoyles, and swans. Guilded paintings adorn the walls. At the end of the corridor is a map of a make-believe world. In the distance are snow-covered mountains, forests of cypresses and parasol pines. There are ships waiting to leave at every harbor, there are places still waiting to be named.

જી

A couple days after I left for Italy that August, a friend told me that my mother had shown up at my apartment on Erie Street. One of the tenants answered the door but he didn't know where I was. My mother spent the night at Agostino's parents'; the following day she disappeared into Chicago's streets. I watched the Perseid meteor shower from a friend's house in Florence that night, *La notte delle stelle scadente*, the Night of the Shooting Stars. For each falling star I cast a wish for her, like I used to in the museum wishing well in Cleveland: Please keep her safe from harm.

My plan had been to find a place in Italy for the fall, then travel to Poland to meet Robert, the medical student I had been seeing before I left. I wanted to live in Poland for the rest of the year while Robert finished school, then we could figure out where to go from there. Robert had told me that work in Poland was scarce, even for Poles. His sister, a doctor, was moonlighting by pumping gas. He had been saying the same thing ever since we got involved, that there was no future for us. We should just enjoy our time together until he went back home.

The night before I left he said, "What will you do in Poland without your sister or your friends?" Robert stayed up late, helping me to pack. In the morning, he looked pale and exhausted. He gave me a farewell gift—a miniature painting he had made of a medieval castle, two lovers floating on a cloud above the spires. We kissed goodbye at the top of the stairs. On his way down, he stopped and turned around for a moment. He looked up at me and smiled the saddest smile I had ever seen. Less than a month later he called me in Italy and broke up with me on the phone.

After that, I had to decide—should I stay or should I go back to Chicago? I had sold or given away nearly everything I owned; I had resigned from the Field Museum and my other jobs. And I suspected that my mother might have even moved to Chicago, maybe to my old neighborhood. I felt I had no choice—Chicago was the past and my future was not in Poland.

෴

I answered an ad in the paper for a roommate in a house on a farm called Cerreto, a forty-minute drive from Florence down Via Aretina, the fast curving road that follows the Arno east of the city. I had no car, so it took almost twice as long by bus and train. My roommates in the downstairs apartment were two women in their thirties, Elisabetta, an art restorer from Milan, and a blond Swedish language teacher named Elsa, who, when I asked where she was from, slapped her chest and said, "I may be from Sweden, but *sono una vera Napolitana*—I am a true Neapolitan!" Elsa laid down the rules the first day: I was not allowed to touch her newspaper, play music in the living room, or record my name on our answering machine. Elisabetta was much kinder but rarely home. I felt most comfortable upstairs, where Gabriella, Massimo, Angelo, and Claudia lived, a group of boisterous forty-somethings. If they noticed I was alone, they'd come downstairs and try to coax me up for dinner.

Beneath the house's eighteenth century walls was a medieval foundation; below that, the remains of an Etruscan tower. The house, and three others on the farm, sat on top of a steep hill embraced by chestnut and fig trees, a lemon grove, and an enormous garden. There were sheep and goats on the land, a pony, chickens, a dog, and twenty-three feral cats. On the hill below were a vineyard and a grove of silver-green olive trees.

On Erie Street, I had two locks, a deadbolt, and a chain on my fourth-floor walk-up apartment. At Cerreto, I didn't even own a key. Beside my bedroom was a little studio with a door that opened onto a flower-lined path, leading to a chicken house. On warm fall days, chickens meandered in from outside, and Stella the farm dog burst in the room wagging her tail, running up to lick my face. She'd sit on the terra-cotta floor beside me, bury her nose in my sleeve, sniff my wrist, and sigh. That was when I missed my mother the most, those brief moments of animal closeness—the warmth of a dog's breath on my skin, the touch of her velvet ear.

Across the path from my studio was a medieval stone house where Sabina and Alfredo—the resident farmers who worked for the owner—lived, along with Alfredo's ninety-year-old mother. Sometimes Alfredo's mother would stop by to offer a slice of *torta di mela* on an old chipped plate, or a few biscotti from her brown leathery hands. Once the family invited me over for a glass of wine. Their house was straight out of Boccaccio—the large open hearth with a big black kettle hanging from an iron hook, a blackened ceiling, an old church calendar with a beatific Madonna and child.

"Where is your family?" Sabina asked. I said my father was dead but my sister was in New York and my mother and grandmother were in Ohio. "*Tutto bene,*" I lied, when they asked after my mother's health. "She's fine."

"We could adopt you," Sabina suggested. She told me how the Lord had decided not to bless them with children, no matter how many times they prayed.

"I'm thirty-one." I said with a laugh. "Too old for that."

"We can still adopt you in Italy. We'll find you a nice husband. Don't worry."

Why would a girl come here without a family if not to make one of her own?

———

I get anxious when I think about the war, being so far from my sister and my friends. And where is my mother? Is she safe? Something inside feels a bit lost and broken. But no matter how sad I feel at times, when I walk down the hill to take the bus to Florence, and the haze lifts off the trees, and I catch a glimpse of a *lepre*, one of the gray-brown hares that scatter across the land, and see a startled pheasant, flushed out from the brush by my footsteps, I don't want to leave. Despite my loneliness and my growing stress about money, I want to stay on this hilltop of grapevines and olives. Without my sister and family around to remind me that she is the writer and I am the art-ist, I start writing stories and poems. I don't want to be the person who gasps in fear whenever she hears the sound of a doorbell or a phone. I just want to lose myself in these hills, in the river winding west to the city of bridges.

I always meet Emilio, the antique dealer, at his workshop, never his store. I've recently begun working for him, restoring ceramics. He is fifty or so, tall and wiry, and when I come to drop off the pieces I have restored, he is bent over his large oak table, a limp hand-rolled cigarette dangling from his thin lips, examining an old print he has just bought for a song. One day I happen to have my portfolio with me when I stop in to pick up a small porcelain figu-rine that needs repair.

"*Mi fai vedere*," he says. "Let's see what you have."

I show him a few paintings, small metaphysical landscapes inhabited with glowing plants and flowers, arches with beasts, tendrils, and leaves. In some I had painted part of a woman, tilting her ear to something she hears in the distance. Emilio leans over my paintings spread out on the table. He holds his cigarette over my work, his ashes dangerously close. "Who is the woman?" He points with his long yellow-stained finger.

The woman's ear is mine; her face resembles my mother. "No one," I say.

"Not bad, these pictures."

Emilio takes a long drag and exhales a cloud of smoke. "Can you do watercolor?"

"Watercolor, egg tempera, gouache. Or oil. Anything."

"Good. I have a job for you."

He hands me some old watercolor paper, a little brown and ragged around the edges, and asks me to copy an Art Nouveau painting of a dancer. He will pay me $200. That is half a month's rent at Cerreto. If I do a good job, there could be more.

"Use the old paper. Americans like anything that looks old. It doesn't have to be exact." He adds, "It doesn't even have to be that good."

Up until now, I have been making six dollars an hour at a part-time job modeling nude for a figure drawing class, taught by a tyrannical professor in an unheated room. Maybe with Emilio, I can make a living wage. When I return to Cerreto, I begin a letter to my sister to tell her of my good fortune. But how should I begin? Rachel has changed her name to Natalia. She says that if she hadn't done it, our mother would find her. My sister wants to start over. She has a tenure-track job teaching English, lives in a new town, has a brand-new life. I write, *Dear Natalia*, at the top of the page, but it feels strange. *Dear Rachel* feels wrong too. Before I left for Italy, my sister had urged me to change my name but I couldn't. The art world is a young person's game. Everything I had done until then had been in my birth name, Myra Herr. What would happen to my career if I became someone else? But my sister would say, "What could happen to both of us if you don't?"

Two years later, my mother will write this in her diary: *I've been thinking of changing my name for over fifty years. I could change the "N" in my first name to an "H"—from Norma to Horma(h). There is a <u>Horma(h)</u>, a city in the Bible, that was marked for destruction. Or perhaps I shall re-name myself Isthmus. Archaic definition: a narrow passage connect two bodies of land. Literal definition: affording little room for place or boundaries.*

Every Wednesday, after I'm done modeling, I cross Santa Trinita to the Oltrarno, the other side of the river, where the artisans work. The streets are incredibly narrow and full of the deafening chatter of *motorini*. It's even louder here than my old neighborhood in Chicago. The city air smells of car exhaust, rotting garbage, grilled meat, and espresso. I stop at a little place called Café Calibria in Piazza Santo Spirito to write, and sip a glass of rose-colored *vin santo*. Afterward, I go to the church and light a candle for my mother. Not that I believe it will do any good; it's just to remind myself that she is still lost in the world.

One day in late October, after the café, I drop off a watercolor at Emilio's. He has been giving me more work lately, more things to copy onto the same antique paper. I ask him why he doesn't want me to use a better paper, something museum-grade without the wood pulp in it that makes it brittle and brown. "These won't last," I say. "I have good paper at home."

Emilio turns his back to me, rolls a cigarette, and lights up without turning back around. "If you don't like the work," he says, "I can easily find someone else."

On my way back toward the river, something catches my eye in the window of an antiquarian shop. It's a small reliquary for a saint's bone. The things people collect, I think. What was in there? One of the eight foreskins of Christ supposedly floating around Europe? I hear a muffled rapping against the window. There's a man with thick salt-and-pepper hair beckoning me to come in. His face is kind; the air is damp and cold, so I go in.

The man had been polishing a silver bowl. "Come in," he says in Italian. He shows me what is inside the bowl—a tiny scorpion curled into a half-moon. He plucks it out and places it on the table. I take two steps back.

"Don't worry, he's dead. My name is Paolo, by the way."

"*Mi chiamo*, Myra," I say, pronouncing my name *MEE*-rah, the way my Italian friends do.

I follow Paolo around as he shows me his rare books and prints, antique pottery, jewelry, and flatware. Paolo looks about forty-five, and is very fit, although his tweed jacket is a bit tight around his waist. He picks up the bowl that had held the scorpion and turns it over.

"English silver, *ottocento*," he says. He motions me to come close. His skin smells like sandalwood. "Can you see that?"

Paolo points to a small stamp at the bottom of the bowl, a tiny crown. He explains how each silver object has a stamp on the bottom—a lion, a crown, a tree, or some other sign. He has to know what each symbol means so he can tell when and where each piece was made. My grandmother used to show me the symbols on the bottoms of her little cups from China, explain which ones were worth more than others and why.

Paolo places the scorpion back in the bowl. "*Sogni d'oro*. Dreams of gold."

I feel embarrassed. Paolo clears his throat. He rubs a spot on the bowl. "I better get going now," I say. "See you around."

"Wait," says Paolo. "Tell me what you like best in my shop."

I take a careful look around again, by myself. Everything is carefully arranged like a cabinet of curiosities. Each book in alphabetical order, the nicer ones with illustrated plates propped open on small wooden stands. The furniture is classic late eighteenth century Tuscany—heavy carved tables and chairs, a rosewood pedestal inlaid with mother-of-pearl, an opulent credenza embellished with gold. I sit down on a red velvet chair and think of my grandma, how she used to take me to Higbee's on Saturdays to see the furniture displays. She'd look at the dining room sets she couldn't afford while I sat on leather couches, among a forest of Japanese screens, both of us dreaming we were living someone else's life.

I walk around his shop again and settle on three things. I lead Paolo to an old mahogany music stand, the reliquary in the window, and then to the scorpion in the bowl. Paolo laughs when I point to the scorpion.

"Wait," I say. "There's one more." I show Paolo an old print I found at the back of his shop. The words at the bottom of the page read, *Penula Antica*. "He looks like Folly," I say. "Or maybe Hermes. His feet have little wings."

"Take it. It's yours."

"I can't do that."

"Of course you can. We can make a trade. You take the print and next time you take me out for a coffee. How's that?"

"That would be nice," I say. When I get home, I see he has slipped another print inside my pack, an engraving of ancient musical instruments. *A presto*, the note says, *see you soon*.

A few days later, I have an altercation with the professor who teaches the figure drawing class. He blows up at me for scratching my nose, for taking a break to pee, for shivering when there's no heat. At the end of the session he refuses to pay and I leave crying. I head in the direction of Paolo's shop. I'm on my Vespa this time, a noisy red one I bought off of a middle-aged Japanese man who had purchased it from a teenage girl. My hair is short now and I'm wearing a black leather jacket and high black boots. But my Vespa betrays my new tough look—it is plastered with Snoopy and I-♥-THE-NEW KIDS ON THE BLOCK stickers no amount of scrubbing will remove.

Paolo asks me out to dinner and I say yes, almost bursting into tears again, grateful for the free meal. Soon I will be out of money if I don't find more work. I remind him of our previous deal, though: the print for coffee later. During our squid ink fettuccine, I find out that he is forty-six, married, and has two kids. His son is eighteen and his daughter is twenty-six, five years younger than me. I block out Robert's face on the stairway, my mother calling after me as I drive away from her in winter. Instead, I notice the laugh lines around Paolo's warm brown eyes; how nice it is to eat a good hot meal.

"I'd like to see you," he says, after our orange and fennel salad.

"Just as friends," I say.

"Of course," he says. "Just as friends."

The next day, at home in Cerreto, I open a letter from Gloria, the woman who takes care of my grandma. She has written to tell me that my mother left the Stuart House apartment and is now homeless. She had contacted Gloria through my grandmother's lawyer to set up a meeting in a restaurant because she isn't allowed to know where my grandma lives. Gloria said in the letter that my mother arrived with two bags, one filled with papers, the other with crumbled-up clothing and a butcher knife. Gloria saw the knife poking out of the bag and made my mother hand it over to her. She had purchased two discount plane tickets for the following week, one for California, the other for Chicago. "You and your minions stole my house from me," she told Gloria. "And I aim to get it and my mother back." The last thing she said to Gloria was that her youngest daughter had changed her hair and face and the other daughter had changed her name.

It's midday in Italy and at Cerreto, the *vendemmia* is in full force: workers gather the turning grapes and olives in the late afternoon sun. In Cleveland or Chicago it's early morning and the city is just waking up. I try to imagine what my mother's life is like now, while I sip my tea and watch the men and women on the hill. A bell is ringing at a homeless shelter, somewhere in a bad part of town. My mother will wake up before everyone else and check beneath her pillow to see if someone's stolen her teeth in the middle of the night. There will be fifty women, or a hundred or more, packed like sardines in a gym. She will gulp down coffee and a donut and go out the door. She'll be dressed in four layers, one for safety, one for warmth, one for gamma rays, and one for just pure luck. She'll find a chair at a library, or a bench in the park, and doze off, dreaming her thoughts are being projected into someone else's dream. When she wakes she'll say to herself, *No matter where I go, where I sleep, I must identify the Enemy or they'll replace my heart with the heart of a Nazi or a pig. I have to know my safety exits in case of fire; know how to crawl on the floor when there's smoke in the room; how to get information from the phone book and the professional manipulators with cannibal teeth. I must walk like I know where I am going, have eyes at the back of my head. If I don't, they'll inject me with poison and dump me far from the city, and there will be water everywhere rushing fast, and I'll be clinging to an old rubber tire, heading down a long river of darkness straight into the leopard's mouth.*

Or maybe she isn't in a shelter. Maybe she's sleeping on the street. Or maybe she's in a halfway house and has a small but clean and tidy bed. Maybe she is dead. I am here, watching men pluck grapes off lush, heavy vines while my mother plucks a tuna sandwich out of a Dumpster four thousand miles away. Would she do that? Would she stoop that low?

The next time I get together with Paolo it's November 2, the Day of the Dead, *il giorno dei morti*, the day Italians place photographs on the headstones of their loved ones. Some people celebrate by making a dish with sweet fava beans they call *ossi dei morti*, "the bones of the dead." If my mother died somewhere, how would I find her bones? It's pouring rain and hard to see; on the way over to Paolo's shop I nearly get run over by a *panini di trippa* truck. I lock my *motorino* outside of Paolo's shop. I've convinced him to go to a gospel concert, a Chicago group is singing at a nearby church. Years ago, I used to go some Sundays to hear South Side choirs in Chicago early in the morning, and then head to the Soul Queen for eggs and grits.

"Gospel music? What kind of music is this?"

"Dance and clap your hands kind of music," I say. "You'll like it."

At the concert, it is clear that Italians do not understand gospel, at least not these Italians. It's a wealthy Florentine crowd, women in furs and gold jewelry, men in Armani suits. No one claps along; everyone is too polite. No encores, nothing. If this were a black church on the South Side of Chicago, we'd all be dancing in the aisles. What's the matter with these people? All of a sudden I am homesick and tears are streaming down my face.

"What's wrong?" asks Paolo.

"No one danced," I say, for lack of words.

How can I explain? I tick off a list in my head of lost people and things: mother, sister, friends, grandma, house, Robert, Ginger, the snapdragons in Grandma's backyard, the Armstrongs from across the street, my old friend Cathy, the Field Museum, Lake Michigan, everything is up for grabs. Paolo puts his arm around me and kisses my face. "Leave your bike," he says. "You can pick it up tomorrow. I'm taking you home."

In the driveway at Cerreto, we make out in his car for over an hour, like teenagers. What am I doing? He is a married man. I've never taken drugs, gotten rip-roaring drunk, stolen anything, not even candy from Kresge's five and dime when I was a kid. Now I'm kissing someone else's husband. All I want to do is hurl myself into a different life as fast as I can, away from what incessantly gnaws at my heart.

"Come to Venice with me," he says, when I gather my things to go inside. "I have to buy some antiques. Please come. You're an artist; you can help me pick things out."

"I'll think about it," I say.

"Don't think too long. I'm going soon."

The next day I return to town to get my bike and drop off another faux-antique watercolor at Emilio's. "Have you ever made an icon?" he asks.

"No, but I could."

"Wait, I have a better idea. An illumination with gold leaf. Can you do gilding? I'll get you the vellum but you pay for the gold. Make a big initial, any letter you want. Something medieval or early Renaissance. You know what I'm saying?"

"I think so."

"You sure you know? I'll pay you a lot more for this kind of thing."

"Fine. Thanks, that's great. I can use the money."

"Don't show anyone, though," says Emilio. "I'm paying you under the table. Let's just keep it a secret, agreed?"

"I'm good at that," I say.

Back home in Cerreto, I am in the kitchen reading a book about illumination, one of Cerreto's new kittens, Puline, upon my lap. I can smell Gabriella's cooking from upstairs, where I plan to go for dinner. Lately, I eat there almost every night. I've just thrown a log in the fire when Elsa walks in the room.

"Well, are you going to Venice with that man?"

"I don't know," I say.

She lets out a little snort. "He's married, huh?"

"Yes," I say, and return to my book.

"Men only want one thing, so it's best to use them as you like. That's what I do. You should do the same."

"Thanks for the advice."

"I don't bother with Swedes or Germans. Especially American men. They're crybabies. I only sleep with Italians. *Southern* Italians. I have a Neapolitan soul."

Here we go again, I think. Neapolitan, my ass. "I have work to do," I say, then add, "By the way, I put my name on the answering machine. There are three of us living here, not just two."

Later, in my studio, I consider the art of illumination; *illumination*, derived from the Latin, *illuminare*: to illuminate or enlighten. What is luminous to me is that I need to make my picture absolutely perfect so Emilio will give me more work. I only have enough money for two more months in Italy, and then what? Go back to Chicago, where my mother probably is? I look out my window at the stars. You can barely see the moon in the city, let alone the stars. I want to stay. But I've never used gold before or painted on vellum or parchment. Emilio will pay for the vellum but I'll have to buy the gold leaf, a burnisher, gesso, and other expensive things.

Illumination originally meant the application of minium, red lead, to decorate a piece of religious text written in black ink. But over time, artist-scribes applied raised and highly burnished gold, embellishing codices with delicate and meticulously painted letters and miniature scenes. They did it to honor God but also to help the reader find his way around the text. The first illuminated manuscript I remember seeing was at the Cleveland Museum of Art with my mother. It was Queen Isabella's Book of Hours, made in fifteenth century Spain. I remember the pages on display were of Christ's crucifixion, but what drew me to the book wasn't the pious scene at the cross but the rich gold border surrounding it, decorated with flowers, butterflies, and birds. Each tiny bloom, wing, and beak looked so real and was rendered in such detail I felt I could crawl right inside the page.

Puline purrs at my feet while I read about how to make something gold: First I outline my drawing in ink, next I paint on gesso where the gold will go. When the gesso is dry, I breathe on the raised letter or design to moisten it so it can receive the thin sheaf of gold I carefully lay down with tweezers. After I apply each layer of gold, I breathe on it and burnish the surface until it glistens in the light. The painting comes after illumination. But what should I paint? I could make the letter *M* for my own name just in case I have to let it go. I will make a beautiful floriated letter, surrounded by an intricate border of flowers and birds, deer and exotic beasts. It will be a historiated letter, like one from an ancient Book of Hours where inside is a miniature scene from a story. In the background I'll paint blue hills and a winding river, a garden, and a sky dotted with birds. Something full of beauty and longing, like Maria Callas singing in my grandmother's basement, like my mother's hands wavering above ivory keys.

After several drawings I am ready to start. Emilio had seen my final sketch and liked it. But when I think of Emilio touching my art with his long yellow fingers, I cringe. I imagine him handing my delicate painting over to a couple of rich loud Americans. Then I hear his voice in my head: *If it's good I'll give you a thousand dollars. But it has to look old.* A thousand American dollars will buy me two more months at Cerreto and food. Massimo from upstairs always says that Florence is a *putana*, a mercantile city only interested in selling her soul. Have I become one of her own?

The day I stop at Emilio's studio to collect money for the vellum I've bought, he's not there. Without the money, I can't afford to buy gold. I pull out his business card to see if his shop address is on it. When I get to his store, the place is closed. Something in the window catches my eye. It's my first Art Nouveau painting of the dancer. I'm happy it's on prominent display. Then I see the sign. ANTICA & AUTENTICA, CIRCA 1900.

Have I been making forgeries?

Had he told me but I was too stupid to understand? "Are you sure you know what I'm saying? I'll pay you a lot more for *this kind of thing.*" The gerbil wheel in my brain starts spinning: If I turn him in he can do the same to me. They'll send me back. And he'll blame me. Tell the police he bought art from me that I said was old. He could play dumb. What should I do? What if he calls, wants to know about the picture I promised?

Later that night, I am thinking of Robert when the phone rings. I jump to answer it but hear Paolo's voice on the answering machine and decide not to pick up. Suddenly I hear a sound like thunder coming from somewhere below the house. My first thought is that it's a bomb. With all this talk of war in the news—Iraqi bomb threats in American schools, the pipe bomb that went off at the American discothèque in Arezzo, only an hour from here—what's next? I tell myself it must be the water heater or gas tank or something else. It couldn't be a bomb.

The TV and lights go off with a pop. I try the phone. Dead. When I hear the second big *ka-boom* I grab my sweater, passport, and Puline. What if there is an explosion and the house catches on fire? The trees could go up in flames. We have no water here; this isn't a city, there's no fire station, no truck of heroes heading to my house to save me. No one is home on the farm; even Sabina, Alfredo, and his mother aren't home. Where has everyone gone? I stand outside in the cold damp night, clutching the small cat to my chest, waiting for someone to drive up the hill and take me home, give me hot milk and honey, read me a story, and put me to bed. But where is home? And whom am I waiting for? It starts to rain. I stand in the driveway and wait until I am thoroughly soaked and feel ridiculous and tired, then go back inside and crawl into bed.

The week before Christmas, Paolo tells me he has bought me a little gift. We are in his shop and his son stops by to say hello. His son is eighteen now, handsome and tall. He is only five years younger than Robert. "He's a good boy," says Paolo, watching his son wave goodbye from the door.

"He might go to war, you know," I say. "He might get drafted to Iraq."

"You are too serious sometimes," says Paolo.

On the way to the restaurant, we pass a tall man from Senegal in a thin jacket, selling handbags on the street. The man calls out to us, "Gucci! Gucci! Armani! Vuitton!" His wares are spread out on a shabby old blanket, probably the same one he covers himself with at night. Does my mother sleep on the street like that? I haven't told a soul here about her, her illness, about how she could be dead and I wouldn't even know.

I want to talk about my mother to someone, anyone, but instead I turn to Paolo and go on a rant about how poor immigrant men from Senegal have to sleep ten to a trailer in Florence and have no legal rights. I tell him that I am now illegal too, unless I get a legitimate full-time job or get married. *Imposter,* says my mother's voice inside my head. *You are the imposter now. You are a forgery. You're not even real.*

"I'm tired," says Paolo. "Can we talk about something else?"

I am tired too.

Later, alone in my room, I take out the print Paolo had given me the first day we met. It smells like his shop, like sandalwood and a faint hint of mold. Is the picture of Hermes, god of dreamers, nomads, and thieves? Or maybe it's the Fool from the tarot, blindsided, ready to step off a cliff. Where to next? I ask myself. Should I stay or should I go? And if I stay, will I have to forge a life that isn't true?

I never call Paolo again or stop by his shop. He phones me once but I don't return his call. One afternoon I see his son near the Duomo. I pull my hood down so he can't recognize me, and feel full of shame. I never call Emilio again either. I avoid walking past his studio and his store. I avoid crossing the river altogether, for everyone seems to know you there, everyone watches who comes and goes. I end up getting a job teaching art history at the American School in Florence and resolve to make my $1,000 the old-fashioned way. With my first paycheck, I buy a small packet of gold leaf and tuck the delicate sheets away for another time, for an illumination of my own, not someone else's.

⁓

In January, America bombs Baghdad. I miss my sister and my grandma, who, by the time I see her again, probably won't remember my name. I miss my mother too and am convinced she is sleeping on a park bench in the snow. I watch Baghdad blow up each night on the television, buildings exploding into bursts of green light. If you didn't know it was a war, you'd think the night-vision sky looked magical, like the Night of the Shooting Stars. Despite the bombing, the streets are filled for some reason with brides; Baghdad defies the West with the oldest ritual in the world. After a month of this, the school I teach at and every other American place closes because of bomb threats. Then one morning Elsa bursts into my bedroom at five in the morning, screaming at me because Puline, the cat, had vomited on her newspaper the night before. In my half-sleep state I think she's my mother; I pull the covers over my face so she can't get to my neck. I want to go home.

The only airline flying out of Florence during the First Gulf War is Yugoslav Airlines. There is one condition if you want to leave the country on their plane. You have to spend four nights in Belgrade as a tourist, even though Yugoslavia is about to go to war too and everything is shut down. At the airport, armed soldiers are crawling all over and customs takes an eternity. Something bad is about to happen and I hope I am gone by the time it does.

I spend all four days sequestered in an ugly state-run hotel taking naps and trying to figure out what to do when I get to Chicago. My last night before I fly back to America, I turn on the television to watch the news. On the screen is a BBC special about starving Kurds displaced by the American-Iraqi war. American helicopters fly low to the ground and drop frozen chickens onto a swarming crowd. Some chickens hit the heads of old men and young mothers holding babies. The men and women fall to the ground as if they have been shot. There aren't enough chickens to go around and the camera pans to a fight starting up between two groups of hysterical men vying for a few frozen birds covered in sand.

I turn the TV off, sick of war and all the heartache in the world, sick of myself. I go down to the hotel restaurant to eat. Will this be the last year I go by my old name? I want someone to say it, Myra, to call out to me so that I'll look up. But there's no one here I know. When the waitress brings me my tea, I hold the slice of lemon up to my nose to breathe it in. I know the next day I will land in wintry Chicago without a place to live, my mother homeless and trying to track me down. I will have to change my name, find a job, and start over again, maybe in a new city. But for the moment, when I close my eyes, I smell the grove of lemon trees at Cerreto heavy with fruit; I smell the rich russet earth, the chestnut trees and pines. I promise myself I will never live anyplace ugly and dangerous again.

Someday, I will live in a quiet green place, off a winding country road. My house will be small but warm, and the rooms awash with light. The floor will be terra-cotta red. My studio will be like the simple room of a scribe, filled with pots of paints and sheaves of paper-thin gold. There will be an arched window in the room with luxuriant vines. Outside, I will have a small, enclosed garden, dense with vegetables and flowers, lavender, basil, and rosemary, the herb of remembrance. And if I look out the window at just the right moment, the garden will be illuminated in the golding hour of the day.

On Love and War

I recently made a rough map of the Arab world, including a scene of the last con-
flagration in Afghanistan—the latest Great American Witch Hunt. In my day,
they went after the artists and writers, the union organizers and Communists.
Now it's people with turbans. Someone's always fighting someone, somewhere. I
remember young men from school, going off to war. I remember Lester Goodman
who I loved, the only boy I ever loved. Lester took me to concerts, to plays. Lester
and I, we could have had a life. When Lester came home from the war I had already
met the bastard father of my girls. Some boys from my neighborhood didn't come
home. They say they died there fighting but I think the U.S. government sent them
to the camps. They did it to the Japanese, why not American Jews? I was lucky. I
could have been somebody's lampshade. Thinking of that old Kashmiri song: Pale
hands I loved beside the Shalimar, Where are you now? . . . Whom do you
lead on rapture's roadway far, Before you agonize them in farewell? *Never*
have I kept The Enemy at bay, nor have I been lucky in love or war.

12

Isn't one's true abode any wild place, any firestorm or night of discontent . . . ?

Gretel Ehrlich, *Islands, the Universe, Home*

A Hand and a Name

I am a refugee, my mother wrote in her diary from 1992. *I'm looking for my children and the key to my home.* In the fall that year, my mother wrote her first letter to me after her disappearance two years before: *Dear Daughter, Today is Yom Kippur, the Day of Atonement. Four more years till the Year of the Rat then eleven more to go. Baruch atah adonai, elohenu melech ha'olam. One may think an enemy has passed, but how can one be sure?* I was traveling in Israel at the time, but she thought I was still living somewhere in Europe: *My only motherly advice to you in travel,* she wrote, *is to bring your own linens, towels and especially washcloths. And consider purchasing a World Atlas and Almanac. By the way, the people here in Chicago are not friendly.*

From her diaries, I learned that when my mother moved to Chicago, she began studying geography and several languages, including Italian, German, Hebrew, and Spanish. She also reviewed the Russian, French, and Yiddish she already knew. It appeared that she was planning on tracking me down overseas. She drew maps and labeled each country in four different languages and made charts with pictures of things she wanted to remember the words for, such as *mother, daughter,* and *lost.* She filled out a passport application but got stuck in the place where they asked for her birth date.

She wrote 1926, the year she was born, then crossed it out and wrote in 1940, then crossed it out again. My mother was also reading a book called *How to Locate Anyone Anywhere Without Leaving Home.* She hired a private detective to hunt me and my sister down, paid him $200, then changed her mind, and hired a different man. She also cut out the weather forecast each week from a section in the *Chicago Tribune* called "Weather for Travelers" and kept track of the rise and fall of the dollar in the rest of the world. Should she stay or should she go?

After I returned from Italy in the winter of '91, I signed a contract with HarperCollins for a children's book series on world cultures, based on the work I had done at the Field Museum. My sister begged me to change my name. Our mother could find us through my books once they came out in stores. The day I went to the courthouse in Chicago, the judge asked me to declare why I was changing my name. "I'm a writer and have decided to take my pen name as my own." How easy it was to lie, make up a different identity with a new Social Security card, new credit cards and picture IDs. What if I had told the truth: "I am changing my name because I don't want my mother to find me. I don't want to take her in and support her, keep vigil all night so she doesn't set my furniture on fire. I am changing my name because I am selfish. I want to be an artist. It's all I've ever wanted to be." When I returned from the courthouse a bouquet of flowers was waiting for me from my sister with a note: *A rose by another name will still be sweet.*

In the summer of '92 I decided to take a three-month break from my book series and go to Hilai, an artists' residency in Israel's Upper Galilee. In exchange for housing, I was expected to do some kind of community cultural project. My plan was to bring together local Arab and Jewish children through writing workshops. I had done a similar project in the 1980s teaching art to American children along with Guatemalan children displaced by the U.S.-Contra conflict.

A couple of weeks before I left town, I spotted a woman walking by the Heartland Café in Rogers Park. She looked just like my mother. Could that be her? It was eighty-five degrees but she was wearing a dirty wool cap and coat, pushing a cart full of garbage bags. Why wouldn't she move to Chicago? Even if she believed I moved to Europe, wouldn't I eventually come back? At the time, I didn't know that she was already living there drawing maps of the Middle East and memorizing the Song of Songs: "I am the rose of Sharon, and the lily of the valleys. As the lily among thorns, so is my love among the daughters." When I boarded the plane for Israel, my mother was beginning her studies in Hebrew and the Kabbala. We had been living parallel lives in the same city for nearly two years without knowing it—me in a quiet basement apartment in the Gold Coast home of my friends Bob and Nancy; my mother in subsidized housing, run by Jesus People, on trash-strewn Wilson Avenue, just a few miles from my home.

∞

A man sits in a refugee camp, cutting pieces of paper for hours. He's never seen a pair of scissors before and the wind rises up from the mountains and blows the tiny slips into the air like flecks of snow, and the man keeps cutting and a silent crowd gathers, and the wind rises again and more slips of paper float away. It's someone else's memory, not mine, a story a friend tells me about the Ethiopian refugee camp next to my apartment in Israel. The scissors had been a gift to the man from his son, whom he had been separated from for ten years. What gift would I give my mother if I could see her once again?

It's a hot August day and I'm walking to the Arab horse stables in Tarshiha, next to the Jewish town of Ma'alot where I am staying. I stop outside the refugee camp and peer in. I can see where the man must have sat all day, making confetti after years of loss. I watch some Falasha children trace their hands with colored chalk on a long concrete wall. When they left Ethiopia they were told about their exodus only an hour before the plane took off and weren't permitted to carry anything except the clothes on their backs. All they had with them were their hands and a name. I haven't seen my mother in two years. What did she carry with her when she left her house behind?

When I arrive at the stables, I run into Dennis, an American journalist who is staying at Hilai. He looks out of place with his blond hair, faded red baseball cap, his big map shoved into his back pocket. On the trail, Dennis lags behind, while I ride on ahead. My horse breaks into a run and Dennis disappears in a cloud of dust. I take the mare down curving roads, galloping hard.

I enter a biblical landscape, beyond the olive groves, tobacco fields, and farms. A lizard darts from beneath a rock; another follows. I lose myself in the movement of the horse, in the red-ocher earth, the open sky. I gallop down goat paths, past rows of tobacco plants beneath the harsh sun, past pheasants, doves, snakes, a mare and its little foal. I don't want the day to end, the machine of muscle, the whirl of hooves below. When I'm in motion I feel safe and free—on a horse, a bicycle, skating on a pond, swimming in the sea.

When I return to the stables, the stable owner's wife offers me *za'atar* on warm pita with thick Arabic coffee, fresh creamy *labneh* and olives. I sit and wait for Dennis in the shade. What would it be like to move here—to a country I feel no love for or attachment to, even though my Jewish friends in America say I should? *I hope you marry a Jew,* my mother always said. *You could honeymoon in the Holy Land.* Growing up, I didn't know any Jews and was even beat up once in St. Mel's playground for "killing Christ." Afterward my mother told me it was because I was one of the Chosen Ones. "Just don't tell anyone," she said. "Next time they'll slit your throat." But on the way home from Tarshiha, it's the Orthodox Jewish kids from the local yeshiva who attack me, bombarding me with stones for wearing shorts on Shabbat.

Later, that evening, I take a walk with Dennis to the edge of town. Ma'alot, a Jewish settlement built in the fifties after the War of Independence (what Palestinians call "The Catastrophe"), is much greener and cooler than the ancient Arab town of Tarshiha, where the stables are. Dennis and I sit on the side of a rocky hill and look out at the distant lights of Peki'in and Lebanon. The southern security zone, the supposed "buffer zone" the Israel Defense Forces (IDF) created to protect northern Israeli Jews from infiltration and attack, is only ten kilometers away. Rows of cypress trees surround us— Lebanon cedar and pine trees planted with money from American Jews. The Arab towns surrounding Ma'alot look like constellations twinkling beyond the hills. A coyote howls nearby. We listen to gunshots over the border and watch the stars. The lights remind me of the lights in the memory room for children at Yad Vashem (meaning "a Hand and a Name"), the Holocaust museum in Jerusalem. The room is made to look like the night sky, one star for every child. I wonder how many stars are in the room; is my mother alive or dead?

"Where do you think the soul goes, Dennis?"

"Is there a soul?"

"I don't know. What do you think?"

"Well, if it does exist, it must die in the body, then live on in people's memories."

"So much nature, so much violence."

"What do you mean?"

"This hillside in Galilee—it's so lush, all these flowers and birds, this valley of trees. But then everywhere you go you see the IDF, thick as locusts. And they're just children. Little kids with AK-47s on their backs."

I want to tell him, or tell anyone, about my mother. But what would be the point? Why burden anyone? Dennis and I talk about war, about Israel/Palestine's complicated past. He tells me he was in prison in the sixties as a conscientious objector while all his buddies went off to Vietnam. He doesn't say much about it, though, and seems like he is holding something in too. We sit in silence again. The gunshots get closer. I think of the shootings on Erie Street where I used to live, my grandfather's basement arsenal, the refugee camps in Gaza and the West Bank where families have lived for generations waiting to return home, and all those souls at Yad Vashem. Do the souls of the children live in the room of stars or do they wander their old streets in Vilnius, Warsaw, Budapest, and Berlin? And the souls of the children who died during the Intifada—where are they now? What if my mother falls dead on the street? How would I know?

When I open up the newspaper the next morning, I read about the bombing of a bus in Jerusalem. Almost all the victims are women and children. It is the year of the Oslo Peace Accord and Israel-Palestine is anything but peaceful. My mother would say it is the Year of the Monkey. The Chinese Year, that is—a year of erratic genius, promiscuity, and a strong will.

After breakfast I hear a knock at the door. It is a young Israeli soldier holding out a bag of moist smelly cheese. I had met him in the town square the first day I arrived in Ma'alot. He saw me exit the cab, staring at my map, looking confused. I had protested his helping me that day, but he insisted on escorting me to Hilai, which was how he knew where I lived. I take the dripping bag from his hand. "Thank you," I say. "Sorry, but I don't have time to talk."

The soldier doesn't smile. He shifts the semiautomatic slung over his shoulder onto his back. When he speaks, his breath reeks of cigarettes and sour milk.

"You come out with me," he says.

"I have a boyfriend," I lie. "A *big* boyfriend." I make a gesture with my hands to show how tall my imaginary boyfriend is. "He is very jealous."

"He is in America," says the soldier. "Etan is here."

An hour later, there is another knock at the door. I think it's the soldier again but it's an elderly Jewish artist named Shalom from across the hall. He invites me over for tea.

His apartment is the mirror image of mine—sterile white walls, small bedroom with a single bed and chair, cramped living room with a hot plate and fridge. Shalom's wife, Nishoma, is busy making tea, their fat yellow Lab sprawled out on the linoleum floor by her feet. Shalom tells me that since World War II, he can't stand being alone. His wife and dog follow him from room to room. "They sit in my studio while I paint," he says. "Even back home in Jerusalem." He laughs and says it's hard to fit the three of them—him, his wife, and Ishi, their dog—all in the single bed at Hilai.

The three of us chat and drink tea for an hour or so. Then Shalom starts telling stories about the war. I'm surprised he is so open about it. He recounts how he lost his entire family in the camps, except for his little sister. He had a young wife (Nishoma is his second wife), an infant son, nine siblings, a mother and father, and other close relatives. They all died. He and his sister were both placed in Dachau. Sometimes his sister, who worked in the kitchen, would steal things—a scrap of bread, a potato—and slip them to her brother through the fence separating the men's camp from the women's. If Shalom was lucky enough to find a tiny piece of paper and pencil stub or piece of coal, he'd make a sketch for her. "I'd tell her it was a beautiful dream and that she should put it under her pillow that night."

Shalom says it was a game they had played since childhood. If one of them woke up from a nightmare, the other would draw a new dream to place beneath the other's pillow. I think of my sister and me in our little room on Triskett Road in Cleveland—her writing stories, me making pictures all day, side by side. I would have drawn a dream for her too.

When the Nazis heard that the Americans were on the way to liberate the camp, they forced the Jews to march in the freezing cold for miles to a clearing in a forest. The remaining survivors were made to dig one giant grave. The SS lined the prisoners up near the edge so they would fall in once they started shooting.

"But the Americans came," says Shalom. "Before the first shots were fired."

How is he able to tell me these things? They say that living through a traumatic childhood is a lot like living through the trauma of war. Here is a man who experienced the worst atrocities and I can't even tell anyone that my mother is mentally ill. Is it shame that makes me hold my secret close?

Shalom says that when the Americans arrived, he had already passed out from hunger and cold. When he woke up, the first thing he saw was a dark empty hole. Even now, he says, he still dreams of falling into that deep abyss. Shalom's story reminds me of what another man told me in Chicago. The man said he survived the war by hiding himself beneath the corpses in a giant mass grave. But I don't tell Shalom. After an hour of this kind of talk, I can tell we are all tired of darkness and death.

"Want to see my drawings?" he asks, and opens up a portfolio leaning against the wall. The pictures are all happy ones—Chagall-like women dancing, flying dogs; exuberant and colorful scenes. Not one trace of sorrow.

The next day the soldier brings me a plate of sticky, rotting figs. He leaves it by my door while I'm at the Arab Community Center, trying to arrange the workshops I want to do with the local children. The day after, the soldier leaves a bag of gooey dates. This time I've been to the Jewish Community Center trying to arrange the same thing. Neither community seems to be able to agree on days and times. Most of the Jewish children are religious and can't meet on Fridays and Saturdays. The Arab kids are all Christians and can't meet on Sundays. And no one can agree on a weekday or a time to meet after school.

One day, while I'm napping, I hear pounding on my door. I wake up with my heart in my throat. My first thought is: She's found me! I crack the door open and there's the soldier again, hands on his hips, gun slung over his back.

"I'm sleeping," I say. "Go away."

"I come back at dinner."

"Thank you, but no."

"We get falafel. You and Etan. I come back."

After he leaves, I go downstairs to the office to talk to the building manager. She laughs and tells me that the army boys are harmless.

"He is stalking me."

"Just because he carries a gun doesn't mean he's a stalker."

"No," I say. "He's really stalking me. You have to do something."

"I'll talk to the boy. But don't worry."

"Tell him to leave me alone or I'll call the police."

"This is Israel." She laughs again. "He *is* the police."

One morning I wake up and write a letter to my mother, even though I have no idea where to send it. For my return address, I write the PO box number a friend has taken out for me in New York. But where do you send mail to a person who's disappeared? I stick the letter in a drawer, sneak downstairs, and head to the soccer field for a game. Through the window, I can see the soldier standing outside the front door of Hilai, so I creep around to the back and hide behind the bushes until the coast is clear.

A Moroccan-Jewish team from Nahariya is playing an Arab team today. I am the only woman in the stands; the men sitting nearby leer at me. The atmosphere is tense. No one cheers for anyone; I've never seen such a grim group of spectators. The men shout obscenities at the players, even their own. It makes me think about the ancient Mayans, who sacrificed the losing team at the end of the game.

A man sitting next to me tells me that there are stabbings at the games. Once, a Jew murdered an Arab and the friends of the dead man went to the town of the murderer the next day and killed him. The police intervened by hosting a reconciliation feast.

"Yet another occasion to roast a sheep," the man says.

"I wonder how many sheep it'll take to bring peace."

"I've been here since 1948," he says. "Don't count on it."

"A cynic, I see."

"Listen, I love this place," he says. "To me, it's home. But if I want peace and quiet, I leave the country."

I tell the man what my friend Nancy said an Israeli cabdriver told her once: "Listen, lady, if you feel safe in a country, you must be on vacation."

"That's a good one," says the man.

"So have you ever been in a war?" I ask.

"Yeah. Fought in '67, the Six-Day War. I was just a kid."

"What happened?"

"Was on my way to Sinai with a couple friends from Eilat. We were on a camping trip. Not too many guns in the car, just the normal amount. We set up camp in the desert for the night and started eating dinner. Out of the blue another friend shows up. He says, 'Listen, guys, you have to go. There's a war.' So we drove eight hours back to Eilat."

"What was it like? The war, I mean."

"Well," he says, "one thing's for sure. You never forget the smell."

The soldier continues to come, early in the morning as I prepare for my day, in the afternoon when I'm napping, and right before dinner. Sometimes I don't answer the door or I yell, "Go away!" I feel like I'm in prison. I can recognize the sound of his footsteps now, the way he creeps up the stairs and shuffles on the landing before he knocks. At night, I use the door chain and the deadbolt and sleep with a knife tucked beneath my pillow, a hammer beneath my bed. If I had a dresser, I'd push it against the door.

In early September, my friend Barbara arrives from Chicago to travel with me for two weeks. She's old enough to be my mother but looks much younger than her age. Barbara has brought a box containing the first four books in my series. They've just come out in the States. The books are all written under my new name, Mira Bartók, not Myra Herr. Barbara snaps a photo of me smiling, holding up my books. Flipping through them is bittersweet. I miss my old name. I've only had my new one for a few months and I'm still not used to the sound. What else will I have to give up now that I'm no longer who I was before? Herodotus talked about an ancient people called the Atarantes who lived in the African desert; a tribe without names or dreams. Now that I've lost my name, will I lose my dreams as well?

I look at the title page of my very first book in the series and feel a little better. I'm glad that I didn't change my first name too much—only from Myra to Mira. I couldn't relinquish it or the story behind my mother giving me the name. She said she had named me for her favorite pianist, Myra Hess, who gave free concerts in London during the Blitz. Sometimes, during concerts, there were deafening sounds outside the National Gallery where Myra Hess played—sirens and terrible explosions. She played without stopping even when a thousand-pound bomb sat outside the building. Once, she gave a man a precious orange to fix the leaky roof so no one would get wet or be distracted from the tenderness of Ravel. I think of Italy and the night America bombed Baghdad, how the sky glowed an eerie dark green on TV, and how, that night, despite the bombs, the city was filled with brides.

The day after she arrives, Barbara and I drive with Dennis to the northwest border of Israel and Lebanon to a place along the coast called Rosh HaNikra. In Hebrew the name means "head of the cave," and in Arabic it is known as Ras-A-Nakura. We have come to see the caves at the foot of the white chalk cliffs. Centuries ago pilgrims carved stairways into the rock so caravans could get through. The labyrinthine network of grottos was formed by seawater pounding against the soft chalk walls for thousands of years.

The weather is perfect: clear sky, low humidity, a cool breeze from the sea. The three of us go into the caves to explore. The water is so translucent that in some places we can see twenty meters down. There are only two tourists in the first grotto we enter—a Swiss woman and her boyfriend. They are kissing beneath an elegant stalactite swirling over them like filigree. Stalagmites rise up around the lovers like crystal towers from the floor of the cave. Athanasius Kircher wrote about these speleothems—stalactites and stalagmites—in his *Mundus Subterraneus*, strange subterranean forms made from water seeping through bedrock. I could lie down and sleep in this cool, dark palace of crystals and chalk, the only sound, my breath and the water dripping from above.

We leave the grotto and search for a refreshment stand. On the beach, looking out at the sea, I feel a weight lifting. It's the relief from the stress of being stalked in Ma'alot, relief from something else too. I become giddy with laughter and want to jump in the waves, release something back into the sea. I picture myself escorting my mother and the soldier to the shore, helping them with their bags into a boat. I say goodbye and push them off toward Cyprus and farther on to Greece.

On the beach, everyone is in love. There are couples everywhere—lovers and soldiers holding hands, kissing, eating ice cream with semiautomatics slung over their shoulders. The sun is setting when we finally leave and drive back to Ma'alot. When we arrive, the town is quiet because it's Shabbat. That night, I have the first good sleep I've had in weeks. The next day I catch the tail end of a story about missiles attacking some spot along the northwestern coast. One of the people killed was a Swiss tourist. Was it the woman we saw kissing in the cave?

It's mid-September when Barbara and I travel to Jerusalem. We meander through the maze of old stone streets to the Western Wall, where Jews have come for centuries to mourn the destruction of the Temple. According to Muslim lore, it is the place Muhammad tethered Buraq, his great winged steed. We stand in an open plaza and watch bearded Orthodox men in black hats daven, shuffling in place, lost in prayer. I find their movements disconcerting. They look like my mother bobbing back and forth because of tardive dyskinesia. I think about how she told me once that before she died, she wanted to travel to Israel with my sister and me. I remember her pile of magazine pictures she kept beside her bed: a photo of the Western Wall, one of Moshe Dayan with his black patched eye, a stern portrait of Golda Meir, and publicity shots of her favorite Jew, Sammy Davis, Jr., standing with the Rat Pack, smoking, holding a martini in his hand.

At their post, above the wall, flanking both sides, soldiers with long-range rifles stand guard. Behind the wall and beyond is the Dome of the Rock; to the left, the ancient stables of Solomon. Visitors stick everything in the cracks of the Western Wall—notes, prayers, money, stones, even chewing gum. I write a wish for my mother on a slip of paper: *Please help her.* I roll it into a tiny scroll and push it into a crack between two big yellow stones. "Just in case," I say to Barbara as we are leaving.

Barbara and I place stones on graves everywhere we go, an old Jewish tradition, and I collect small stones from the ground to take back home. I take them from every place I visit in Israel. On the walls surrounding one cemetery, there are holes from rockets and gunshots. In the Orthodox part of Jerusalem, a young boy hurls a pebble at my back for carrying a bag on Shabbat. I've also forgotten to conceal my hair beneath a scarf or a wig. We walk toward East Jerusalem, into the bowels of the medina. Barbara and I wander down streets of stone buildings and boarded up stores; almost every shop is closed, for some reason. "Must be a holiday," I suggest.

My face is tanned and could pass for anything here—an Italian tourist, a Greek, even an Arab. But people can somehow tell that Barbara is an American Jew. Suddenly it is raining pebbles upon our heads. A group of Palestinian boys sitting on a ledge have launched an attack. The stones are much smaller than the ones the Orthodox kids throw at me in Ma'alot but who knows which way things could turn?

"Let's get out of here," I say. We shield our heads with our hands and run.

We go into what appears to be the only open shop in the neighborhood, a small general store. "Why is everything closed?" I ask the man behind the counter.

"Muhammad ascended to heaven today," he says. "It's a holiday."

"What now?" I ask Barbara. "Should we go back?"

Out of nowhere a mass of Israeli soldiers barrels toward us down the street, holding their guns above their heads, shouting. A group of terrified children scatter out of the way. We lean up against a wall, not sure what to do, which way to turn. We scan the street for signs of life and commerce.

"There's a place," says Barbara.

Across the road is a store with a light on inside. We knock and a woman around fifty, with short gray hair and glasses, unlocks the door and hurries us in. "Come and sit down. I'm closed right now but you can stay here till they're gone. I'll make some tea."

All around us there are exquisite tiles, cups and pots, platters and plates decorated with birds, vines and flowers, and fanciful trees heavy with fruit. The shop floors are covered with rich burgundy rugs. The woman returns from a room in the back and sets out a tray of tea and dates. "If you don't mind watching me work, you can stay as long as you like. My name is Amani."

She sits at a tidy worktable and goes back to glazing a traditional Palestinian tiled mural. Barbara and I sip sugary mint tea and watch delicate birds emerge from her tiny brush.

"What's going on outside?" I ask. "The soldiers, the closed shops? A man said it was a holiday."

"No holiday today." Amani frowns. She plucks a sprig of mint from her glass of tea and goes behind the counter to get something. "Is it too much mint for you? I can make you more if you like. Here. Try one of these." She offers me a date.

"Why are there soldiers?"

Her face clouds over again. "It's not a good day. It's the tenth anniversary of the Sabra and Shatila massacre in the Palestinian refugee camps in Lebanon."

"Did Israel invade the camps?" I ask.

"No, but they allowed it to happen. It was a confusing and brutal mess. Anyway, everyone around here closes down on this day, but of course the army has to put on its little show."

"So what happened in '82? Were you there?"

"Let me show you around the studio," she says, avoiding my eyes. Later, she doesn't talk anymore about Sabra and Shatila but tells us a little about how the Jews came and took over her ancestral home. She was only a small child when her family had to flee. When they could finally return there were strangers living in their house.

"Don't get me wrong," she says. "I have nothing against the Jews. It's the government and their policies I don't like."

Everyone I meet in this country, young or old, seems to have lost something—a son, a daughter, a family, a house.

When dusk falls, things quiet down outside. Barbara and I decide to go back to our hotel.

"Just a minute," says Amani, and goes behind the counter. "Here. Take this. You might need it." She hands me a small silver charm in the shape of hand pointed downward. "It's a *khamsa*—for good luck. And here's a chain for it. If you hang it around your neck it will protect you."

I think of Toda, her ashen fingerprints on mirrors to keep away the Evil Eye, her clumps of black tea leaves, glowing icons, and herbs. "*Shukran*," I say.

"You are welcome," says Amani. "Be safe. *Bissalama*."

It's hard parting ways with Barbara. She has always been, like Nancy, my *mameleh*, my surrogate mother. After she leaves, my thoughts return to my real mother. Where is she? Why do my letters come back? The soldier in Ma'alot continues to stalk me but in my dreams it is my mother who is the stalker. In one dream, she follows me to town, hides behind bushes at Hilai, carries an AK-47 on her back. She whispers to me in my ear, *All you have left is a hand and a name and the name isn't even yours.* I wake up sweating, my hand, palm outward, protecting my face.

Behind Hilai there's a bomb shelter painted with bright flowers and geometric designs. It looks like an ugly psychedelic rock album cover from the sixties. I try to imagine what people do here during bomb raids, how they climb inside, put on gas masks and cover their heads with their hands. It reminds me of our bomb drills at Riverside Elementary School in Cleveland, how we had to crouch below our desks when the special bell rang. "Duck and cover!" our teacher would shout, and we'd hit the floor. Something ominous was coming from above, from the slate-colored clouds, heavy with rain, or from a missile far away—who knew where it would land and when? A sickly yellow cat lives out behind the bomb shelter. I leave him bowls of water and food. One day, as I'm setting down a bowl of kibble, Etan steps out from behind a tree.

"Why you don't come with me?"

"You have to leave me alone. Do you understand? *Leave me alone.*"

Etan grabs my shoulder, his gun peeking over his back.

"Let me go," I say, trying to pull his hand off. He finally backs off.

"I am here, not American boyfriend. I come back later. Then you go with me."

Etan turns abruptly and walks off toward his base across the street. The cat creeps toward the bowl with his tail between his legs. I step back so he can eat in peace. He gulps down the kibble but keeps a watchful eye on me. Even the cats here are mistrustful and afraid.

I'm getting close to the end of my time in Ma'alot. It's October and most of the people I've met have left and gone back home—Dennis, Shalom, other artists and writers who stayed at Hilai. Barbara has left as well. In the end, my idealistic dream of doing Arab and Jewish workshops has failed—I had to do them separately in two different schools. In the Arab school, almost all the stories the kids wrote were about meeting a stranger on a road carrying a gun. In the Jewish school, most kids wrote about meeting a strange man with a bomb or a knife. If the children think this way here, in a relatively safe zone, how can there be hope for peace?

One day I go on a hike by myself. I know I'm not supposed to do that around here, but I feel stuck inside Hilai and the town, especially with the soldier always lurking about. In my hiking-in-Israel guidebook, the rules are clear: (1) have a hat, sunscreen, and rest often in the shade; (2) water, water, water, and bring your own; (3) watch out for scorpions and snakes; (4) watch out for wild animals, including leopards; (5) watch out for live minefields; (6) watch out for remnants of military anything; (7) never be alone.

I bring a hat, a sandwich, and water and that's it. My day is grand—no soldier, no distant sounds of gunshots, no scorpions, leopards, or mines. I eat a peaceful lunch on a hill and draw in the shade of a tree. It's twilight when I head back to Ma'alot, tired but content. But as soon as I get to Hilai, something feels wrong. The light outside the door isn't on, and it always is. I don't hear a thing. I try the front door. It's not locked; someone has forced it open. I slip inside without making a sound, careful not to let the door slam shut. I know that no one is in the building, since everyone has left town, but why is the hallway so dark? I tiptoe up a couple stairs, far enough to get a glimpse of my door and the landing. The red safety light barely illuminates the stairwell. I sense someone is there but can't see a thing. Then I spot the shadow of a man.

The soldier is leaning against the wall to the left of my door, hidden from view so I can't see him when I walk up the stairs. He presses his body against the wall, AK-47 in his arms, not swung over his back like it usually is when he walks through town. He is holding it in the position he has been trained to use when it's time to shoot. I inch quietly toward the exit, open it slowly, and shut it carefully behind. I am twelve years old and my grandfather is pointing a pistol at my mother's head; I am five and he is shooting a rifle off by my feet. *Girls should be seen and not heard.* As my mother would say, *War is war.* I run like hell.

I tear past bomb shelters and the ugly concrete fountain where the children play, through the park, and past unfamiliar streets. I keep running and running until I finally have to stop to catch my breath in a deserted parking lot. I hear a small clanking sound, like someone kicking a can. I see a figure, a man, walking toward me. The man speeds up; so do I. My chest is heavy from running so fast but I have to keep going—but where? Which way?

I find myself at the entrance to a forest. A woman at Hilai had warned me, "Whatever you do, don't go into the forest," just like in a fairy tale. She said she heard there had been snipers there. I had only been in the forest once, with a violinist named Lily from town. We had cut through the forest to meet some friends of hers on the other side. Could I find those people again?

I sprint through cypresses and pines. I can't tell if he's behind me. I wander without direction but can't stop moving. Finally, I stumble into a ravine. My body makes a soft thud against the damp earth. Should I stay here among the roots and the worms? Should I keep on going into the night? The forest is silent and black. I hear an owl and the wind in the trees. It feels good to lie in the soft fragrant earth. I feel invisible, like when I hid in the woods behind my grandparents' house. Will I always have to hide? I think of Lily, the violinist, how, when the Nazis invaded the Netherlands a Dutch family hid her in a small cupboard behind a wall. Lily said she was separated from her mother from the time she was three till she was eight. Her mother could only come to visit her once. She made a drawing of her daughter's small hands, reaching out from behind the shelves.

Everywhere around me there are dark trees and sinking moss; beyond the forest, a desert of burning stones. What is it I have learned to love? My closest companion has been a horse; my bedfellow, fear; my pillow, fevered sleep.

I wait for half an hour or maybe it's only fifteen minutes or maybe I've been there all day. Time is suspended beneath the shadowy trees. The Holocaust survivor I knew in Chicago who survived the end of the war by hiding under those dead bodies—he said he focused his mind on the feel of the mud in his hands, the rich dark earth below him. He said he knew the earth was alive with roots and burrowing things. He imagined himself a plant, dormant, waiting to be born.

I pick myself up, climb out of the ravine, and keep on running. Somewhere along the way, I lose a shoe. I slow down, hobbling, with one shoed foot, the other bare. I can feel the cool silver chain around my neck where the little hand, the *khamsa*, dangles. There is no one here but me, I decide, except for all the nocturnal beasts and birds. I hear a coyote howl and then the other members of the pack, one by one, picking up the song. There is the sky, the trees, the soft mossy ground—if I sleep here, no harm will come.

I relax and slow down to a normal gait. The North Star flickers through the trees leading me to an opening and the glow of streetlights. It's the neighborhood Lily had taken me to before. A museum curator and his family live there; I remember their collection of curiosities from around the world, carpets from Turkey, Moroccan bowls, woodcarvings and masks. I can't recall the number but remember their name, Kesos, written on a sign in front. I find it almost immediately—a vine circling their family name, which means "ivy." The windows are lit up so bright I feel a pang, a longing to be in a house full of music, people, and light.

I knock hard. The family welcomes me for dinner. It turns out they are friends with the soldier Etan's superior officer. The father makes a call and the officer comes right over to talk. The next day, the soldier is sent away to another base.

On one of my last days in Ma'alot, I am walking through town with Lily, the violinist. She brings Arab and Jewish children together each week by teaching them Suzuki violin. I finally begin to feel safe, now that I am leaving. And especially with Lily, even though she is very shy and small. As we walk through the market in town, we suddenly hear the sound of children calling her name, "Lily, Lily, *musica, musica!*" We turn and see a group of Falashas from the Ethiopian refugee camp, holding something high above their heads, a rough-hewn instrument made from wood and wire. They gather close around us. "Look, Lily," they cry. "We made violin!"

They follow us all the way back to Hilai, singing and calling out Lily's name, their hands waving in the air.

When I returned to Chicago that fall, I finished transferring everything to my new name. My mother's first letter addressed to the "old" me arrived two months after I got back. She had shown up at Nancy's husband's office downtown and told him that she was now living on the North Side. She gave him a Chicago PO box number and said to pass on the information. My mother insisted he tell her where I lived but he refused. Enclosed with the letter was, of all things, a crude map she had drawn of the Middle East.

In her first letter, the one she began with: *Dear Daughter, Today is Yom Kippur . . .* my mother quoted from the Song of Songs: *For, lo, the winter is past, the rain is over and gone; The flowers appear on the earth; the time of the singing of birds is come.* On the back was a drawing of a plant. In her sketch the sky is sunny and raining at the same time. *I am living day to day,* she wrote. *Where are you? So many changes have occurred over the past thirty years or more! Countries achieving independence, countries joining, countries splitting apart. How is it overseas? I can't wait until we are together again. I fear your sister is in a war zone, hiding. Someday,* before I become blind, I would like to see the enchanted cities of the world. The reading I've done suggests that the state of California will join the sea, sooner than expected.

At the end of her letter, my mother wrote: *Baruch atah adonai, elohenu melech ha'olam. I am teaching myself Hebrew among other things. Did you know that green plants are primary producers, the first link in the food chain? Did you know that photosynthesis makes things from light?*

In my memory palace, I place my mother's map in an empty sun-filled room the color of sand. I place it next to the *khamsa*, the little hand charm the woman in East Jerusalem gave me. Next to it is a photograph of me in the desert on a horse, squinting at the sun. The horse is tall and chestnut-brown; the rider is still harboring a secret.

On Love and Forgetting

I have forgotten everything I have ever learned. My left hand looks like an over ripe banana and I have momentarily misplaced the continent of Africa yet again. I closely guard what I carry and never ever say, "I'll be back." Sometimes, in my room, I am soothed by the FM radio playing Spanish music I like, especially Navarra. It always reminds me of my unused erotic life, that is, unused by me. The Question at hand is: Why did I pick a lemon in the garden of love where only peaches grow?

Many fathers are gone. Some leave, some are left. Some return, unknown and hungry. Only the dog remembers.

Nick Flynn, *Another Bullshit Night in Suck City*

Rabbits

My first memory is not about my mother.

It's the summer of 1962; I am three years old and my sister is four. A friend of our father's from Chicago has lent us a house near the Indiana Dunes by Lake Michigan so our father can take a break from the city and finish his second book, *The Amnesiacs*. My sister and I find a family of lizards inside the mailbox in front of the house, half hidden by wild asparagus, beach grass, and flowers. We feed the lizards lettuce and bugs and take them out to play. When our parents divorce and we move to Cleveland the following year, I will lie and tell children in my kindergarten class that I used to raise baby dinosaurs by the sea.

I have three big black dogs with pointy ears. Sometimes the dogs and I slide down a dune to the lake and race along the beach. I collect things that wash up onshore and put them in a bag—shells, driftwood, colored glass. One day the dogs and I follow the sound of birds into the woods. I can't find the birds; they are hiding in the thick of the leaves. When I get tired I take a nap beneath a tree. The dogs curl up beside me, their breath steady and warm. When I wake up, each has a bloody rabbit in its mouth. I carry the rabbits home so my father can save them, but he is angry and grabs them from my hands.

The picture left indelible in my brain: A tall dark man tossing three dead rabbits over a dune. It's a scene in slow motion, like a soldier's parting embrace. The man's face is tight and determined as he looks straight ahead. One by one the rabbits sail through the air, landing somewhere below, into the tangle of blackberry brambles, onto a sandy path, or farther out to the deep waters of Lake Michigan.

When he's done the man turns, walks in long strides toward the small white house. His hands are stained with blood. He opens the door and goes inside. The little girl slips by unseen. She watches the man open the refrigerator and pour a glass of cool white milk. The girl creeps back outside. Clouds gather. The girl kneels at the edge of a dune. In my palace of memories, the rabbits are safe, hiding in an alcove. Above them hangs a memento—a lock of my mother's hair; below are the keys to my father's secret life.

When I came across my mother's diaries, I found an undated document my mother had written by hand. Part of it was devoted to her life with my father: *My first week in Los Angeles I met Paul Herr and thereafter from the late 40s until 1963, he was the dominant person in my life. I bring this up as technically it could be said that it was an arranged kidnap. Those years I did typing for him; cared for the apartment and worked in an office. I paid for my own clothes and some of the household items. However, I might say that I did have periods of amnesia that lasted a very long time. After we divorced I had no advisor, my furniture disappeared and I reported increasing blindness. I returned to Cleveland to live near my parents. Support checks came six years and then they stopped. I applied for Welfare in 1969. My hospitalizations in Cleveland, beginning in 1964, I attribute to outer environment. At the deepest level, it was a war zone and that should be taken into consideration.*

In the same box, I also found a letter from my father to my grandparents. In his letter, dated July 18, 1960, he describes the evening he and my mother spent with a top editor from Random House and his wife in Manhattan. The editor had offered him a three-book deal based on having read only half of my father's first novel. At the fancy dinner in New York, there is talk of television and radio shows, of big features in magazines. "As guests of Mr. Geis and his wife," my father writes, "Norma and I dined on caviar, champagne, and duck." He goes on to say, "I am very tired of working all day at some difficult job and doing my real work at night. Now I feel free, and it is a very fine feeling." He closes the letter with the only reference to my sister and I that I have ever seen: "The children are well and growing like weeds. Myra is talking. She also climbs like a monkey. Love, Paul."

Who was my father? Why did he disappear?

Years before Katrina stampeded into New Orleans I decided to go down to Louisiana to look for my father's grave. It was 1994 and I had been living near Boston for about a year. The stress of living in the same city as my mother had gotten to be too much so I moved east, not far from Cambridge. What spurred the decision to look for my father's grave was the sudden death of a close friend's father. At the funeral, I decided that I wanted to know the end of my own father's story. I also needed a break. I had been working over fifty hours a week on my book series for children, holed up in my apartment writing for months.

I knew my sister's spring break from her teaching job was coming up so I checked out flights from Boston Logan. She could drive down from Canton, New York, and we could fly out together. I called up Natalia and told her how much fun it would be to go on vacation, just the two of us, a whole week in New Orleans.

"A sister vacation," she said. "I love the idea!"

"There's one small hitch, though—I want to find our father's house and grave."

"Whatever I can do to help," said Natalia. "But just so you know, I made peace with all that years ago."

The night before we left, I pulled out the map I bought of New Orleans and looked for Napoleon Boulevard, my father's last home, not far from the Garden District. I had gotten his address from a copy of the coroner's report my mother had sent me years ago in 1986 when she first found out about his death. The boardinghouse my father had lived in was only a few blocks from my sister's and my B&B. Natalia and I could even walk there. Then I found St. Rosalie Cemetery, just west of the city of Kenner, inside Jefferson Parish. I used the legend on my map to measure the distance to the cemetery from our father's house. Paul Herr was buried off Route 61, not far from the river, only fourteen miles from bed to grave.

Our first day in town, Natalia and I eat breakfast at an open-air café; we drink café au lait and devour hot doughy beignets like two messy girls, powdered sugar on our faces and our hands. We stroll past pink and yellow antebellum houses with fluted pillars and lacey iron gates, beneath a canopy of rambling trees, their green leafy arms stretched out across wide boulevards. "Those are called live oaks," my sister informs me. "They stay green all year-round." She has done her homework about where we are and I haven't read one single word about this place. I try to keep up with her when we walk. I am slower, more prone to meandering; she moves with a fast clip, hands clasped behind her back, body forward, a professor lost in her thoughts.

"So when do you want to look for the grave?" I ask.

"Let's go later in the week. I'd like to have a little vacation first."

While my sister is getting coffee, I people watch in Jackson Square: A beautiful dark-eyed child in a bright red stroller stares into my eyes, while his parents shout at each other in spitfire Italian between bites of muffuletta sandwiches. A woman with long white hair, tattered sundress, and gauze patch over one eye, Mardi Gras beads around her neck, walks in circles around my bench, singing old chansons. She is my mother; she is everyone's mother, half blind, and lost. An emaciated man without a shirt stumbles by, drunk in the middle of the day, talking to God about a devil in Congo Square. He is my father, drunken nomad, unknown, hungry, and lost. An unfamiliar world is stretched out before me: crowds of tourists and palm readers at every corner, tap dancers, fiddlers, psychics, and shops where people can buy gris-gris and spells. I've only been in Boston a year but I could pick up and move here too; this place is as good as any other. The air is warm and full of music, and there's a river that leads to secret oceans, enchanted worlds. Any place could be my home. Was that how my father chose this place? Just a random temperate place, a place as good as any?

Before my sister and I left for New Orleans, I wrote my mother at her most recent post office box to ask if she would tell me more about our father. Did he have other children? Did he ever marry again? My mother wrote back: *Your father was a drunk and a louse. I remember nothing else about our years together. I was kidnapped and given chemicals to forget.*

My sister has a New Orleans guidebook she consults daily. She circles things she wants to see: the tomb of voodoo priestess Marie Laveau, the Musée Conti Wax Museum, Preservation Hall, the all day/all night Café du Monde, and the best places to eat chicken étouffée. I follow her lead but am more interested in things we see and hear by chance—the ancient washboard player with the scar across his cheek, the tap-dancing boys at the corner of Bourbon and Toulouse, the zydeco accordion I hear wafting down an alleyway.

On day three of our trip my sister and I shop for flowery dresses, the kind we'd never buy back home. It's difficult not to think of my mother, somewhere on the streets of Chicago, or some other large city, carrying her possessions in a cart. Or storing them somewhere in some cold, dark room. It's hard not to think of things that she might need. When I am in a store, I can't get her out of my mind: Should I buy my mother the cheap gloves or the expensive insulated ones? The nice ones will keep her warmer when she's waiting outside a shelter, but what if someone steals them? The cheap ones will be easier to wash. How does a homeless person wash her clothes?

I look around at all the ruffled dresses in the shop—the big straw hats with bows, espadrilles in every color of the rainbow. Why shouldn't I get her something frivolous? Why should it always be easy-to-clean socks and shirts, sweaters you don't have to wash by hand, sturdy hats that can withstand the snow and rain?

"Can I help you?" asks the clerk. "Is there something that you need?"

"No, thank you," I say. But the woman is annoyingly cheerful and pushy;

keeps following me around, picking out things for me to try on. I feel like
asking her if she has something festive for a woman who is homeless but I
hold my tongue.

Natalia and I try on one dress after another. My sister is ebullient in
clothing stores; she is in her element, happy and content. She loves fine fab-
rics, the latest colors and styles, wearing something stunning and new. Why
shouldn't she? Why shouldn't I?

"Now, that looks fabulous!" the clerk says to me, as I step out of the dress-
ing room in a breezy summer dress. "Go look at yourself in the mirror!"

I stare at myself in the tight frilly dress and am surprised at how good it
looks. My mother would approve. *Try being a little more feminine. Use a little lipstick and get a new bra, put some rouge on your cheeks.* I buy the dress and choose
a summer hat for my mother. And a little chiffon scarf with splashes of red,
yellow, and green. "That scarf is perfect for you," says the clerk.

"Thanks," I say, imagining it around my mother's soft, slender neck.

Later that night, I call up William, the tall, thin poet I had just started dating. We had met in line at the post office in Cambridge. On our first date, he
told me his life story—how he had to keep his whereabouts secret from his
parents who he said were abusive, how his siblings, all eight of them, were
either religious fanatics or drunks. I surprised myself by telling him the story
about my mother. We stayed up all night, and in the morning we knew some
mysterious and irreversible bond had been forged. The night before I left for
New Orleans, we lay on my bed holding hands, staring up at the glow-in-
the-dark galaxy I had painted on my ceiling. He cautioned me about digging
too deeply in the past. He said, "Sometimes its best to just turn your back on
it all and walk away."

On the phone, while my sister is reading in bed, I sit in the kitchen of our
B&B and tell William about the live oaks, the dogwoods in bloom, and the
redwing blackbird I spotted on our second day. I tell him that I want to go
deep into the bayou and find an alligator. Or maybe a panther, if there are
any left.

"How are the sisters getting along?"

"Great," I say. "I just hope she's having fun. I like to get lost but she prefers to have a plan."

"Have you seen your father's grave yet?"

"Nope."

"Good luck. It might be tough."

My sister hasn't met William yet but I plan on arranging something soon. I know she's nervous about him being a poet who is currently unemployed, but hopefully, she'll come around. She better because, after all, he and I have so many plans for the future: art and poetry collaborations, children's books we want to write together, a poetry reading series we want to start. I know she's worried about me but I want her to understand that William's and my creative projects mean more to me than a pension plan or a brand-new car. And when I'm around him, I don't feel as much guilt about running away from my mother. "How can you possibly help her?" he insists. "She would destroy your life." I haven't felt this way about anyone since Robert. Maybe this is the man with whom I will start a family. We are both thirty-five and don't have that many years left to decide. Maybe that's part of why I wanted to come to New Orleans. If we do start a family, shouldn't I know more about my own?

Back in the room, my sister looks up sleepily from her bed. "Who was that on the phone?"

"William," I say.

Natalia's face clouds over. "Well," she says. "Let's get an early start tomorrow. We have to leave soon and there's a lot I'd want to do."

"I know, Nat. And there's still the house and the grave. Don't forget."

Years before my trip to New Orleans, when I was twenty-one, I found out that Social Security would forward a letter from me to my father if I gave them his number. I wrote a short letter to him, telling him that I was an artist and my sister was a writer, and that our mother was still quite ill. I promised that if he wrote back, I wouldn't reveal his address to her if he didn't want me to. What if he had another family? What if I had siblings scattered across the country?

It struck me then that I had never once seen a photograph of my grand-parents on my father's side of the family. I had no idea what their names were, what they looked like, only what my mother said my father had told her when they got married—that his father had been a general in the Hungarian army and that his mother was a gypsy dancer. She said he left home at fifteen because he hated his father and the town of Mulberry, Indiana, where he was born.

Had my mother made up my father's story? No one ever talked about him, so how was I to know? My grandmother always said the same thing—he was a genius but couldn't drive more than a half hour without having a drink. But they were a beautiful couple, she'd say. He was tall and handsome and your mother, what a looker!

I rarely thought about my parents as a couple. But when I did, I imagined them a little like F. Scott and Zelda Fitzgerald. Paul, my brilliant boozy father, holding court each night with Chicago's intellectual elite—Saul Bellow, Nelson Algren, and the rest of his South Side literary pals—and my mother, Norma, exotic, beautiful, and mad, and perhaps even more brilliant than Paul. My father's first book, *Journey Not to End*, was compared to Camus when it came out in 1961. Two years later, by the time he and my mother divorced, he had already finished his second novel, was on to his third, and was writing a play with Nelson Algren. My father was a painter as well. I imagined their dinner parties, everyone drinking each other under the table while my mother, sober yet not of this world, played Chopin or Gershwin or Monk on their rented black baby grand. And then in the middle of dinner—a sudden strange outburst, perhaps, a string of obscenities muttered under her breath, or something more theatrical, a little violent. Had her volatility been the source of my father's inspiration? Or had it driven him to drink even more?

Right after my mother sold the family house in 1989, I got a call from my mother's old landlord who owned the apartment she and my father had rented on the South Side of Chicago in the late fifties. He was an old man but still owned the same building where I was born. "Your mother called me about an apartment," he said, after explaining who he was. "She put you down as a reference. She sounded really bad."

He said, "She used to come to the door with a black eye, her arms all bruised up. I felt sorry for her. Your father was a very troubled man."

The only other person who told me something about my parents' life together was the late great Studs Terkel, who interviewed my father on his radio show when his first book came out. In 1987, the year after I found out my father died, I heard Studs was doing a book-signing in Chicago, so I went. I introduced myself to him and asked if he remembered a writer in the early sixties named Paul Herr.

"I interviewed him years ago," said Studs. "I remember him quite well."

"He was my father. But I never really knew him."

"Your father was a brilliant man," said Studs. "I remember your mother too. How is she now? I remember her being quite ill. She was a lovely woman and a gifted musician."

"Thanks for asking," I said. "My mother is still pretty sick. But I always have hope."

Studs asked what happened to my father. He said that he was a great writer. I told him that he passed away in 1980. "Bad heart," I said.

"I'm sorry for your loss," he said. "Please give your mother my best."

If I could track down that interview and listen to my father's voice, would I remember the voice of the man who tossed three rabbits over the edge of a dune? How far back does the memory of sound go?

༄

On Friday, the day before we fly back, my sister and I finally rent a car to look for our father's grave. First we visit his place on Napoleon Boulevard. Natalia is wearing a bright flowery skirt and mustard-colored blouse. I look like a funereal tomboy—baseball cap, black tank top and pants. In the photos we took that day, my sister is frowning, standing on the red steps in front of the peach-colored boardinghouse where our father rented a one-room flat. She is clutching the key to the rental car in her hand, her large overstuffed handbag held close to her side. I look smug and falsely confident: hand on my hip, body relaxed.

"Should we knock?" I ask. "It doesn't look like anyone is home, though."

"No. It's too weird. What would we say?"

"You're right," I say, relieved.

"Okay," says Natalia. "So we saw where he lived. Let's go."

Before we get in the car I turn back to look at the front porch one more time. What happened before he stumbled out the door that morning at 9:40 a.m.? Had he just popped open a beer? Did he think of us that day? Had the letter I sent through Social Security arrived? His death certificate said he died of marked fatty liver, cardiomyopathy, chronic pancreatitis. Miserable alcoholic, I say to myself. What a sad, sad man.

"I expected a dilapidated house in a bad neighborhood," says Natalia, starting up the car. "But this is pretty nice."

"I know. I wonder what was inside his room."

"Can we go now?"

"Yeah," I say. "Let's hit the road."

In 1994, although I have my license, I have never owned a car, so Natalia must take care of all of the driving. She has only been driving for four years and has rarely driven in a city. My sister is five-foot-four and tries to sit up as tall as she can in the seat. She drives under the speeding limit, leaning forward to see, like my grandma used to do in her white Chevrolet. "I hope you know your way to the cemetery," she says.

"Don't worry. We've got a map. We just head west to Kenner. I think if we keep following this road we'll hit the highway."

"You *think?*"

"Don't worry, Nat. It's hard to get lost when you have a map."

"You're the navigator, so don't screw up."

When we leave the outskirts of the city it turns out that I am not the best navigator after all. I'm not a driver but a subway taker, a bike rider, and long-distance walker. I don't know how to use dead reckoning like the old explorers did, or even follow our map. We wander down industrial streets west of New Orleans and past factories and slums. Natalia gets more and more nervous. After driving around in circles, we find ourselves way off track, beneath an overpass, in a desolate section of town. My sister begins to cry.

"We're lost!" she says, sobbing. "Where are we?"

"I don't know, Nat. But it's okay. We'll figure it out."

"It's not okay. We're really lost."

"Nattie, why are you crying? So we're lost. I'll ask directions. Don't worry."

"You wanted to do this! Not me. I did this for you."

Tears are streaming down her face.

"Let's pull in here," I say. "I'll find someone to ask."

We turn into what looks like a fly-by-night mechanic's shop. Both of us have to pee, we are thirsty, we can't read the stupid map, and my sister is on the verge of hysterics. "I can't believe we're lost," she cries.

I haven't seen her like this in years. The last time was the day our mother went after me with the broken bottle.

"Why is this happening to me?" she says. "Why am I crying?"

I smooth Natalia's hair and wipe her wet face. I feel terrible. This whole day has been stressful for her, trying to drive in a new city, with no help from me, then getting lost. But it isn't just that.

"Why is this happening to me?" she asks again.

"Nattie, until now, most of my life I've barely thought of our father. I was too little when he left. You've said all along you were doing this for me but you're really the one who remembers him. And now I'm dragging you to his grave."

"You think that's why?" she asks. She sobs even harder.

"Nattie, it's okay to feel bad. You don't have to be perfect all the time. Let's just try to move on. You'll be okay."

I make a face that always makes her laugh, no matter what, a secret look I only share with her and her alone. My sister breaks a tiny smile, then cries a little more, then stops. She lets out a long sigh.

"I'm really, really tired," she says.

"I know. But we'll get there. Let me ask someone inside where the hell we are."

When we arrive at St. Rosalie Cemetery in Kenner, I get out and Natalia stays planted in her seat. She looks a bit shaken and scared. I lean against the passenger door and look at my father's final home. An elderly black man takes out his garbage from the back of his house. The man glances at me, then carries on with his work. Surrounding the small fenced-in field of mounds are sad yards with plastic baby pools, broken lawn furniture, and trash. On the ground at the entrance there is an Arby's wrapper, a hubcap, and rusty chicken wire.

"I'm going in," I say.

"I'll stay in the car."

"You sure you don't want to come?"

"I don't like it here. It creeps me out. Try to hurry up."

Is she afraid of the neighborhood or the graves? The dark place of despair she might enter if she walked across the field of scattered bottles, buried bones, and trash? I wish I hadn't convinced her to come. Sometimes things are better left buried, as William would say.

"Don't worry, Nat, I'll try to be quick."

I am holding a letter I wrote to my father for this purpose, with a snapshot that must have been taken right before our parents' divorce. I have a moment of regret—it's the only copy I own of the photo and now I'm going to stick it on a dead man's grave. And it's the only photograph of just the three of us, my father, my sister, and me. I am in a pink dress, dangling my one-eyed teddy bear by its leg. Our father grins at the camera but my sister and I aren't smiling. We look lost, tired, and cranky. Not unlike how we look now. The letter is simple. I wrote that I forgave him for not helping us and for never trying to find us again. I don't know what else to say. I signed it, *Love, Myra*. I used my old name. What do the dead care about names, anyway?

When I pass through the gate I am confronted with a dilemma. Which grave to place my letter on? None of them have headstones or even small markers with names. I hadn't thought of that. Of course they would be nameless. This is a potter's field for the unidentified poor. I walk around and consider the mounds. There aren't that many; it's a small field. Whom did he share this lot with, who were the other men without families? I can't imagine women here, only homeless men or drunks, solitary creatures of the night. Then again, my mother could end up in a place like this.

I pick the cleanest grave with the softest grass and whisper, "Hello. Is that you in there?" The air is a little sticky, still, and warm. I place the envelope on top of the grave and stand back. A breeze rustles the paper and it moves half an inch. Who knows, it might just blow that letter away to another grave, or out into the street. What then? All of a sudden it strikes me as absurd, walking around these unmarked graves, not knowing which one contains my father's bones. Absurd and sad. What if there was a flood? Would his body float away? Someday my father could end up at the bottom of the sea or on some distant shore.

I scan the yard of graves again. It's not such a bad place after all. Melancholy, but still, quite peaceful. I'm glad I came. I feel like I have left a burden behind, not a heavy one, but a burden just the same. I go back to the car where my sister is waiting. She rolls down her window.

"Can we please leave?"

"Are you sure you don't want to go in?"

"I'm sure. Can we go back now?"

"Let's go see something beautiful, Nattie. We rented the car for the whole day. Tomorrow we have to go home. Let's go see the bayou. I promise, we won't get lost."

"I know. *We have a map.*"

My sister and I head south.

Natalia and I turn off the highway and drive down a lonely sunless road, a dense forest on either side. I am trying to take us to one of the state parks, a big green blotch on my map. As we travel farther into the bayou, there are fewer and fewer places to stop. No gas stations or stores. Not even a McDonald's. My sister grips the steering wheel. Her knuckles are white. "Are we going the right way?"

"Well," I say, "We have some options."

"I don't want to hear options. I want to know if we're going the right way."

"Okay, I'm lost again. But I know there's a state park nearby. Let's find a place to eat lunch and ask for directions."

The customers at the diner, all of them middle-aged white men, stare at my sister and me when we walk through the door. Some turn around in their booths to get a good look. Natalia and I order shrimp gumbo. This is years before I realize that I have an allergy to shellfish. After lunch I start to feel queasy. We drive in silence for a while, then suddenly I grab my sister's arm.

"Pull over! Now!"

I lose my lunch all over the road.

"Are you okay? Should we go back? We should go back."

"No, Nat. I'll be fine. We've gone this far, please, let's keep going. I have a feeling we're almost there."

We follow the directions the waitress had given us at the diner: "You can't get there from here if you girls are looking for road signs." She had said we have to look for changes in the shape of the land, not the names of streets. Now I am getting nervous. I can't tell if we are going the right way and soon it will be dark. Natalia and I drive past swamplands and thick dark forests. Bald cypresses, I wonder? The waitress had said something about cypress trees. I don't know my trees well but in my head I tick off the names of Louisiana plants to calm myself: *ground orchid, bull tongue, saw grass, lotus, spike rush, banana lily.* Then the birds: *ibis, egret, wood duck, redwing blackbird, great blue heron.* I can't remember the Latin names except for the heron: *Ardea herodias.*

I have to puke again. We pull off the side of the road.

"Where the hell are we?" asks Natalia. "We're lost again and now you're sick. You told me you knew the way."

"Nat, we are so close. I just know it. That woman said it was only twenty minutes away or less. She said it's a state park and easy to find. Please let's just keep going for another few miles. If we don't find it in fifteen minutes, we can turn around, okay?"

My sister puts the car in drive and clutches even more tightly to the steering wheel. I name all the Louisiana creatures I can recall: *nutria, possum, raccoon, black bear, armadillo, alligator, silver-haired bat, swamp rat, turtle, deer.*

It's almost five when we see the sign for the park. The air is a cloak of steamy wool; we are hot and tired, and the sun will be setting soon. Natalia is reluctant to get out of the car, but finally does. I put my arm around her. "Come on, Nat. Let's take a little walk."

Thankfully, the signs into the wooded swamp are well marked. We walk along a raised wooden path, brackish waters bubbling up on either side. Steam rises off the slick carpet of algae. I can hear a gurgling sound below and the call of some bird in the trees. Something slaps the surface of the swamp. I look down to see a small reptilian eye.

"Nattie!" I whisper. "It's a baby alligator—look!"

The creature comes right up to the boardwalk, then sinks low in the water so we can just see the top of its head and eyes. Its eyelids slide back and forth from left to right, like a secret door. I've never seen an alligator in the wild and wonder if its mouth is big enough to bite my foot off, even though it's just a juvenile. If my mother were here she would warn us about the hurricane that could come and sweep us away, or the man with a gun who is lurking in the woods, waiting to abduct us, but I don't think of her at all, or our father in his grave, or anything else—just this little ancient head peering up at me, water lilies parting around his body as he moves, the sound of a bird I don't know, and my sister beside me.

I take her hand and we walk a little farther, a little deeper into the swamp. We don't really have much time to go far; dusk is starting to settle in. We stop again and look at the endless swamp encricled by trees. Spanish moss, *Tillandsia usneoides*, is beardlike and prolific here. Early settlers had thought the moss resembled the bearded Spaniards who had once explored the region, and gave it its name, but it isn't really a moss at all, or even a parasite. *Tillandsia* is an epiphyte, a plant that derives its nutrients not from where it is planted but from the air. My sister and I are epiphytes too, like the abundant green canopy dripping down from the trees above our heads.

"We should go," says Natalia.

"Just a couple minutes. Then we'll head back."

"It's beautiful. I feel so peaceful."

"Me too, Nattie."

Then, from somewhere up in the canopy, we hear a whooshing, flapping sound of wings. We look across the slow green water to see a flash of gray-blue and black alight upon the mucky bank. It's a great blue heron, *Ardea herodias*. He is magnificent—his black feathery crown, his smoky gray and black cape across his shoulders and wings. Natalia and I stare at the bird in silence until it lifts its great wings and flies up into the tangle of darkening green. We listen to the heron's high bright call, as if it is saying, *Nothing to be afraid of, nothing at all.* Then I understand—this is the Louisiana lagniappe, the unexpected gift. It's not what is lost but what is left—my sister, this bird, these trees, this falling light. We turn and head back to the car. This time, driving out of the bayou toward New Orleans, Natalia and I don't get lost once.

Over the next couple years, information about our father surfaces: he once lived on a farm in Tuscany, not far from my beloved Cerreto. And, as it turned out, he wasn't Hungarian after all. His parents were Dutch-German chicken farmers from Indiana who could trace their roots back to the founder of the Mennonites. He had two sisters, now deceased; one lived in Chicago when I lived there but I never knew about her. A few months later, we discovered that my sister and I did indeed have other siblings, at least one—a half-brother named Greg. He was our father's first child, from the first of three marriages; our mother was his last wife. My father was allergic to feathers like me. I wondered how he felt about shrimp and clams. What else did we share? What other secrets did he keep?

Here is what I do know: when the landlady cleared out my father's room, all that was there were six identical brown suits, six pairs of brown shoes, a dusty typewriter without paper, and a large stash of empty beer bottles and cans. No letters, no diaries or books, no manuscripts, nothing. No address book of family and friends, no photographs in frames. No evidence of a life.

I think of those shoes sometimes, and New Orleans. Those bright red steps leading up to the porch where he fell in winter. Was his house swept away when Katrina came to town? And what happened to those six pairs of shoes? Did someone wear them after him, even though they say it's bad luck to wear a dead man's shoes? And the ones he wore in potter's field? I imagine they were scuffed and out of style, heels black and low. What's a shoe anyway but just a piece of skin cut from a cow fed from buttercups and clover? A shoe is only stardust, DNA, a host for microbes and the prolific larvae of carrion beetles. A thousand years from now my father's shoes will rest in what was once a rushing river. They'll be mute and peaceful in the loam, not like shoes at all but something that feeds the moles and millipedes, bacteria perhaps, or some kind of fungus made from leather, the shifting of the earth, and time.

And what of the rabbits? My sister remembers them too. But she says there were no black dogs in Indiana in our house by the lake. I hope, in a way, that they didn't exist, that each day I left to wander the woods and bleaching sands of Lake Michigan, I dreamed my woodland guardians into being.

Winter in Paradiso

It's Winter in Paradiso, but this past week there's been a rise in temperature. In fact, it makes me suspicious of ill intent. Soon I will tell all about secret crimes of infancy, drugs to know me out, and the taking of my childhood home. But for now, I spend my time resting, drawing and listening to the radio. Lately they have been talking about global warming. The scientists have really loused things up. The TV at the motel last night cautioned tornado warnings but onscreen showed an avalanche and a fist projecting out from under the snow! Who was buried there? Where are my girls? The manipulators have had a lifetime ball on my defects. Last week I went to see the doctor. He said I have hemorrhoids. The tests were painful; I have chronic fatigue and feel uprooted as a homemaker. In the meantime, I'm just a kid again, living month to month. I sustained some injuries of late, general neglect of water that burned my body and caused lentigo, facial cysts, boils, and then another fall at the train station that was caused by the negligence of others. Also supposedly by water. They always blame it on "water," on something else. But how can you explain the small dead rat I found in a drainpipe the other day? Who put that there to warn me of what's to come? You've got to have eyes at the back of your head, especially if you're blind. When the snow falls, no one sees your cane. It's white against white in winter—you slip and fall and next thing you know you're following the White Rabbit down into his hole.

14

I distrust the forest, or any wilderness, as a place to live. Living in the wilderness,
you may well fall asleep on your feet or go mad.

Annie Dillard, "Why I Live Where I Live"

Oracle Bone

The room I conjure is made of ice—the walls, chairs, table, and bed. On the table—a fragment of bone and a little snow globe. I shake the globe and a blizzard swirls above an Arctic village. I crawl inside it and look up: a fiery comet, a sapphire sky full of flickering stars. A memory shimmers under a carpet of snow:

November 1996. My husband, William, and I are flying over the Arctic Ocean toward the northern coast of Norway. I watch the sky turn from red to royal blue to black at two p.m. Below are icy mountains and the sea. Someone on the plane is talking about an avalanche near Tromsø that happened earlier that day. I am moving to a place where you could get killed by snow. Who would bother to follow me here? Not even my mother. I take out my journal but as soon as I put pen to paper, William asks me to take dictation for a poem. "You can write later," he says. "This is going to be a good one." What would my mother think of this tall, gaunt man beside me? *Never trust a writer*, she would say. *He looks like a Nazi. Is there a parachute on the plane?*

It's been almost seven years since I last saw her. She'd be surprised to know I've been married for over a year. My husband and I are on our way to Norway because I got a Fulbright to study the cultural history of the Sámi, an indigenous people who used to be known as Lapps. Over the past five years I had gotten tired of writing educational books for children and wanted to work on a project for adults; more specifically, do research in an inaccessible place. To find my new home on a map, my mother would have to place her finger on the North Pole and trace a line through Svalbard and the frigid sea, down to the sixty-ninth parallel to a place called Kautokeino.

Later, on the two-hour drive from the airport to our new home, I have to pee, so Ristiina, the dark-haired Sámi woman who is driving, stops the car to let me out. William is sleeping in the backseat. A blizzard starts up while I squat, freezing in the darkness, next to a giant snowdrift. A desolate and pristine place engulfs me: dwarf birch trees of ice, an endless white horizon. The moon is a ghostly orb, circled by a ring of red clouds. Within a minute it disappears behind a veil of driving snow. That night, at Ristiina's house, I learn to pronounce my first Sámi words: *mánná, čáhci, monni, áhkku, mánnu*—baby, water, egg, grandmother, moon. "Tell us about your family," they ask. "What are their names?"

The Sámi call the period from mid-November to mid-January the Dark Time, or Skabma Dálvi—the Beautiful Darkness. Most of the day, the sky is a deep indigo blue, even in the morning. It is so hard to know when to wake up, when to work, when to eat a meal. I think of my mother and wonder how the season affects the mentally ill here. At all hours of day or night I can hear snowmobiles in the distance, an occasional car or shout from a child, and the howling wind. The land disappears into the horizon; the church, looming just beyond the hill, is lit up like a casino. On Heargadievvá Street women pass by on foot sleds, their red Sámi bonnets bobbing up and down in the wind, fur boots with curled-up toes, pushing and sliding their sleds. Some women carry a small child on the sled with them, and fly down the little hill toward town.

Sometimes, if I'm up early, I watch William sleep. His long pale face is peaceful while he dreams. I try to be quiet so he doesn't wake. Once he does, who knows if he'll be happy or sad?

As snow piles up around our house, my thoughts often drift out to the open tundra where the reindeer search for lichen, and to the hills beyond where the bears are, and the foxes and wolverines. I think about the bears, sleeping in the hills, how people here say the bears sleep till May. I wish William would sleep until May, then wake up refreshed and not angry—or irritated, jealous, or depressed. Ever since we got married, I've noticed he follows a cycle of moods that is much too familiar. Three weeks up, one week down, two weeks up, two weeks down. Then it starts all over again. Is it the darkness or something else?

A woman in town told me about how a man and woman went skiing in the hills once and came across a big hole in the earth. They were tourists from the States, newlyweds, like William and me. They had wanted an Arctic honeymoon: total December darkness, a sled ride at Christmas, the northern lights. The man stuck his ski pole down the hole to see what was there and out came a bear. It mauled the couple to death. People say that there's really nothing to be afraid of around here, though. The wolves are all gone now, and you'd have to be pretty stupid to wake up a sleeping bear. But if my mother were here, she'd say there is no safe place on earth. She'd probably say what she says in one of her diaries that I find years later: *Be careful, wherever you are. Value your own mouth, hate privately, and pray for yourself. When distressed, see if you can remember all the bones in the body. Recite them alphabetically by name. Stay calm and always watch your back.*

When I think about those bears, it reminds me of what Ristiina told me about the war. "People had to leave in a hurry," she said. "The Germans were coming." She said that when the Nazis retreated from northern Norway, families had to flee their homes because soldiers were burning everything to the ground. The Nazis told the Sámi to evacuate and take all their reindeer to a place called Helig Skøg, Holy Wood, where the soldiers planned to slaughter all the animals for their troops. The Nazis didn't know that there were two Helig Skøgen, one in the west and one in the east. There was no way that the Sámi were going to let anyone tell them what to do with their herds. Ristiina said that when the Germans gave the orders to go east, her grandfather loaded up their sleds and the family set off for the west. From a distance Ristiina's family could see their house go up in flames. They traveled all day long until the winds became too strong. There were no trees for protection, but the winds were so fierce they had to set up their *lávvú* on the tundra. In the morning Ristiina's family awoke, buried alive in snow. The wind had entered their tent during the night and had ripped the entrance flap wide open. It took nearly all day for them to dig out their own bodies, their sleds and belongings.

Ristiina's mother, who was a young woman at the time, told her, "I am seventy-five years old but only have fifty-five years of memory." She said she doesn't remember anything that happened before the night she was buried in snow; she said the snow erased her memory. In her letters to me, my mother says something erased her memory too—Nazis sending in gas, aliens taking on the form of people she loved. She says that evildoers never really die, they just *metal horse themselves into another costume.* She writes: *It is very much out in the open now that I have a formidable enemy. At that hospital in 1990 they stole my teeth, my house, my memory. Presently, I draw only when I feel very acutely my muteness. Nobody hears a mute but I hear myself. Of my life at the piano, I shall say nothing for the time being. Enclosed you will find a picture I drew of two little goats. I also made a chart of nuclear power plants in the U.S. I hope it proves helpful to you in your endeavors, wherever you are. Love, Mom.*

And William, who, every few days, only seems happy in sleep—what to do about him? I have taken to making my own charts, a hidden log of his moods. I store it with my mother's charts, the ones that predict hurricanes and earthquakes, and nuclear plants built along unsteady faults.

When I'm out with Ristiina, who is my helpful and good-natured guide and cultural "informant," I feel happy and excited about my research, especially if William stays home to write. Ristiina drives me around to visit her family and friends, helping me collect stories from elders. Sometimes, though, it's difficult to drive with all the reindeer in the road. By late December, the town is surrounded by the large herds the Sámi had followed down from the coast. "For us, the reindeer was the alpha and the omega," said Ristiina one day, while we sat in her car, waiting for a female reindeer to move. "Less than thirty years ago, when I was a kid, we had no cars, no roads in winter. We didn't even use money. If people wanted milk from my family, I'd give them some from our cow, then make a mark on the bottom of a bucket. That way I knew how much reindeer meat they owed us, or how many skins."

Ristiina's headlights illumined some reindeer near the road, the front of their bodies buried deep in snow as they tried to dig for lichen. Food is very scarce in winter, and difficult to reach. Ristiina went on, "The reindeer was the center of our lives—our identity, our clothing and transportation, our food. We wore reindeer clothes; reindeer pulled our sledges. And distance meant much more than it does now. People got around on foot or skis or sled. Everything and everyone was far away. And back then," Ristiina added, "there were wolves. So if you walked a long way by yourself, you had better be prepared."

When I returned home, William was pleasant and cheerful. He had dinner waiting for me, and fresh-baked bread. I secretly marked a smiley face on my little chart hidden beneath my desk. Later, after dinner, William and I took a walk through a snowy field. Halfway through, the snow got so deep it came up to William's knees. December snow is soft in the Arctic; it can trap you and make you sink. William trudged ahead while I tried to follow in his big footsteps. When we stopped to rest I noticed strange wisps of clouds moving rapidly across the sky.

"What's that?" I asked.

"What's what?"

"Look up."

The clouds had changed from white to shimmering green in an instant, then to twisting ribbons of magenta light swirling around the stars.

"It's the northern lights."

We stood, half buried in snow, holding each other's mittened hand, trying to balance against the wind. My hand slipped out of his and I let myself fall back into the snow. William fell too, laughing. We stayed like that for a long time, watching the sky. Things aren't so bad all the time, I thought. Maybe I should stop keeping that stupid little chart.

"Now I know why people believed the aurora borealis were gods," I said.

"Can you believe we live here?" said William. "We can't forget this day, in the snow, lying here like this."

"We won't forget." William and I huddled closer together, my head upon his puffy-down-coated chest. "You know what the Sámi say about talking when the northern lights are out?" I said.

"What?"

"If you speak when they're above you, they will think you're talking to them. It's bad luck. They scoop you up and take you into the sky and you never return."

"We better be quiet, then," said William.

"I could stay here all night."

"Shh," said William. "Watch out or they'll take you away."

That night, about one in the morning, we awoke to the sound of crying. At first I thought it was an injured dog. We got on our coats and went out to investigate. Our entrance was in the back of the duplex; a single mother with three kids lived upstairs in the front. Standing outside her door was the woman's youngest child, a boy of around seven. He had a pile of snow on his head three inches high. How long had he been out there? He was shaking from the cold. "Hvor er din mor?" I asked in Norwegian, then asked him again in Sámi. He didn't say a word. I asked if he wanted to come inside our house but he just kept crying. Then, a few moments later, his mother drove up with the boy's older brother and sister.

A blond woman stumbled out of the car, drunk. When William and I asked why her boy was standing in the snow at that hour, she laughed and said she just forgot him. The woman staggered inside; the children followed her in, eyes to the ground. I said to William, "Let's keep an eye on her. With a mother like that, you could freeze to death and no one would know."

Friends from Chicago write to tell me that there have been sightings of my mother in the city. She's been visiting my old haunts and asking about me—at the women's clinic I went to for checkups, the gallery where I had my first show, museums where I worked. A friend in New York now manages my post office box but rarely checks it for mail. The first letter I get in Kautokeino arrives three months late:

> Dear Myra,
> We are now in autumn, under the sign of Virgo. One may think an enemy has passed, but how can one be sure? The newspapers daily tell of fabrications—there are many underhanded activities going on. Yesterday an arsonist burned a chair in my room. They come in while I'm sleeping. My eye condition is worsening and even if they are there, I can't see them. When I wake up my furniture is on fire. Please help me. I am very desirous of getting back in my house. But I need the keys. Do you have them? If you don't, do you know who does? Please respond ASAP. Mother. P.S. Although I am not of the Christian persuasion, I have been reading the Bible as of late, especially Revelation. I have recently read that the voice of the turtle is heard in the land. But if that is true, who wants to hear the turtle?

Some mornings I walk in darkness to the post office and wait my turn in line, longing for news from home, longing and dreading it. Can she find me? How could she? But if she did, could she come this far? Is her coat warm enough? Does she have enough to eat? My mother writes me about her "Jesus Freak landlords" who run the subsidized apartment building she lives in, as she says, only for the short term, when she's not sleeping at the bus station or on the train. *They're not too bad. They leave you alone if you don't want to talk.* She sometimes ends her letters with: *If you give me your address, I'll give you mine,* trying to strike up a deal. At the start of the New Year, in 1997, my mother is still living in Chicago, but sometimes she takes the bus back to Cleveland and spends a couple nights sleeping outside in her old backyard. My mother, who once was terrified that a backpack could strangle me to death, now uses one, with a sleeping bag and a canteen. Does the current owner realize she's there? Or is the house vacant now? I picture her buried in snow beneath the magnolia tree I used to climb; I imagine someone finding her in spring, the way dead mice are discovered after the first warm thaw, or little voles, or the runt from a litter of foxes.

I send my mother gifts from Norway via my friend in New York—warm Sámi mittens, a red and white hat, and a scarf I knitted with thick Norwegian wool. *Where are you?* she writes back. *You don't tell me anything of your life. Do you write your own letters or does someone write them for you?* My mother sends me clothes she buys at the Salvation Army, smelling of cigarettes and mold. She keeps making her charts of earthquakes and all the nuclear power plants in the world. One day a children's book about trees arrives. It has pictures of fat squirrels and smiling boys wearing red plaid shirts, like something out of the 1950s. There are chubby robins building nests. In every picture the sun shines down upon life in the canopy. This becomes a great source of hope for me, the fact that my mother is thinking about trees.

Another week, a box of broken teacups arrives. *These were your grandmother's,* she writes. *They are of no use to me.* They were the cups and saucers my grandma collected from the time China was occupied by Japan. She liked to take them out of the glass case and show the little pearlescent cups to me, turn them over in her hand. At the bottom of each one was the Chinese symbol for longevity and a special ideogram that meant "Occupied China." She had a passion for things that survived a war: photographs, teacups, jewelry smuggled abroad.

My mother sends me a shoe box full of Grandma's precious cups and saucers, unprotected—no paper, no bubble wrap to stop them from turning into shards. They had endured a great war and had crossed two oceans. What could I do with a box of shattered cups? I write *Occupied China cups* across the lid and stick the box below my desk, the same place I put my mother's letters and her charts of future disasters, my own charts of William's mercurial moods.

The sun finally returns in the middle of Oððajagemánnu, the Month of the New Year. I run outside mid-January to catch its fleeting light. The sky is on fire just above the blue-white horizon. I turn my face up and feel warmth for the first time since I arrived. But the feeling is brief. After a few minutes the sun is swallowed by darkness. The sky is like William. A month ago his mood would change gradually every other week. Now he's cheerful one moment and five minutes later he can go into a rage. Something is very wrong. I saw signs of it before we left—sudden jealous outbursts, his angry pronouncement one day that he refused to have children. His laying down of laws one by one: no alcohol in the house, then no meat, then no travel unless we are together. Is it seasonal affective disorder? Will he get better when the sun comes to stay? I write long lyrical epistolary essays to friends back home and include his beautiful poems about our life on the tundra. Before I send them, William edits out the darker things—hints of my unrest, my small jabs of irony.

One morning, I run into Ristiina at the post office. I tell her that I had just read that Stállu, the Sámi ogre, was a shape-shifter. "Was he the worst of the bad guys?"

"Stállu is pretty bad," says Ristiina "but he's also very stupid. The Sámi always outsmart him in stories. I think the worst were the Tchudit. But they were real. The Tchudit were tall black-cloaked invaders from the east who pillaged towns, killing every man, woman, child, and beast in sight. Didn't matter who was in their way. They destroyed everything and stole what they could find."

After Ristiina and I part ways, I stop to look at three large figures someone has made out of snow. The giant sculptures are the three Sámi goddesses of childbirth, motherhood, and the home. My favorite is Uksáhkká, who lives in the hearth and protects children and pregnant women. In some ancient stories, she appears as a knot in a rope that, when untied, unleashes a fierce and powerful wind. Some call her the "second mother." Years before the Sámi were successfully Christianized, they offered sacrifices to her and other deities at sacred sites. They left fish fat, animal bones, antlers, wooden figures, and silver, even trees. They turned the tree upside down and buried its branches in the ground. Sometimes a reindeer was slaughtered and given back to the earth.

The summer before William and I moved to Kautokeino, I had been invited to come and speak at a conference on indigenous education. The day before the conference, I went hiking along the Arctic coast and came across a crevice at the foot of a mountain. I shone my flashlight inside and saw the bottom was littered with hundreds of bones. They seemed to be placed in some kind of a pattern. Had they been arranged to tell a story or to foretell the future?

Every time I open a letter from my mother I can hear her calling me across the ocean: *Can you help me? Can we all go back home, be together again? Can you help me find the key?* She will ask me that until she dies. While she keeps looking for the keys to her lost home, I keep looking for the meaning of all those bones. Will my future always be determined by someone else's needs?

☙❧

In late January, Ristiina invites us to Finland to see her aunt, who she says is a great storyteller. William likes Ristiina a lot and I can tell that he tries really hard to be in a better mood when she is around. She is the reason why we have a washing machine, an oven, and just about everything else. I would never have gotten so deeply involved in Sámi society without her. She sets people at ease so they open up and tell me stories: folktales, stories about the war or supernatural beings, family histories, anything they feel comfortable talking to me about.

When she stops by to pick us up, Ristiina says that we can go to an ice hotel for coffee on our way to Finland if we like. She had taken William and me to one once before. Everything was made of ice—chairs, tables, walls, and bed. But at the last minute, William says he doesn't want to go. Ristiina goes back out to the car to let us work things out between us. I've told her a little about his mood swings.

"Okay," I say. "Get some good work done and don't worry about dinner."

"You're still going?"

"Why wouldn't I?"

"I can't believe you'd go without me. I just can't believe it."

"It'll be nice for you to have some time alone," I say.

"Nice for *you*, you mean."

"I'll try to be back by dinnertime, but I can't promise."

"You can't promise anything, can you?"

William follows me to the door. "I wanted to make love this morning but you had gone for a walk. Alone."

"Sorry," I say. "I didn't know."

"Well. Now you do."

I stand on my toes to kiss him but he turns his face so that my mouth kisses air.

In Finland, Ristiina and I sit by the fire while her aunt tells me stories. It's twilight when we start to drive back from the Finish border. We are quiet for a while, then Ristiina asks, "Is your *guoibme* okay? I haven't seen him in town lately. Is he sick?"

"He's getting more depressed. I'm not sure what's wrong, to tell you the truth."

"He'll cheer up when there's more light," says Ristiina.

Suddenly I hear the *la la la la lo lo* of a *yoik*, the chantlike poetry-song of the Sámi, coming from someone walking out on the tundra, but it's too dark to see a soul. It sounds like a baby crying, somewhere in the thickening fog. It sounds like the little boy we found in the snow. Ristiina slows to a complete stop, turns to me, and whispers, "*Gula! Gula!*"

"Listen to what?"

"Something bad happened here."

"Where?"

Ristiina shows me a spot in the landscape that, to me, looks like any other. "That's where my aunt saw the *eahparaš*. There."

The *eahparaš* are the forgotten ghost babies of the tundra, children abandoned by their parents, due to poverty or some kind of family scandal.

"Their spirits cry because they're left outside to die," says Ristiina. "They wander the earth until they are given a proper name."

Ristiina says a family lived in a farmhouse on the land. The family was happy until the woman's first husband died, after which she married another man. The man got his stepdaughter pregnant when she was thirteen. After she had the baby, he took the newborn and strangled it. He secretly buried the child in front of their house.

"Nobody knew," says Ristiina, "until one day when my aunt was out driving. She heard a baby crying. She looked out her rearview mirror and saw a naked infant crawling across the road, disappearing into a bush."

It was twenty degrees below that night. Ristiina's aunt knew that it had

to be an *eahparaš*. "No human baby could survive naked like that in the snow.
My aunt, she knew something really bad happened at that place."

Ristiina tells me that her aunt called the police and they investigated the
matter. Should I call the police about the woman upstairs? Sometimes she
leaves her children home alone for a day or two at a time. The oldest is only
twelve. And when she's home she has loud parties that go on until morning. William and I can hear the children crying and loud fights. How much
should we get involved?

"The stepfather confessed," says Ristiina. "He took the police to where he
had buried the child." She says the child was hidden in the exact spot where
her aunt had seen the apparition. The authorities put the man in prison and
the family moved away. If I call the police on the woman upstairs, will they
take her children away? Will they split them up? My biggest fear when I was
young was that someone would find out about our mother and take me away
from my sister. As Ristiina starts the car up to head back home, she says, "My
aunt and I hear that baby every time we pass this place."

When I return home, I don't invite Ristiina in, which would be the Sámi
thing to do. I should offer her coffee, let her warm up a little from our trip,
but I say good night and trudge up the walk to our door. Thankfully, I have
remembered my key. The last couple weeks, William has been locking our
door, which no one does around here. He can't handle guests, and in this
town people drop by uninvited, sometimes late at night.

The apartment is pitch-black. I get that feeling I used to get when I'd
come home from school and see my mother, sitting in the dark, the shades
drawn, a lit cigarette in her hand. I switch on the living room light and follow a whimpering sound coming from the bedroom. It sounds like the ghost
baby Ristiina and I had heard on the road and at first I think it is William,
joking around. But then I see him curled up in a fetal position on the bed.

"What's wrong? Are you sick?"

He starts to moan.

"What's going on?"

William yanks the covers over his head and tosses frantically beneath them. All of a sudden he lets out a sharp cry, like an animal that has just been shot. He starts to sob. Upstairs, another party is just getting started. I can feel the stereo's bass thumping in my bones. Someone throws something heavy on to the floor. A man is laughing, then shouting, something made of glass shatters, a child cries out. William moans again.

"Stop it," I say. "I can't stand this."

He throws off the covers, sits up, and spews a stream of nonsense words and phrases, as if in a trance. William sounds like the patients in my mother's psych ward. He goes on for several minutes, then, just as suddenly, quiets down. The noise continues upstairs.

"What is going on?" I ask. "Talk to me."

William says in a flat voice, "I can't talk about it. I'm not allowed."

"Not allowed?"

"I can't tell you what's wrong. There's a gag rule."

"*A gag rule?* What are you talking about?"

"I can't say anything. You won't talk to me."

"I'm talking to you now."

"No, you're not. You're judging me."

"You're crazy."

"You *left* me this morning. You met someone. Who was it?"

"Christ, what is your problem?" I say. "I feel like I'm in prison."

"*I* am not the oppressor, *you* are."

I slam the bedroom door and go into the large closet off the kitchen that serves as my office. I check my calendar. It has been filled with little black dots for weeks where I marked down William's foul moods. The month before, sixteen days out of thirty had been horrendous, the rest had been like being around Stállu, who can transform into an unbearable dark weight at the bottom of a boat.

I go back to the bedroom. "I'm going out. Don't wait up."

"Where? Who are you going to meet? You can't leave me!"

Who are your associates? Is that sperm on your leg? Did a man touch you there? Does your sister sleep with the mob?

"I am going out," I say. "Alone. I can't breathe in here."

"If you go—if you go I'll . . ."

If you go I'll kill myself! Someone is going to kidnap you out there!

I shut the door and walk out. I wander around outside for an hour or so, then make my way over to Kru's Pub. It's way below zero and I've forgotten my long johns; my legs are turning numb. Since William and I have been together I have paid for just about everything. I am beginning to wonder if he is seriously ill. What if he won't get a job when we get back to the States? My sister had warned me that William could be trouble. What if he needs full-time care?

I stare at the red tablecloth, my cup of red hibiscus tea, a piece of cake on a bright red napkin. Everything looks blood-red, the color from my dream last night. I was trying to wash out my blood from my mother's dress, then her dress transformed into William's shirt in my hands. No matter how far I go, I spin around at the slightest noise, thinking I will see her there, her hair wild as grass, begging me for the keys. Now I spin around whenever William enters the room.

૭૭

In February, the aurora borealis swirls above the tundra and town nearly every night. There is electricity in the air, there are sudden snowstorms in the middle of brilliant, clear days. The sun stays longer in the sky and radiant clouds appear out of nowhere, within each cloud a rainbow. I remember what Ristiina said about the light and hope that maybe the sun will help William's moods. At the post office, a letter my mother wrote in late autumn has finally arrived.

> *Dear Daughter,*
> *No, the burnt chair was not caused by smoking. That was arson. Enough said.*
> *Some people would love to sell my birthright but I tell you this: The Wolf is in*
> *my house. No disclosures as yet. Offhand, I can't think of anyone in the world*
> *to trust. It appears to be a new ballgame. A little bird told me they even bid on*
> *stolen letters. On a brighter note, I have started to look at art again. I thought of*
> *you on a recent visit to the Cleveland Museum of Art. I had never noticed before*
> *the feet of "The Thinker" were blown off and there was blood in the bed of a*
> *famous nude lady. I am still going blind. A white cane means blindness. I sweat it*

out but can wait no longer. I need my keys. Please come home immediately. They still send up gas from below, but I now possess information that can incriminate them.

  Mother

When I return to the house, William is peacefully writing at his desk. He smiles when I come in and gets up to hug me. We've been getting along for five days in a row and I'm starting to think that maybe things aren't so bad. We've been talking again about creative projects we want to do together when we get back to the States. Maybe I've been too harsh. The extremities of this place would be hard on anyone. During early polar expeditions, didn't icebound crews get "wind sickness"? Go crazy from the eternal days of night?

"We need to do something about the kids upstairs," he says. "I think she hits the kids. While you were gone, there was a big fight up there. I think we should report her to social services and let them check it out."

We spend the rest of the morning at a social services office in town, filing a report and talking to a social worker. I can't wait to get out of there. Here I am, four thousand miles from home, and once again I'm back in a social worker's office. I wonder if the system is any better over here. The man is nice but seems vague and reticent when we ask him what he intends to do. William and I leave feeling dissatisfied and wary. "Well," I say, "what more can we do? We reported her. It's up to the authorities now."

The next day, the air is bitterly cold when William and I set out for the Sámi Museum, where I do some of my research. William's mood has shifted once again. We are both on edge. The night before, the children's sobbing had woken us up. The mother showed up at our doorstep early that morning, drunk and surly. Someone must have told her that we had reported her to the authorities. She shouted obscenities at us and said we'd be sorry for what we did.

When we arrive at the museum, the door is open and the place empty. It's like that here—people leave doors open, offices empty and unguarded. "I hope that man doesn't show up," says William, referring to the museum director, a balding man in his fifties. When he's like this, William is jealous of anyone, even Ristiina. William wipes his fogged-up glasses clean with the special lens cloth he keeps folded neatly in his breast pocket. Before we left Boston, I bought him his glasses. I bought his coat, his boots, his gloves, his hat and socks, his plane ticket to Norway. What was I thinking, that he was a child? He tucks his lens cloth back into his pocket and takes out a notebook and pen.

"I'm going to draw in the other room," I say. I feel my neck tightening. Does he have to follow me wherever I go? William finds a spot in a corner to write. I go to a different room and sit on the floor in front of a glass case filled with reindeer shoes from the last three hundred years. Finally I relax. With my pencil, I follow the contour of an eighteenth century shoe of a child. Who wore this little boot? The boy we found in the snow wore shoes just like this one. I remember a Sámi word: *ruw'ga*, the cry of a reindeer calf when it's separated from its mother. The shoe makes me think of another artifact taken from a small child. In the fall, right before we moved to Kautokeino, William and I flew to England to see my sister and her husband for a few days. Natalia was on sabbatical while her husband ran their school's London program.

One day, when William was sick in bed with the flu, I decided to go draw in a museum. William begged me to stay and take care of him but I pretended I couldn't hear him and hurried out the door. I took the train to the British Library and began my journey in a room of illuminated manuscripts. Looking up at all those ancient books, I felt at peace, like I was on the shore of a vast and beautiful sea. In another room I found my mother's favorite book: *Alice in Wonderland* propped open to the White Rabbit and Alice in a tête-à-tête, their figures surrounded by Lilliputian waves of hand-printed words. I wandered through the galleries until finally, exhausted, I spied a bench in front of a case of artifacts and sat down.

I closed my eyes a minute to rest. When I opened them, I noticed a small bone, nestled on a piece of faded red velvet. The label said that it was an oracle bone made from human remains, used for divination in China during the twelfth century. After all its years of use predicting births, deaths, wars, famine, and prosperity, and its second life as a sleeping relic, the bone still glowed white like a pearl. When I took a closer look, I noticed a faint inscription carved into the bone. Later, in a catalogue, I discovered it was the ancient Chinese character for "child." Had the bone been used to foretell the birth of a child or had someone taken it from a child, offered up as a sacrifice so someone else's future could be told?

"I'm ready to go," says William. I gasp and spin around. I look up at this stranger, my husband, towering above.

"I just started drawing."

"People will come back soon," says William. "I don't want to be around when they do."

Something is brooding beneath his face. His eyes have that faraway flat look, the kind my mother used to get before an episode. I wonder if, in another time, the Sámi would say that William's real self had been kidnapped by the Uldat, the hidden people below the earth, and replaced with an evil changeling. The ancient Sámi would have said I needed a magic silver knife, the help of a shaman, and a large herd of reindeer to use as a bargaining chip.

"I'll pack up my things," I say. "I guess I'll finish this another time."

When we get home, there is dog excrement smeared all over our door. In front of our entrance, in the snow, someone has dribbled *Americans Go Home* in urine. "It's her," I say. "We have to report this."

"I know," says William, his face softer now. "This has to stop."

In March, the month the Sámi call Njučkamánnu, the Month of the Swans, we find out that although we have made several calls to social services, they still have not paid the woman upstairs a visit. But somehow she knows about our reports. News travels fast in this town. One afternoon we forget to lock the door and she barges into our apartment drunk and screaming. We finally get her out and head down to the social worker's office once again. He apologizes for the delay. They will certainly look into the matter soon. "If you don't," William warns, "something really bad is going to happen and you'll be responsible."

In April, the Month of Hard Snow, Čuokamánnu, it is even more difficult for the reindeer to find food. The surface of the snow is too frozen to dig through in many places. Things are hard for humans as well—the light in April is blinding, bouncing off the bright white ground. Neither William nor I can sleep. And the woman upstairs stays up all night partying. Her parties spill out into the streets, even though the temperature rarely gets above fifteen degrees. As the woman's behavior worsens, William's does as well. He spends more and more time locked up inside. If I say something to him he snaps back. If I get a letter from a male friend, he throws it in my face, saying, "Why don't you just go fuck the guy when you get back home?" I try to skip out of the house early in the morning before he wakes up.

One day he announces, "I don't want to go back to America. I want us to find a cabin somewhere on the tundra and stay."

"I thought you hated it here. And, besides, who's going to fund your idea? My money runs out in May."

"I don't get it. All you care about is money."

"What's not to get? It's simple. You refuse to work and I pay for everything."

"I'm a poet! How dare you?"

"Even Walt Whitman had to eat."

We don't talk for two days, but then one night his mood shifts and I find him in the kitchen, cheerfully making pizza. He tells me he wants to go out to Kru's afterward for dessert. But during dinner, we hear someone pounding on our door. I crack the door open, thinking maybe it's the police. The blond woman and a dark-haired heavyset man with a knife burst in. Both are drunk. Apparently, social services had finally come to call. From her garbled shouting I realize that she has to appear in court the next month. I grab my cell phone, run to the bathroom, and lock myself in, while William pushes past the two intruders to go next door for help. It's January 1990 all over again.

A blizzard is starting and I can't get a signal unless I stand in the bathtub and hold the phone above my head. I put it on speakerphone and call the police. Outside the door I can hear the woman and her friend breaking things inside our apartment. I am trembling all over. What if no one comes?

Finally, a policeman shows up. They all know each other; who knows, maybe they were old buddies at school. Small-town life is the same all over. The couple calms down, they say something about how foreigners come here and try to get in their business. The cop gives the man and woman a light warning, then leads them back upstairs. When William returns with a neighbor, our place is quiet and everyone has gone. We push a heavy chair against the door, clean up the mess the couple had made, and go to bed.

The storm that had been brewing continues throughout the night. William and I fall asleep to the sound of shutters slapping against our windows, as if Stállu were trying to force his way in. The next morning, neither of us can hear a thing, not even the wind. I pull the curtains back to see that we are completely buried in snow. Our house is set low in the ground, so the blizzard had caused giant snowdrifts to press against our windows and door. I had left our shovel outside the day before, so William and I have to dig a hole with our hands through the bedroom window in order to get out. William boosts me up and I crawl through the hole first, then he follows. We stand outside and survey the land. I can't recognize a thing—not one ski track, or animal or human footprint. The bushes in the backyard have disappeared; everything is changed.

"Things will turn out okay," says William. He is almost his old self again, whatever that self is. He puts his arm around me.

"Will it?" I ask, shivering, his arm a dead weight upon my shoulder.

He pulls out our shovel from beneath the snow. "I changed my mind. I think I want to go home. It's just that I don't know where that is right now."

"Neither do I," I say. "But I know it's not here."

The next day, William and I move out. I feel like I am abandoning the children upstairs. I have been their watchdog and now I've given up. But I'm too afraid to stay, and so is William. Ristiina helps us move into a small two-room dormitory apartment at the Sámi College and we never see the blond woman or her children again.

At the end of April, Gloria, the woman who took care of my grandma, called to tell me that she had died. "She passed in her sleep, honey. She was just sitting up, real peaceful. Don't worry. She wasn't in pain. I sure loved Annie. She was like family to me."

Gloria told me that she had lost my number, and hadn't been able to find it until just now, a couple days after my grandma's death. She didn't know how to reach my sister. "We just had to go ahead and put her in the ground," she said. "God rest her soul."

There was too much static on the line and I could barely hear her. "I'll call you tomorrow," I said. "Thank you for taking such good care of her all these years."

I lay down on the couch, stunned. My grandmother had been ninety-two years old, but I thought she would be there when I got back. I had visited her in Cleveland right before I left. Her Alzheimer's was so advanced that she didn't know who I was and just babbled nonsense, pulling threads out of her sweater and flipping through an old checkbook from a decade before. In Sámi stories, the dead walk on the ceiling of a world turned upside down, their feet following the footsteps of the living. I walked in circles in our little dormitory room and imagined my grandfather, father, and grandma walking below, around and around beneath my feet. Who would tell me about my mother, should she pass away? I lay down on the bed and began to cry. William came in from the other room and held me for a while until his face clouded over and his eyes grew distant and mean, and within the space of an hour, Stallú became a dark weight at the bottom of a boat once again.

∽

The day before we fly home in early May, another letter arrives from my mother:

> Dear Myra,
> If you are in possession of keys to the house or know who is holding them, please send. I have left the Jesus Hotel and am moving from place to place, using the sleeping bag I bought. I've suffered some disfigurement, blindness and an injured foot. This is urgent. This is my life story. They are trying to steal my memory. I will keep making posters of their intent. Enclosed is a picture of where the next cyclones will hit. It looks like, from my calculations, that you are still safe in your

*corner of the world. Please take two days off and come home immediately to help
look for the keys. If I have a couch by then you can sleep on it. Mother. P.S. Be
careful. The Wolf is in the house.*

My mother has been ending many of her recent letters with the phrase
"the wolf is in the house." When I first arrived in Norway, people told me that
there weren't any wolves left, save for one lone female, passing through on her
way back to Russia. They said that no one has really seen her, but everyone
knows she is there. A friend in town says she heard the last wolf when she
was ten and lost in the woods. Twenty years later, she heard it again. The loss
of the wolf is like the loss of a mother. Somewhere she roams in memory, in
darkness. Our bond with her is inexplicable, before the beginning of time.
She is fierce love; she is sorrow. She is a howling in the wilderness we can
never see, calling us home. She is what we fear—and what we long to return
to—the heat of the cave and animal closeness, before all civilization and
reason. Was it right for me to try to separate the mother from her children
upstairs? Should someone have come to take my sister and me away? The
wolf is the dark heart of winter. She is the hot breath of life, red eyes searching for her child at twilight in the snow. How long will I wait to hear my
mother's voice? Will I ever hear it again?

Back in the dormitory, I finish packing for William because he is too
depressed to get out of bed. When he finally gets up, I tell him that I'm worried because I've just been to the bank and we are almost out of money. But
he doesn't care or even seem know what that means. *You will have to get a job
when we return*, I say. *Do you even know what a job is?* He throws a book at me
from across the room, goes into the bathroom, and slams the door. I remember what the Norwegian explorer Roald Amundsen once said about being
alone in the Arctic: "The country here is one single glacier. To go it alone is
pure madness. Two roped together, absolutely necessary." Maybe Amundsen
was wrong.

Who knows how things will turn out with William? At the moment,
the future is not looking that bright. If my aunt Toda were here, she'd sit
me right down and read the tea leaves in the bottom of my cup. I think of
the little oracle bone from China. What does my future hold for me? Will

I let someone else's sickness determine how I spend each day? I decide then and there that when we get back, there will be new rules, and that I will set the agenda, not him. If things don't change soon, I will leave. William will have to see a therapist, get a job, and even take medication if he has to. If he doesn't, I will hide from him too, just like I hide from my mother. Whatever it takes to be safe.

As I gather my own things for our trip back to the states, I remember a story about the Tchudit, the legendary marauders Ristiina told me about. One day, the Tchudit came to a nearby river and hid behind some bushes. There was a girl on shore who was going to swim to an island where her family was. As the girl started out at the riverbank, the Tchudit grabbed her and demanded she lead them to her people. She told them to follow her while she swam across to her island home. It was night and she pushed a torch before her. She told them to follow the light. They began swimming after her, deeper into the dark river. "How far?" asked one of the men. "We're almost there," said the girl. The Tchudit swam even harder toward the light. As they got closer to the island, the girl let go of the light and let the water carry the torch so the Tchudit would follow it instead of her. They continued to follow the torch, until finally the swift river pulled it and the Tchudit out to sea. By morning, they all had drowned.

And the girl? Some say she made it back to her island home that night. Her family held a great feast, and they celebrated till dawn. But I like to think that she too was carried off to sea—where she can still be found, at the bottom of a canyon, moving the bones into the shape of her future.

Part III

Palimpsest

. . . you scrape, and find—simplest of mysteries,
forgotten all this time, but not quite lost—

Jared Carter, "Palimpsest"

I Am Slowly Healing

The Navajo say that when a person becomes sick he or she has fallen out of harmony with nature. The healer uses a sand painting to cure the sick person. The sick person sits inside the painting to absorb its beauty. Then a part of the painting is poured on the diseased areas of the patient's body. After they finish, they destroy the painting and bury it so the illness of the person can't bring evil to others. I made some pictures this year but am not going to destroy them. Especially the ones of the two white goats, the macaque monkey holding a potted plant that is a self portrait and the picture of the five little dress-up trolls with hats. There is a nice one in pastels of a woman and a dog too. I think the woman is my mother but I can't be sure.

    I am slowly healing.

. . . loving kindness, let me approach you sleeping,
let me touch your shawl of blindness,
your hems of breathing and breathing . . .

Dara Wier, "If After All Excuses Suddenly There is
Never Again a Need for Any Afterall"

In the Palace of Kalachakra

Natalia and I are driving down Route 68 heading southeast toward the Carry Falls Reservoir, away from her town of Canton, New York. It's been raining for days. Most of the snow has disappeared but the air still feels damp and cold. I look out the window and all I can see thick brown mud, a blue-gray sky. There's no one else on the road except for a man lumbering along in a rusty red tractor.

"You okay?" my sister asks. "Sure you're up for a hike?"

"I'm fine. Just a little tired. It'll pass."

The art gallery at my sister's university has hired me for several weeks to help with an exhibit on Tibetan sacred art. It's my first time back to work after a two-month rest. At the beginning of the year, I slipped and fell on the ice in Northampton, Massachusetts, where William and I had moved to just before we got divorced. A woman passing by found me lying in the road. I had been unconscious for at least several minutes, and because of that I received priority care in the ER. By March, I still had a few cognitive problems and short-term memory loss but was well on my way to recovery.

Natalia doesn't ask me about William and I don't offer any information. What's there to say? I see him sometimes in town and when he notices me, he crosses the street and pretends we are strangers. Better that, I think, than him begging me to come back. I had worried that I'd have to hide from him but it appears as if he is trying to hide from me. Not so with my mother, however. In the spring of 1999, she is still trying to track me down.

Nine years have passed since my sister and I last saw her. In a letter she wrote not long after my fall on the ice, she said that she had moved back to Cleveland and was searching for my drawing *Help Is On the Way: I am consumed in getting the White Horse back. Then, when we reach the next plateau, I'll change my name to Helen R. Keller and go by the name of Rachel. I am also thinking of pronouncing your father's name HUR from now on, and dropping the sound of HARE. I am tired of using a name that sounds like a rabbit. What do you think?* She informed me that she orders my sister's graduate thesis every few months from interlibrary loan. She makes corrections on Natalia's book of short stories, then sends it back. She believes that she is communicating with my sister through the book. She sends me copies of some of the pages with her suggestions: *Remove first line on page 36* or *If you cut the introduction to this manuscript, I believe it will be publishable.* I know this would probably upset Natalia, so I don't mention it. Instead, in the car, I chat about the mundane. "Been raining a lot up here, huh?" "Yep," she says. "It's mud season. Hope you brought good boots."

My first day at work, before the tour groups arrive, I watch two Tibetan monks in maroon and yellow robes, one thin and solemn, the other round and robust, circle a white platform in the middle of the main gallery. The two men bow and chant in deep overtones. After their prayers, they sit across from one another on a large blue square on top of the platform, lean in, and start their work. They are building the Palace of Kalachakra, the most sacred of all Tibetan mandalas, made from colored sand. They believe it has the power to create healing and peace.

The Kalachakra mandala is a symbolic depiction of a five-story palace where an incarnation of the Buddha of Compassion is believed to reside.

As part of a Tibetan monk's training, he must learn three thousand different mandala designs by heart, but Kalachakra is said to be the most complex of them all. They say that if a monk can complete this one, the rest will seem easy. In Sanskrit, *Kalachakra* means "Wheel of Time"; some call it the Subterranean World, the same term Athanasius Kircher used to describe his underground world of caves. The story goes that the historical Buddha entrusted the Kalachakra tantra, the sacred teachings, to the King of Shambhala, who took the tantra with him to his subterranean kingdom where all beings live in harmony without sickness or death.

In one of my mother's recent letters, she wrote: *Well, I'm not doing too bad, considering. I guess as long as one doesn't have cancer, heart disease, kidney disease, tuberculosis, diabetes, multiple sclerosis, hepatitis, shingles, malnutrition or AIDS, they are doing pretty well. How's your health, by the way?* I hadn't told her about my fall on the ice. I still struggle with a few things, including concentration and memory, but other than that, I am on the mend, so why upset her? I wrote back: My health is great. I rarely even get a cold. But thanks for asking.

From the center of the square, the monks draw white lines with chalk to map out their design. Afterward, they begin sprinkling tiny pieces of crushed colored stone from *chakpus*, long metal cones they rub together to control the flow of sand. The sound of *chakpus* echoes like a pealing bell throughout the room. The monks work slowly, meticulously guiding the threads of sand from memory. In the next three weeks, they will build a great palace, filled with dharma wheels and elephants, lions and lotus flowers, protective deities, wind horses, and shells.

I approach to the white velvet rope surrounding the platform. The monks are deep in concentration. They wear surgical masks as they work; just one sneeze could send a hundred deities flying. The chubbier monk looks up and smiles. "I'm Tenzin," he says. He comes out from behind the rope to greet me. He bows, then nods toward his colleague. "He's Tenzin too. You can tell us apart because I'm the fat one." The other monk keeps working, *chakpus* ringing in his graceful and patient hands.

"Not so fat," I say.

He laughs. "What do they call you?"

"Mira," I say.

"*Tashi delek, Mira*," he says. "Maybe we can have tea together soon."

Over the next week, after leading tours all day, I hang around the gallery until closing in case community members or students want to ask me, or the monks, any questions. Although I've read up on Tibetan sacred art, I feel like an imposter. It's not like when I worked at the Field Museum and could answer questions about the origin of some ceremonial mask. Here people ask what path they should be on, as if I were some kind of spiritual guide. A middle-aged woman with a toddler asks me if I think there is life after death; an unemployed Vietnam vet pulls me aside and wants to know if the mandala will help with his depression. The exhibit is drawing in people who have never been in the gallery before—unemployed factory workers, disabled vets, North Country women with sad, weathered faces. They approach me with a lost look in their eyes. At the heart of the Kalachakra is the lesson of compassion. I want to tell them, What do I know about compassion? I abandoned my mother to the streets. Instead, I invite them to hear the monks.

Each morning, the two Tenzins lead a sitting meditation. Afterward, they give a brief talk about Buddhism's "Four Noble Truths": First, one must come to understand that he causes much of his own suffering. That's easy enough to digest, except maybe when it comes to my mother. She suffers from biology, from crossed wires, from too many voices in her head. I have always known deep down there is great love and sweetness inside her, her true self she had at birth, but schizophrenia devours it every day. The second Noble Truth is that one must look for the cause of one's pain. Where to begin with that one? Third, the looking brings confidence to end one's own misery, and finally, the monks tell us, a wish arises to find a path to peace.

I go every day to hear them. As a rule, I'm not one to join a spiritual group, or any group, for that matter. I'm suspicious of the crowd that gathers, suspicious of gurus or spiritual guides. But the Tenzins are humble and remind those of us who come to listen that they have no answers, only suggestions on how to find some kind of inner peace. The Tenzins always end by talking about compassion and how we must try to eliminate the suffering of all sentient beings. And what of my mother? In her letters, she says she is trying to figure out what part of her suffering is caused by "outside" influences and what is caused from within. She writes: *I am bleeding from below, I can't control my bladder, I am blind and have lost all of my teeth. Sometimes I can't tell if it is night or day.* Well, as they say, everyone is guaranteed the right to be deprived of the pursuit of happiness. What does Buddhism have to say about a schizophrenic woman who sleeps at the airport and covers her face in zinc oxide at night to ward off gamma rays from another planet? And how can I help her, be compassionate to her, but not put myself in harm's way? I'd like to ask the monks—Should I see her again? What can I do? Is there any hope for her, or does hope just bite the tail of fear?

It's the beginning of April and I have gotten into an easy Monday-through-Friday routine. I lead one to three tour groups in the morning, grab a quick lunch, then return for my next round of tours. One day the more rotund and cheerful of the monks, Tenzin Y., asks if I want to join them in the cafeteria. At lunch, he orders the special of the day—roast turkey, mashed potatoes, salad, and soup.

"You guys eat meat?"

"Of course we do."

"I thought there was some kind of rule or something."

"Everything is good. Especially cake."

We find a table and sit down. I look across at the other monk's plate, a small dish of macaroni and vegetables. Both monks bow before they eat. I am growing fond of these two men. Despite their robes and rituals, they are anything but off-putting or annoyingly pious.

"Anyone can learn to watch his or her mind," says Tenzin Y. "Christians, Jews, Muslims, atheists, anyone. To pay attention to how one creates one's own suffering, that is the point. To end the suffering of others—even more important."

Tenzin G. is quiet during lunch. When he finishes, he gets up quietly, bows, and goes back to work. After he leaves, I ask Tenzin Y. about what he hopes the impact of the mandala will be on the community.

"The Kalachakra plants a seed of motivation in the mind of those who see it. The most important part of creating a mandala is the motivation behind it. Motivation eventually leads to compassion."

I want to ask him about my mother. What about her suffering, the suffering of the mentally ill? How can I help her if I am too afraid to see her face-to-face? Instead, I ask him if he was born in Tibet.

"No," he says. "Dharamsala, where His Holiness lives."

"What about Tenzin G.?"

"He came over the mountains."

"The Himalayas?"

"Yes. He came as a child to India, after China invaded Tibet."

"Like the Dalai Lama."

"Yes," says Tenzin Y. "And many small children. They still cross that way by foot."

"And Tenzin G.—did he cross over the mountains on foot?"

Tenzin Y. nods, his smile gone. "It was a very long and difficult journey."

❧

In my mother's April journal, she writes:

The poet said April is the cruelest month. It seems so. I am trying to think constructively about cooking again. I learned how to cook at the Recovery Center before Reagan closed everything down for the poor. I would like to make a dish called Turley Tava. I've never prepared it, but will. Maybe it's something like Hungarian goulash only it goes inside the stove: very small of quantity lamb, eggplant, fresh tomatoes, onions, yellow string beans and white potatoes. Stuffed peppers are good to make too. And meatless casseroles—tuna, mushroom, pasta. And salmon cakes. I would make those too if I had a home. I have always been partial to salmon cakes.

At my sister's, the three of us take turns cooking. It's quiet and relaxing to dine with them after being with the public all day. But sometimes I wonder if my mother digs in garbage bins for food. Has her life gotten so low? I worry about whether or not she has enough to eat, if she has shelter. I know I won't mention my concerns to Natalia. What can she do? What can either of us do? In the evenings, Natalia, her husband, Kerry, and I watch a movie or read in the sitting room. There are so many rooms in their house—five rooms upstairs, five rooms below. I wander through the house, not sure where to sit. Where does my mother sit—on a park bench? On the cold hard ground?

One day, a group from a local women's shelter appears at the gallery. The women range in age from nineteen to seventy-three. The oldest is the same age as my mother.

"I've never been in here before," says a middle-aged woman with blond curly hair, arms crossed in front. "It's not my kind of thing."

The women hang up their coats and congregate in the hallway. "Are we allowed to smoke?" asks the seventy-three-year-old. "Anyone got a cigarette?"

"Just look around," I say, "then we'll talk in a few minutes about what's on display."

"This is a waste of my fucking time," says a young woman with short-cropped hair, tattoos up and down her arms. A couple women snicker.

"Walk around a bit. If you don't like anything, you don't have to stay after that."

These women didn't choose to come here; they're only here because some social worker cajoled them into coming. What do I have to offer them? And the older woman—is that how my mother looks now, stooped shoulders, favoring one leg, sitting down every few minutes because her emphysema makes it hard for her to breathe?

"I want a cigarette. Where the hell can I smoke?" she says again.

"You got coffee here? I'd like a cup of hot coffee," says another, whose left hand and wrist are bandaged. Did her husband do that? Did she try to kill herself? These women don't need me, they need money and a place to live.

"Let me show you something," I say.

I take them into a room filled with ritual objects and *thangka* paintings, painted scrolls traditionally used for meditation and healing. They walk around awhile, then meet me by the altar the monks have set up. I explain to them the story of Buddha, who was called Siddhartha before his enlighten-ment, and how, after a cloistered life of luxury, he stepped outside his palace one day and saw an old man, a sick man, a corpse, and a starving man who had rejected the material world. I tell them how Siddhartha was so struck with all the pain and misery he saw that he renounced his riches and set out to find a cure for human suffering.

"He left all that money?" asks the youngest, a girl with long dark brown braids. She could be me at twenty-two. "He gave up all those jewels? What a dumb-ass!" Everyone laughs. "So what happened next?"

"For years he wandered. First he denied himself everything, like that starving man he met his first day out in the world. Then, later, he wasn't so hard on himself. He found a middle path between poverty and the life he had led before." I tell the women about Siddhartha sitting under the Bodhi Tree and meditating until he found the root of all suffering.

"What'd he find?" asks Nancy, a woman about my age, pushing forty.

I try to explain meditation to the women. I tell them how it might help them to just sit sometimes, be still and watch their breath. I tell them, "It helps calm down the gerbil living inside your brain."

We go into the main exhibition room and I introduce the women to the monks. The women seem intimidated, for some reason, and don't ask questions. They watch the two Tenzins for a while, but aren't that interested in the mandala. Most want to see the photographs they passed by when they first came in, so we return to the main hall. The pictures are from a contemporary series called "Tibetans in Exile." I ask each of them to pick out a photo and tell the group what she thinks is going on. Nancy selects a portrait of an elderly monk holding several implements of torture. He stole them from his captors when he was being held and tortured by Chinese guards.

"Why did you pick that one?" I ask.

"The label said he was beat with those things," she says. "Just look at his face. You can tell it really happened. It's in his eyes."

Another woman picks a photo of three little boys in Dharamsala, India. The caption below says that the children crossed over the mountains all the way to India by foot.

"I got three kids," the woman says. Pat is her name. "I took them with me when I left."

I tell the women how many children make the journey over the Himalayas alone. I show them photographs of the mountains and explain how treacherous they are, especially in winter.

"Their mothers let them go alone like that?" asks Pat.

"Their parents might be in prison for speaking out against the government," I say. "Or they might have gotten killed. Some of the children lose fingers and toes from frostbite. But many of them make it to safety. I don't know how but they do."

I start to ask the women what I ask every group I take through this exhibit, even children: "If you had to leave your home in a hurry, what would you take with you?" and then I realize, for these women, the question isn't hypothetical at all. They tell me they grabbed their children first, what money they had, and that's about it.

"I wore the clothes on my back," says the seventy-three-year-old. She still won't give her name. "Didn't take a thing," she says. "My husband had a gun."

I scooped up photographs of strangers and a piece of rosin. Natalia grabbed my mother's address book so she couldn't find the phone numbers of Natalia's friends. My mother will obsess about her missing book for years. *Do you know where my address book is?* She will ask in her letters. *I have lost the addresses and numbers of all my friends and loved ones. Some had unpublished numbers. How will I ever find them?*

I've kept the women way past my usual hour-long tour. My mother could be in this group. She'd be outside right now, agitated, puffing on a cigarette. "It's time to go," I say. "But come back anytime. Just look for me. The show will be up for a while."

They gather their coats and I tell them where they can get coffee and a snack, where to buy cigarettes nearby. One woman is missing, though, a quiet one in her late twenties, with wavy light brown hair and a bright pink hoodie. I retrace our steps. The mandala room is empty now except for the Tenzins, working steadily in the center of the room. I return to the room with the altar. The missing woman is standing in front of a *thangka* of Green Tara, one of the divine bodhisattvas, a female Buddha in the making. The woman spins around and gasps when she hears me enter. PTSD, most likely. I would have done the same.

"Who is she?" she asks.

"Her name is Tara. She's a goddess."

"Awesome. I got a friend named Tara."

"Her name means 'to cross over,' like you cross a bridge over a stream. She helps people cross over difficult places. They call her the Swift Liberator sometimes because she stands for freedom from pain and suffering."

"I like her. I wish I could take her home."

"She's a kind of mother figure because she's so compassionate. There's a story about how she was born from a tear falling from Buddha's eye. Some people meditate on her image to help them overcome fear."

"Do you do that?"

"Not really," I say. "Listen, the gallery's closing but you can come back another time. I can tell you more about her then."

"Thanks," she says.

"See you again maybe."

"Yeah. Maybe. 'Bye."

Before I leave for the day, I stop to look in on the monks. I pause in front of a grainy 1959 black-and-white photo of a young Dalai Lama in disguise on horseback, fleeing his homeland. He looks vulnerable in the picture, so small on his horse in the immense Tibetan landscape at dusk. When the Dalai Lama left the Potala Palace in the night as the Chinese were advancing, he said to his companions, "I see a safe journey. I see a safe return." I wonder if the woman in the pink hoodie will come back. I wonder if I will return as well, to the place of my origin, to the mother I left behind.

෴

It is almost mid-April and the monks are close to completion. From the side, looking at it at eye-level, the mandala resembles a giant cake. It's hard to believe that soon the monks will sweep it all away—the colorful rooms and animals, the protective rings of fire and water, the secret Sanskrit prayers. I feel sad about leaving and saying goodbye to the monks, especially Tenzin Y. When I'm around them, I feel more at ease in the present moment, more accepting of the fact that I don't know what to do about my mother *today*. I also feel, when I'm with them, that I have the potential to do something compassionate and brave. But what that is, I don't know. Will I feel the same when I return?

After the Tenzins leave for the day, I climb a ladder a workman had forgotten to put away. From above, the mandala is a perfect architectural plan and easy to imagine as a five-story palace. There are circles within circles, each one a mandala, each mandala surrounded by a square representing a palace room. In my mind, I enter one of the doors at the first level, the mandala of the body, and walk through transparent walls. I climb up glistening steps to the second level, the mandala of speech, surrounded by five multicolored walls. Up another set of steps and I'm at the third level of the mind, encircled by three more walls. Farther in, on the fourth level, is the room of consciousness. Is this a map of the human brain? Everything here is ordered, like a Bach cantata, a nautilis shell, the petals of a rose. On this platform is yet another room—the center where the monks first began, the mandala of enlightenment—happiness, freedom from suffering, compassion, freedom from pain. They say that Kalachakra resides here, upon an eight-petaled lotus. I peer down into the mandala of enlightenment; it is the smallest one of all. Is there something in that tiny room for me, for my mother, or is it just another beautiful thing to be swept away?

Close to the outer rings, I see a tiny smudge. I climb down a couple rungs. An insect has died in the sand, perhaps a fly, but I can't tell. I climb down another step. It is a fly embedded in a secret Sanskrit word. Will they leave it there or try to pick it out? Even in this realm of ordered beauty there is something a little off, a fact I somehow find comforting.

The friend who manages my post office box in New York forwards a letter to me from my mother one day. *Dear Myra*, she writes, *I hope you know that you are the only friend I have in the world, and that I don't know where I'll be in the near future but I'm sure to be alone.* She says she has decided to let me have her address and hopes I will do the same. She wants to see me quite badly. She tells me she hasn't been that well and is living in subsidized housing for "women in transition" in Cleveland. *You can call me in the evening on the public phone, after five. I look forward to your call.*

I decide to decide later about what to do, after I return to Massachusetts. Maybe I'll write the director of the place. Or should I call? Do I have the courage? She doesn't have to know I called. Maybe she has a social worker now, someone who can help. It's possible that social services in Cleveland have improved since 1990. There is always a sliver of hope in me, the hope that I can still save her and see her again.

∾

The monks have finally finished. Everyone from the school and surrounding community is invited to the closing ceremony. We place flowers and little bowls of water on altars at each cardinal direction of Kalachakra. The two Tenzins circle the palace and chant, turning the ritual bell and *varja* in their hands.

Dozens of people pour into the gallery. I recognize two women from the shelter but the one I talked to about Green Tara is not in the crowd. The Tenzins invite a couple of us up so they can give us gifts. Tenzin Y. places a white *khatag* around my neck and bows. He calls me Mira·la, adding an honorific ending to my name. It sounds like what my grandma used to call me in Hebrew when I was young—Miraleh.

The monks pinch special places in the sand. Then, with steady hands, they guide the *varjas* and mark lines through the palace, dragging them to the outer edges of the design. They sweep the sand to the center, the place where they began, and then, when all of the rooms and deities and elephants and flowers, jewels, horses, shells, waves, wheels, words, and protective flames have dissolved into a pile of colored dust (including the little dead fly), the two monks scoop the pile up and pour it into an urn. With all the colors blended now, the sand resembles the gray ashes of someone's cremated remains.

We head to the river, a hundred people or more. It's a quiet but joyous procession through Canton. We pass beneath the movie theater's marquee, which advertises the film *Life Is Beautiful*, and walk in the spring air to the banks of the Grasse River. We sit in silence while the two monks enter the river and wade up to their knees. They chant for several minutes then tip over the urn. We watch as the water takes the fallen palace and carries it away.

The next day, I stop by the gallery. The blue platform still bears faint traces of chalk; soon that too will be washed away. Tenzin Y. is gathering his tools.

"Tenzin-la, I was just wondering—why toss the sand in the river? Why not over a hill, or bury it in the ground?"

"Oh, that is easy," he says. "We sprinkle colors on the water because it delights the magical beings who live below."

"Magical beings?"

"The colors make them happy."

A group of professors and gallery staff arrive to say goodbye. I want to ask Tenzin about these water creatures—if this is something he really believes in or if it is a myth. I want to ask him what he thinks I should do about my mother, now that I know where she is.

"Tenzin-la . . ."

"You have another question for me."

"Yes . . . I mean, no—not really, I guess. I just hope we see each other again."

"Don't worry, Mira-la. I see a safe journey. *Tujechhe.*"

"*Tujechhe*, Tenzin-la. Goodbye."

When I get back to Massachusetts, a letter is sitting in my post office box:

Dear Daughter,

I'm still waiting for your call. I don't know how much longer I'll stay here and I want to ask you a favor. There's an art show at Cleveland State University. I never submitted anything before. I brought in a large picture called "Going Places" and a small one of a girl named Nancy who comes in here to cook. They accepted them both. I went to your big art exhibit in Chicago once. Can you come to mine? I wonder if you are receiving my mail or if you are in some kind of detention. I need to see you even if it is a screen appearance. Lately I've been through hell. Your old picture, "Selective Forgetfulness," is still missing and many other things from the house. What other dirty tricks will be played on me this day?

Norma—"Mom."

She asked me to come to her art show. What should I do? How long will she stay in that place? If I lose her again to the streets, what then? The day the monks tossed Kalachakra into the river, I watched colored sand that had once been palace rooms of red, yellow, blue, and green sink below, forming a final mandala on the surface of the water. A few rippling circles spread outward, and then, in an instant, they were gone. "May I be a protector for those without one," said the Buddha of Compassion. "May I be a bridge, a boat, a ship for all who wish to cross the water. May I be a shelter for those without a home." I finally have an address for my mother. Can I find her safe and permanent refuge? I don't know if I can see her again, for in my dreams she still holds a broken bottle to my neck. But can I find her a place where she has enough to eat and a quiet room, and people to watch over her every day? The Buddha of Compassion said, "How is life precious? O ignorant one, do not fall asleep now."

Could I be a bridge, a boat, a ship?

Five months later, at the end of September, a truck driver falls asleep and goes hurtling down the New York Thruway right into my car. When the doctor at the hospital in Schenectady discovers that I had only been unconscious for a few moments, he briefly checks my neck, asks me a couple curt questions, and sends me home. The man I had been dating at the time, who had been driving my car and who had sustained mild whiplash, finds a rental car and drives me back to Massachusetts. I call my sister to tell her I had an accident but am fine.

The next day, I wake up in a fog. I wander from room to room, not sure what I'm looking for. I call a friend, then put the phone in the freezer. I boil water for tea and leave the burner on for most of the morning. I try to read the paper but the words blur together and nothing makes sense. When I talk, some words get stuck and can't come out. All I want to do is sleep. I can't remember what happened the day before, or the day before that. Or what I did ten minutes ago. When I go see my primary care doctor the following week, he says I look and sound fine. "Nothing to worry about," he says, patting me on the back. "It's just a little concussion. You were only out a few moments," he says, "so it can't be that bad. You'll be back on your feet in a few weeks, tops."

How we measure the severity of head trauma has a lot to do with a rather flawed system called the Glasgow Coma Scale. Doctors look at how long a person has been unconscious, how well he or she responds to stimuli such as voice commands and touch. If a person is only unconscious momentarily or not at all, he or she is often given cursory neurological examination and sent home, which was what happened to me. But even though my doctor says I'll be fine, something isn't right in my head. I can't seem to focus and can barely read. Going to the grocery store is now a harrowing experience. I can't bear the music they play and all those bright lights. I can no longer find my way out of the store without help. I find myself standing in an aisle, crying and confused. Then I get lost walking the two blocks home. And those sounds on the street—so many people talking, dogs barking, and people honking horns, children shouting—the world around me is unbearable. All those voices coming at me wherever I go. This must be what my mother feels, this relentless assault to her brain.

In an accident like mine, a *coup-contrecoup*, your brain rings back and forth like a bell inside your skull. As a result, the back and front of the brain can get serious contusions, causing a cascade of problems. The prefrontal cortex is the seat of executive functioning, problem-solving, emotions, and concentration. This is one part among many that isn't working but I am so out of it that I don't really notice or understand what is going on. Even though I look and seem fine. On the day I move into my new apartment a couple weeks after my accident, I have no idea how to put things away. Two friends come over to help. "Here is where the cups go," they say. "Here is a good place for your books." One friend sees the confused look on my face. She puts her arms around me and says, "Do you want me to post little signs so you know where things are?"

Not long after I move in, I break up with the guy who had been driving my car and try to simplify my life. Over the next few months, I cover all my bookshelves in white sheets; I can't read right now anyway, so why bother having books? All those colorful spines and titles are distracting and make my head throb. I take down the art my friends had helped hang and stick my CDs in a box. The slightest sound can give me a migraine even if the sound is a favorite piece by Bach. If this is supposed to be a "mild" brain injury, then why do I get lost on familiar streets?

My sister sends me money to buy a secondhand car. That way, I widen my chances of finding a job and can also drive to my medical appointments. But I quickly find that I can't drive farther than fifteen or twenty miles without getting lost. I try returning to my freelance work writing educational copy for magazines, and to my other job, teaching art to adults. I find that writing only one page can take several days and then afterward I have no recall of what I wrote. When I try to teach, just one short class makes me a zombie for days. All I want to do is sleep. One by one I lose my jobs. And my creative projects—my children's books, my short stories and essays, and a memoir I started about the Sámi—I stick inside a box. I don't even remember writing them. After I use up all my savings, I live on credit cards and start applying for grants. My new boyfriend, Doug, a musician, helps me out a little with bills, but he can only do so much, what with having to support his two teenage girls. But having him around makes life much easier. He drives me to doctor appointments, reminds me where I put things, walks me to places so I don't get lost.

You'll be better soon, my doctor assures me. I write my mother and tell her the same. It's been months since I've written her or even checked my post office box. "I had an accident," I say in my letter. "But the doctor says I'll be fine." My letter comes back "Addressee Unknown," just like ten years ago in 1990 when my mother first disappeared. A fuzzy memory rises to the surface—didn't she say she was living in a place with a phone? I search for her letter and find it. I think about the monks for the first time in ages. I wonder what Tenzin Y. would say. Maybe he'd say that this is the moment for me to be brave, to walk across the mountains. I call the number. "She left months ago," says the woman on the other end. "She didn't leave a forwarding address. Left her room in a hell of a state, though. Set two chairs on fire. We had to kick her out."

One day, while hiking on a trail with Doug, my legs suddenly give out. I feel jolts of electrical pain everywhere—in my legs, my arms, behind my eyes, my tongue, my feet and hands. The pain is excruciating and escalates over the next few weeks. I don't know if it's my spine, since I had injured my back in the accident, or if it's my brain. Along with the pain and the feeling of hot lava that's been there from the start, I feel other odd sensations now, like ants crawling up my arms and raindrops falling all over my body. When I sit down in a restaurant, I tell the server that there is a leak in the ceiling and that water is dripping on my head. I tell her she better get a bucket; she looks at me as if I'm nuts. At night, I can't control my legs and I wake up in pain. Doug is beside himself and doesn't know what to do. He comforts me and rubs my legs. Massage is the only thing that seems to help but I can't afford the treatments. The neurologist puts me on antiseizure medication that makes me groggy all the time. My world becomes flat and gray. Was this what my mother felt when she took her meds? I get scanned and probed and X-rayed but all my tests come back borderline normal. Finally, the neurologist announces that he can't find a single thing wrong with me. He tells me that it must be all in my head. I turn to him and say, "Well, Doctor, where else would it be?" and walk out.

The new doctor I find believes me. He explains that, with the kind of TBI, traumatic brain injury, that I have—a diffuse axonal injury—there can be widespread damage that is undetectable in fMRIs and other tests. In an accident like mine, the rapid acceleration and deceleration of the brain within the skull causes the axons, the parts of nerve cells that allow neurons to send messages, to become disrupted. Tissue slides over tissue, and shearing, swelling, and microscopic bleeding can occur. Cells can also die, which causes swelling, decreasing blood flow to the brain. The shearing can release chemicals, contributing to further damage. "You need to see a neuropsychologist and get in rehab," he says. "You should have gone right after the accident. Have you ever tried meditating? Some people swear it helps."

After months of silence, I finally get a letter from my mother, with her new post office box number. She is back to sleeping in motels and shelters, airports and bus stations, and park benches when it isn't too cold. The letter is more disturbing than usual to read because the way she writes reminds me of my own damaged brain:

> Dear Daughter,
> Painted my Reebok shoes today with yellow and black, thinking of a pirate flag. Of study, I am reviewing tree identification. One looks not just at leaves but general shape of tree. Deciduous trees, as opposed to Evergreens, shed leaves annually. Not to be confused with deciduas, lining of the uterus, cast off by pregnant females in childbirth. I feel great unfamiliarity with the Midwest where I have lived most of my years. Strange feeling I was born in New York, or was there in my infancy. My memory is impaired due to chemicals and gas. Thinking I am on edge today because I have "so they, so he" thought interference. My Post Office box is always empty. I eat lunch at a shelter on the east side. What I am wondering now is: In England, if a Queen dies, Is there royal ascent or is the throne left vacant? When are you coming home?
> Love, Mom.

When I write her back, I am so out of it that I make a grave mistake. I write Mira Bartók and my real street as my return address. She writes immediately. *Is that your real address? Did you change your name?* I shoot another letter off to her. "No, it's just an old friend from school," I write. "I have a new post office box. Don't write there anymore. She's not such a reliable friend." Fortunately, she believes my lie.

By 2001, I can't keep up with health insurance or daily bills anymore. The first lawyer I hire tells me that my lawsuit against the trucking company won't be settled for years, so I best find some way to survive. Finally, after maxing out my credit cards I end up, like my mother, on disability and welfare. I receive $850 a month from the government to live on. I wonder who gets more, my mother or me.

My new neurologist tells me that even so-called "mild" traumatic brain injuries, MBTIs, can cause lasting damage. But he's optimistic. Cells can regenerate; new pathways can be formed, detouring around damaged spots. He insists I go to a rehab center. "You need to start monitoring your progress," he says. "And exercise your brain."

At a brain trauma center in Springfield the doctor asks me, "What's a proverb?" I stutter out an answer: "A word that means something b-b-but I can't explain what it means." What is the speed of light, she asks, what direction does the sun set, what was Mahatma Gandhi known for? Pretty damn fast, I say, the light I mean, making light of my damaged brain, my loss of multiplication tables, my memory of what I ate for lunch that day. I am taking a cognitive test to see what my deficits are and am stuck on two words—*peace* and *light*. For the first time in ages I think of the Palace of Kalachakra, the monks making all those rooms of color from tiny grains of sand, only to sweep them away after three short weeks.

"Let's move on," says the doctor.

But move on to where? When all is said and done and the cards and blocks and lists of related fruits and vegetables, and animals beginning with the letter B, and all the sequences of numbers, going backward and forward, are put away and the test is completed, the score tabulated, filed, and assessed, my thoughts will still be a gaggle of noisy geese. I'll still be unable to work and my mother, who will soon turn seventy-five, will still be homeless and begging me to take her in. I have yet to answer the question I wanted to ask Tenzin Y. the day the monks dismantled their palace: should I find my mother and see her again?

While struggling to read a short story one afternoon, I get fixated on the word *birdsong*. It looks like *bridge-song* to me, and I can't get the image of birds on a bridge out of my mind. I can't follow words and sentences in a straight row anymore, even when I try what my new doctor suggests: place a piece of paper below each line so my eyes don't skip too far ahead. I am frustrated and feel like crying. But even though the emotion is there, nothing comes out of my eyes. *B-b-b-birdsong*, I stutter to the empty room. I am tired and want to give up. Who am I now, if I can't be the person I was before? My brain is just a field of scattering deer, a birdsong is a bridge of wings, there are ants crawling in and out of my ears. Why can't I just accept it and move on? What about the monks—did I learn nothing at all? Tenzin Y. said to me once that the only thing we know for certain is that things will change, sometimes in an instant. Their palace was like my brain is now, a palimpsest—an illuminated manuscript that has been scraped away, over and over again, so something can be created anew. When buildings are rebuilt, wherever spaces are shuffled or destroyed, ghost shadows still remain. These too are palimpsests. What's important is the impulse to go on, to create, even if tomorrow you can't remember what it was you made the day before.

I finally begin to write again, a little each day. My neuropsychologist suggests that I start drawing too. I hang a card above my desk that says, "Remember what you love." Then, in September, two airplanes hit the World Trade Center. The personal consequence is that my mother loses her home, where she has been sleeping in baggage claim at Cleveland Hopkins International Airport off and on for weeks. Everyone is kicked out—of airports, bus stations, train depots, the Rapid Transit that my mother rides long into the night. Where will she go now?

Months later, my mother sends me copies of some of her medical reports. I had asked her to send them because she had complained of so many ailments—blindness, vascular disease, heart problems, stroke, rectal bleeding—and I wanted to know if any were true. Enclosed, along with the files, is a police report and part of a long document from a mental institution where apparently she had been kept for observation a couple weeks after the 9/11 attacks. The hospital document stated that while the owner of my grandparents' old house on West 148th Street was out of town, my mother somehow convinced a locksmith that her own house had been robbed. She paid him to change all the locks. The owner, who had lived there for the last few years, came home to find a strange woman pacing in his living room, smoking and talking to herself. After she was arrested, they put her in restraints and brought her to the hospital for observation. When they asked her if she had any children, she told them, "I don't have any kids. I had an adopted daughter once but she lives in another state."

Some of her other medical files validate how ill she really is. She definitely has something wrong with her gastrointestinal system—all the alarming signs are there—but she refuses to be X-rayed or examined without her clothes. Her heart shows signs of irregularity and she does indeed suffer from vascular disease, which is why it's so hard for her to walk. Her partial blindness is due to cataracts, though, and can be repaired if she agrees to have the operation. But try telling that to a woman who thinks the Nazis had removed her womb. There must be something I can do but I can't figure out what it is.

I live in a cramped duplex with Doug out in the country and although my condition has improved it's clear that there are many problems that will never go away. Weeks blur into months and years. I've lost the order of things. To the outside world, however, I show a different face than the one I show with Doug at home. Children of the mentally ill learn early on how not to be a bother, especially if they grew up with neglect. As my sister insisted once, when she was in severe pain after injuring her ankle, "This isn't me! This is not who I am!"

Then one day, a gift from my mother arrives in the mail. It's Chanukah 2004. In the box is a pair of a small child's blue slippers, decorated with gold stars and moons, and a plush toy owl with a little cap. For my mother's return address, there is a real one on a real street—the shelter on Payne Avenue. *I live in pain on Payne*, she says on the enclosed card. It's the first thing she sends me with the Community Women's Shelter's address. *Very good holiday recognition at Shelter*, she writes. *We were given each two boxes, presents, and an envelope with five dollars. But I am feeling very bombarded by events, insights of past months and days. I feel very much hated by unknown parties. When will you come see your old lady again? They sometimes have extra cots in the large room downstairs. Or you can take my bed and I can sleep on a mat on the floor. Love, Mom.*

She mentions a social worker named Melissa who helps her out. She's from an organization called MHS, Mental Health Services for Homeless Persons, Inc. I write back and ask if I have permission to contact her social worker. She writes to say of course, but can I please come to Cleveland to help her find her keys? My mother says, *I'm seventy-eight years old and I want to go home*. I want to see her again too. I've already lost her once, and have, at least for a time, lost myself. I don't want to lose her again. But I decide I can only see her if she is in some kind of supervised setting. Otherwise, she'll try to come home with me. I contact the social worker and we begin the long process of finding my mother a permanent home. Which, in the end, turns out to be a quiet dark room in a hospice ward.

Finally, I have built a palace within my palace, made from bits of colored sand. One breath could sweep it all away. It is protected by blue waves and fire, by elephants and incandescent shells, lotus flowers and horses, cryptic words and prayers. But the palace cannot possibly last; it will, like everything else, eventually disappear. It is the essence of memory, ephemeral as sleep, unsettled as the sea.

Last Page

Nov. 16, '06 Receive package (box) from Myra.

Nov. 20, '06 In all day.

Nov. 21, '06 Tuesday

Sagittarius Nov. 22–Dec. 21

Wednesday, Nov. 22, '06

Chica—drink of Peru

Hecuba—Wife of Priam

Baroque Palace—?

16

Through birds, through fire, but not through glass . . . that we came to earth to live is untrue; we come to sleep, to dream.

Aztec

Into the Land of Birds and Fire

I awoke to an old familiar smell—stale cigarettes, musty paper, and perfume. My baby book was next to me in the hotel bed, propped open to a photograph of my sister in a playpen, reaching toward someone, a woman's body just beyond the picture frame. My sister's face is beaming, her tiny fingers grasping for the woman's hand holding a brush. It was Saturday, two days before Christmas 2006.

Natalia and I rushed through breakfast to get to the hospital early in case they decided to move our mother to a nursing home that day. The hospital needed the bed and our mother needed to be in hospice care. When we arrived at the hospital, we found out that they had made arrangements to send her to the worst nursing home in the city, full of drug addicts, the criminally insane, and Cleveland's neglected poor. Melissa, the woman who had been my mother's social worker before Tim, told me they were sending her there because she was homeless. I called up the hospital's social worker in charge.

"My mother is not going to that place," I said. "Do not move her until I find a better one. Is that clear?"

Natalia stayed at the hospital while Cathy and I went to look at two other nursing homes. I almost settled on the first place, a cheerful hospice center that looked like a condo, but changed my mind when I saw the crucifixes hanging in every room. There was also an unlocked door right by the first-floor room she would be given if she moved there. I was still convinced my mother would get up out of bed, walk outside, and disappear into the streets. After all these years of hiding from her, I was terrified she would leave. Finally I chose a place called The Westlake Healthcare Center in Westlake, Ohio. This one looked exactly like a nursing home. It smelled like one too: that faint mingling of urine, iodine, cafeteria food, and coffee. But the staff was warm and friendly and security was tight. My mother could have her own room on their well-monitored second floor.

After we get our mother settled in to her new home, I run around to stores, collecting things for her room—a lamp, socks, toiletries, nightgowns. For the last seventeen years I have been shopping for my mother, searching for warm practical things she can wear on the streets, looking for art supplies on sale, museum calendars, little postcards she might like, the occasional box of chocolates. It hits me in the store that this is the very last time I will shop for her. I run out of Sears crying.

I head over to the bank, where I discover my mother has saved $50,000 from when she sold the house. She spent only $10,000 in seventeen years and most of it on storage space at U-Haul. "I was saving it for you girls," she tells me when I return from my errands. I contact a lawyer so I can get power of attorney to manage her financial and medical affairs. The lawyer drives over to the hospital to explain to our mother what the documents mean. Our mother is willing to sign the medical forms but refuses to sign the POA. She glares suspiciously at the three of us, the lawyer, my sister, and me. Here we go again, I think.

"Let me try," says my sister. "I think I can get her to sign."

"I doubt she'll agree," I say, "But she better. Otherwise, how will we pay for this place?" I leave the room. When I come back a few minutes later, my mother is signing the forms. "How in the world did you get her to sign?"

"I don't know," says Natalia, "I talked to her. She just did."

The next day, on Christmas Eve, Natalia will be going back to Canton to spend the weekend with her husband and stepsons. Doug will arrive from Massachusetts the same day she leaves. I am looking forward to seeing him but am very stressed about all the things I still have to take care of before Christmas, when everything shuts down: call up hospice to make sure someone can stop by over the holidays, deal with people from Medicaid and Medicare, and so on.

"Why don't you just stop a second and sit down?" says Natalia.

"I've got a lot of things to do now that I have POA."

What I don't say is, *You would never want this job. You would never take it on.* And then I think about what Doug always says: "I understand your sister. I'm a lot like her. I would have left long ago. She does what she does in order to survive. It's in her nature. It's in mine too."

I start fussing with my mother's tray, tidying up, ticking off things I need to do.

"Stop for five minutes," says Natalia. "I know you have all these 'important' things to do. But can you just stop for a second and sit with her? Why don't we give her one of her presents now?"

Natalia looks completely spent. What has she carried these seventeen years? What have I? If I am to be really truthful, there is something in my nature as well, something that, like Natalia, and even our mother, made me choose my freedom and creative life above all else. Maybe I can only help her now because I know there will be an end—a week, two weeks, at most a month. Perhaps there is something restless in our shared DNA. Would our mother really have been happier medicated in some kind of supervised home or hospital ward? We would have been happier, but would she? Would she have studied ancient geology? Memorized all of the state flowers and birds, the bones in the body? Would she have studied the movements of the stars?

"You're right, Nat," I say. "I need to stop."

Our mother is too weak to unwrap her gifts, so we take the soft flannel nightgowns out of the box for her. "For me?" she says, surprised. "They're beautiful. You girls shouldn't have."

For everything we give her, she is overwhelmed with gratitude. We open Chanukah and Christmas cards women have sent from the shelter and show them to her, then hang them on the wall by her bed. Cathy had brought over a large red begonia in bloom and some homemade cookies. She had left a small lamp, a framed embroidery she had made, and a plush burgundy-flowered rug. Our mother's room is beginning to look homey. The light is soft and her radio is playing Debussy quietly in the background.

I go into the dining hall to heat up a snack in the microwave, and sit down for a minute to take a break. I can't remember ever feeling this tired. An elderly man hobbles up to me, confused.

"I got a bed," he says.

"You do?"

"I got a bed—but no home."

"I'm so sorry."

"I got a bed but no home. Do you know where I should go now? Do you know what they did to my home?"

"I don't know," I say. "Should I get someone to help you?"

"I got a bed," he says again, and sits down, lost.

When I return to the room, my mother says, "Have you been to the house yet?"

"Yes," I lie once again. "Everything is fine. Everything is just like it was."

"Good," she says. "I hope we can go soon. I want to get the hell out of here."

Later in the day, some women from the shelter on Payne Avenue come to visit. Renée, an African-American in her forties, who used to live at the shelter but volunteers there now, is the driver. All of the women who come are black, except for Crystal, who sits in the corner of our mother's sweltering room, wearing three coats, two hats, and a scarf. She sits without saying much, sipping from her can of Coke.

"I haven't known your mama long," says Cheryl, a tall thin woman the same age as me. "But she made a big impression. I couldn't be with my own mother when she was dying."

Lucille, a vivacious woman in her thirties, tells Natalia and me how she came up to Cleveland from South Carolina to flee her husband.

"I was living in my car," she says. "I'd been picking cotton since I was five years old. I'm not afraid to work. I got kids back down there but I had to get out. I met Miss Norma my first night at the shelter. It was Thanksgiving and I wanted to be with my kids. Miss Norma gave me such a warm greeting when I walked in. I saw her and saw how old she was and knew if she could make it, so could I."

The women congregate around her bed. They massage her feet and hands, offer her spoonfuls of applesauce, and treat her like a baby. They love her and see in her a kind of wisdom I never imagined she had. In my mother's diaries she sometimes wrote: *I miss my women terribly.* Which women? The ones from the shelter on Payne, or my sister and me? Or did she long for her own mother whom she didn't believe was dead, or her lost friends from childhood, the ones listed in the address book she searched for these long years?

The women gather around her bed while birds gather on the golf course and parking lot in front. According to Cathy, a few years ago much of Westlake was a forest surrounded by wetlands. Now the nursing home sits in the middle of a soulless beige subdivision, surrounded by a shopping center, golf course, hospital, nursing home, funeral parlor, mall, and cemetery. The only green is the empty golf course out in front.

The women chat about shelter gossip, rub lotion on my mother's face while she sleeps, fluff her pillows, brush her hair. I indulge in a Hollywood fantasy: the old house is somehow empty or we pay the family who lives there to leave for a few weeks. We gather some of our mother's furniture from U-Haul and set it up inside. We make it look just like it did in 1990, but nice and neat. I hang up my picture of the big white horse I found in my mother's storage room. My sister and I move our mother back into her old house; the women from the shelter come too. We take turns cooking. In the evenings, we watch animal shows on TV or listen to the radio. She gets to die in her old bed, what used to be our grandfather's, the first room on the left at the top of the stairs.

"Myra?" My mother has just woken up from a nap. "When can I go home?"

"Soon," I say. "You have to get better first. Now, will you look who's here? Look who came to visit you all the way from the east side."

After the women leave, I tell my mother I am going out to take a little walk.

"Don't go out there!" she says. "It will be dark soon. It's dangerous!"

"It's safe. Don't worry."

"You could get kidnapped. Don't go!"

"I'll just take a quick walk with one of the aides," I lie. "I won't go alone."

"Come back right away. Don't wander far. You could get injured, or worse."

It's warm for December and has been raining. I walk along the muddy path surrounding the golf course. Along the path I notice animals tracks—not just from dogs but wilder things—rabbits, raccoons, and foxes. I wonder if there are bears too, and coyotes that refuse to leave. Where do they hide? Everything is flat here; there is no place to go. Before I go back in the building I spy a hawk perched high on a telephone pole, and geese taking flight.

When I return, my mother is staring at the giant white teddy bear we brought back from U-Haul. It's propped up on a chair in the corner where Crystal had been. Natalia is getting her hair cut, trying to carve out an hour or two of normalcy, so my mother and I are alone.

"What's that?" she asks.

"You had it at U-Haul. Rachel thought it would be nice to have him here."

"What should we name him?"

"What do you think?"

She pauses. "Brian."

"Brian?"

"He's a friend of Santa's. The man who brings the gifts."

"Okay. Brian it shall be."

"Is Rachel's husband Santa Claus?"

"No, he's an English professor."

"He's not Santa? She showed me a picture of a man with a beard."

"Nope. He's not Santa."

"Oh. Well, maybe I should give Brian to Rachel's husband as a holiday gift."

"That's very generous of you. But let's just keep him here for now. He sort of cheers up the place."

∽

I've set up an appointment to meet a local funeral director that evening. I want to get all of her arrangements out of the way so I don't have to think about it on the day she dies. Natalia stays with our mother while I go to meet him in the dining hall. The elderly director seems uncomfortable. Is it because he knows my mother is homeless?

"Thanks for coming down so close to Christmas," I say. "I really appreciate it."

"It's no problem," he says. "It's my job."

"My sister and I decided that we are going to cremate her. I can't really ask her because she's incapacitated but I think it's what she would want."

The man goes over the prices for cremation, shows me a fancy brochure of urns for her what he calls her "cremains." *Cremains?*

The pictures he shows me resemble the canopic jars from ancient Egypt that held the sacred organs of the deceased. They remind me of the urn that contained the fallen Palace of Kalachakra.

"That's okay," I say. "I'm an artist. I'll make something for her myself."

"What about the funeral?" he asks. "We have a lovely chapel we can offer you for a service. We can even get a minister if you like—Catholic, Baptist, Methodist. Even Pentecostal. And there's quite a lovely little organ, if you want to sing some hymns."

He tells me the price.

"My mom was, I mean is, Jewish."

"Oh," he says, fumbling with another brochure. "Well, I'm sure we can find a . . . Jewish minister, if you like."

"A rabbi."

"Yes, I mean rabbi. My apologies."

"She's not religious, though," I say. "So that part doesn't matter."

Am I wrong to cremate her? Would it make her think of Auschwitz if she knew? The graveyards in Israel come back to me, how Barbara and I searched for tombs, placed small rocks on the headstones of strangers. Is that what my mother would prefer, to be placed in a box in the earth, or to leave this place by fire?

"The cost is quite reasonable," says the man. "For a service, that is. It can be an hour long for two hundred fifty dollars. Longer ones are extra."

I am about to say yes to the chapel, for lack of a better idea, but then I remember all the women at the shelter, how far away they are from Westlake.

"I'm going to have a memorial for her at a women's shelter in Cleveland," I say. "It was my mother's last home. That way visitors can stay as long as they like."

The funeral director clears his throat. "Her body is cremated in twenty-four hours. Two to three days later, the obit will appear. If you give me a short bio I can have our secretary write one up for your mother."

I think about what my mother's bio might read like: *Norma Kurap Herr: Born into poverty during the Depression, child prodigy slated for Carnegie Hall, lost her mind when America dropped the bomb, wife of aspiring alcoholic writer, homeless schizophrenic for seventeen years, spent last years in a shelter for homeless women.*

"Thank you, but I'll write it myself."

"What about her cremains? Do you want me to send them, since you're from out of town?"

I imagine my mother's ashes getting lost in the mail, ending up on someone else's doorstep or, worse, lying in a puddle below a bridge in Indiana. I imagine them circumnavigating the globe.

"Thanks, but my sister and I will pick them up before we leave town."

When I return to the room I tell Natalia to take a break for a while. She has been by our mother's side all day. "Go call Kerry or take a nap in the lounge. Stay as long as you like," I say. "I'll be here when you get back."

Since my mother arrived at Westlake, she seems to be doing a bit better. I wonder if she'll hang on longer than we previously thought. She doesn't seem to be in that much pain, although she is extremely weak and tired all the time. When she needs to urinate, she has to be assisted the few feet to the bathroom very slowly. One of the aides usually helps her, and sometimes my sister and I help too.

After Natalia leaves the room, my mother wakes up. "I have to make a pee-pee," she says. I ring for the aide. She runs in to tell me she just got an emergency call and can't come till later. "I'll be fine," I say. "I've done this before. Go."

After my mother's finished, I lift up her nightgown and wipe her like a baby as she stands, straddling the toilet, clinging to my arms.

"What are these?" she asks, looking down at the stomas and the ileostomy bag that drains out her bile.

"Nothing for you to worry about. They're just from the operation," I say. "They're not going to be there forever. Now, let's go real slow. Just hold on to me."

I walk backward toward the bed, my mother facing me, holding on to my shoulders. She stops after a few small steps, overcome with fatigue. I wrap my arms around her and feel her frail body lean in to mine.

"So tired," she says.

"Let's wait a second," I say. "We'll go when you're ready. There's no rush."

When was the last time we did this, held each other close, that embrace you give your mother when you walk through the door, that parting hug on your way out? Was it seventeen years? Was it more?

We stay in the middle of the room for a long time, holding on to each other. I wrap my arms around her tighter. My mother closes her eyes and relaxes into my embrace. A nurse comes in to take my mother's stats.

"Is she okay?"

"Yeah," I say. "She's fine. It's just that I realized—I haven't hugged my mother in seventeen years."

"I'll come back later," says the nurse.

"Thanks," I say. "That would be great, if you don't mind. I think I want to stay here for a while."

My mother and I stand like that for as long as she can bear to stand, and then we make our way slowly back to the bed.

On Sunday, Christmas Eve day, Natalia leaves and Doug arrives. "I'm so glad you came," I say, as we hug at the airport. "I couldn't imagine her dying without having met you."

We drive directly to the Westlake Healthcare Center and go up to her room. My mother is wide awake. "Mommy," I say. "This is my fiancé, Doug."

She eyes Doug with suspicion, but forces a smile and nods. She waves to him from the bed like a queen, then motions me to come closer so she can whisper in my ear.

"Your sister is kind of dumb, isn't she?"

"Why do you say that?"

"She has yet to produce a man."

"But Mom, she's married. Her husband is in New York."

"Well, I haven't seen him, have you? How do we know he really exists?"

Doug and I spend a quiet day by her side. My mother eats two bites of macaroni and cheese at dinner, then falls into a deep sleep. When she wakes up, she announces, "I want to watch the news. I want to see what's going on in the world."

I flip through the news stations and it is all bad—murders, kidnappings, rapes, hurricanes, the Iraq War, and beached whales. I try the other stations and there's nothing but reality shows, Spanish soap operas, or reruns of *Law & Order*—until I find the Animal Planet channel.

"Look," I say. "It's a tiger and a baby deer."

The show is about animal "friends," unlikely companionships between predators and prey. There's a young female tiger curling up to sleep with a baby deer that has lost its mother. My mother is transfixed. She stares at the tiger and the little deer on the screen. What is she thinking? I'm reminded of her tiger picture in the clock, her Chinese astrology charts. *I am a Tiger,* she once wrote. *Your sister is a Rooster, and you are a Pig. I think we are compatible but I can't be sure. Tiger people are sensitive, given to deep thinking, capable of great sympathy. They cannot make up their minds and often arrive at sound decisions too late. Tiger people are suspicious of others, but can be powerful and brave. They say Pigs, however, are the bravest of all.*

A commercial for Oscar Meyer wieners comes on TV; a happy family at a cookout stands around the grill smiling.

"I would like ... I would like ..." my mother starts to say.

"What?" I ask. "What can I get you?"

"What can we get you, Norma?" asks Doug.

My mother points at her lap and speaks very slowly. "I would like ... a hot dog ... right here ... for me ... now. Just a plain one, please."

"Let me go look," I say to Doug. "You stay here with her. I know the staff."

It's after dinner on Christmas Eve and the kitchen is closed. I run around the nursing home, trying to see if anyone has any hot dogs. Nothing. I drive around the neighborhood. All the places nearby are closed. I return an hour later empty-handed.

"I'm so sorry," I say. "Nothing is open. It's Christmas Eve."

"That's okay. I'm fine without."

"Listen, is there anything you want me to do, you know, anything you want me to take care of for you, besides the house?" I can't bring myself to say, Do you have any last requests?

"Yes," she says. "One thing I'd like you to do."

"What's that?"

"There's a man named Willard Gaylin, a psychiatrist in New York. I used to know him. I want you to track him down."

"Who is he?"

"We knew each other years ago. He's very famous now. He wrote a lot of books that helped me."

"What do you want me to say?"

"Tell him what happened. He'll know what to do."

"Okay," I say. "I'll tell him you're here. How do you know him?"

"It's not important. Let's just say that after the war, it was not necessarily a champagne bottle-breaking period for everyone."

I have no idea what she means, but images flood my brain. That old picture of my mother holding the bottle to my neck comes back to me, and another, a woman breaking a bottle against the bow of a ship, christening a voyage. I imagine my mother clinking glasses with this mysterious man, Willard Gaylin, at the end of the war.

"I'll remember that," I say. "I'll do my best."

———————

I know I need a couple days of rest or I'll have what I call a brain freeze. I've been running on adrenaline and need to stop. I fly back to Massachusetts with Doug on Tuesday, the day after Christmas. I sleep for two days straight. I can barely talk, and when I do, I stutter and can't find the words for things. When I return to Cleveland, I move into an Extended Stay Hotel close to the nursing home so Natalia and I can be there at a minute's notice. My sister returns right before New Year's weekend.

It has been nearly three weeks after our mother's surgery and her weight is dropping. I am struck with a macabre thought, one among many—that my grandfather weighed his age too when he died. He was eighty years old, weighed eighty pounds, and died in 1980 on December 18, the day I arrived in Cleveland. If my mother had figured all this out, no doubt there would have been a conspiracy attached to the facts.

My mother only takes a couple sips of water now and one or two bites of food at mealtime. Mostly, she moves the food around with her gums and then spits it out. She has been concerned all these years with people steal-ing her teeth and now refuses to put them in. "I don't need them," she tells me. "I'm not hungry anymore." The hospice staff tells us it's normal, that we shouldn't force her to eat. It's the body's natural state of letting go.

"This is how we leave our bodies," I say to Natalia, remembering the year before when Doug and I kept vigil all night while his mother, Shirley, passed away. "Look at her skin, how mottled it's getting. Feel how cold she is. She won't be with us long."

As terrible as her dying is, it fascinates me. I want to study the process, draw it, and understand its mystery. But still, I am unbearably sad. So is Natalia. She sits by our mother, stroking her hand and crying. I start crying too.

Our mother is bewildered. "Why are you crying?" she asks. I don't think she knows that she is dying, or does she, somewhere deep inside?

"I'm so sorry," I say.

"Why are you sorry?"

Where do I begin? How could she understand? "I'm sorry you're sick," I say.

"I'll be fine. I just need to go home."

When I was in my twenties, I made an etching called "Into the Land of Birds and Fire." The print had six sections with an image in each one. Beneath each image was a line of text. The last image was a picture of a hand reaching into a woman's chest to pull out her heart, or perhaps the hand was putting the heart back in. My mother wrote to me about the print once when she was homeless: *I am continuously inspired by your print, "Into the Land of Birds and Fire," especially "Geographies of the Seed."* She always liked when I combined pictures with words in my art.

I have so many things I want to say. I sit on my mother's bed. There's just no time. "I never told you this, but I published some books for children. Now I'm writing a book for adults."

"I believe it," she says.

"The book will have drawings too. I can't seem to do anything without pictures."

"You can do anything you put your mind to. I always had faith in you."

Later, I peek at one of her journals when Natalia and I are back at the Extended Stay Hotel. I find this: *What I respect most in this world are those who can combine words and pictures together in the same book or piece of art. If I believed in reincarnation, I'd come back and try my hand at that kind of thing.*

The nursing home is quiet on New Year's Eve day. Natalia and I get there early so we have all day with our mother. She sleeps most of the time now. We sit on either side of the bed, watching her. I kiss her forehead softly. She slowly opens her eyes.

"Happy New Year, Mommy," Natalia and I say in unison.

"Do you want anything special today?" I ask.

"I want something . . . but I don't remember what it is."

"What does it look like?" I ask.

"I can't remember the name. It's for a holiday."

"Something to celebrate?" asks Natalia.

"Yes. It's pink."

"What do you mean?" I ask.

"You know. Something pink. For ladies; ladies drink it." She looks at Natalia. "You made me one once. You know what it is."

"An umbrella drink!"

"I don't need an umbrella. I'm inside."

"That's what they're called," I say. "We'll find one for you."

"Don't bother if it's too much trouble. Just a little sip of something pink."

Later, Natalia and I run out to look for a liquor store. There is only one open in the vicinity. We buy a nip bottle of grenadine.

"It's all we could find," I say. "But have a sip. Let's make a toast."

"I don't feel like it now," she says.

"Happy New Year," I say.

My sister holds up our mother's head while I help her take a sip. "Sorry, no umbrella," I say. "But at least it's pink." The grenadine dribbles out of her mouth onto her nightgown.

"I'm not in the mood for happy new year," she says. "Maybe later."

"Okay," I say. "Maybe later."

Four days after New Year's, on Friday, a hard lump appears on our mother's neck.

"It's her lymph node," says Natalia, distraught. "Is it a tumor?"

Our mother rubs the lump and moans. "It hurts," she cries. "Help me. Please."

She is very distressed. We are very distressed. It's the first time she's been in real pain, as far as we know. We talk to the staff, increase her pain meds. I call the shelter and tell them only two people can come today, no more. It has to be quiet in the room.

Renée and Cheryl come and the four of us whisper around the bed. I run out at noon to get some lunch for everyone; on my way back I stop to look at the rain-sodden golf course in front. The hawk has returned, and the geese. I have never seen so many geese in my life. The course looks like it must have before the developers came, a marsh of birds enveloped by trees. Then I notice something to the left of the geese. It's a great blue heron, standing on one leg, like the one I saw in the bayou with my sister. I take a couple steps toward it. The bird ruffles its feathers, and lifts up into the air.

As the day goes by, the lump grows larger. Her pain is getting worse and nothing seems to be working. Natalia and I kiss her face, her hands; we are helpless.

"No more kisses!" she says, pushing us away. "No more!"

We call the emergency hospice nurse to come to the nursing home and check her. We are afraid she's going to die that night.

Evening falls and my sister and I wait for the on-call hospice nurse. Outside, a terrible storm is raging. There's been an accident on the highway but even without the accident or the rain, the nurse is coming from over sixty miles away. Natalia and I don't know what to do. My sister turns to me, her face streaked with tears, and says, "I'd give anything, anything at all, just to have one more day with her."

"I know," I say. "I don't know what to do."

We haven't had our mother for seventeen years and now that we finally have her, she could be gone by morning.

My sister has been in the room all day. Her eyes are bloodshot and she's been wearing the same outfit for three days in a row. "You need a break," I say. "Go call Kerry or get something to drink in the dining room. Just get out for a while."

"You're right," she says. "I'll be back soon."

After my sister leaves, my mother looks up at the ceiling in terror.

"What is it?" I ask. I look up to where she is staring but there's nothing there. My mother doesn't say a word. She raises her arms as if she's reaching up to touch something or someone. Books on death and dying tell us that at the end of one's life, often a person sees his or her loved ones floating above them, or they see light or some other vision. But my mother has always had visions, has always seen people who weren't there. What is it she is staring at now? I don't want my sister to find her like this.

My mother is terrified. I grab her hands and pull her arms down to her lap.

"Don't worry," I say. "It's okay."

She makes a sweeping gesture with her hand across her lap. "No more of this," she says. "No more."

"No more of what?"

"No more of *this*."

My mother is mumbling now, looking off to the side at someone who isn't there.

"What are you saying, Mommy?"

"He says . . . he says . . ."

"What does he say?"

"He says . . . he says . . . he says—he has to go now."

"He does? What else does he say? Where is he going? Tell me what he says. Mommy? *Mommy?*"

But she doesn't answer. She never speaks again.

It is a long night of waiting, of being present, nothing but sitting and counting her breath. There is no white horse in an indigo sky coming to save her in my mind, or Kircher and his Subterranean World, or fossils trapped in rocks. There are no crows taking flight, fairy tales, wild horses, wolves, or red and yellow firebirds. There is no palace of memories, no memories at all, just one moment, then the next, and then the next one. To sit beside the dying is like meditation—sometimes there is only the thought of ending pain, of how slow the breath is and how labored. You begin to count the breath, going in and out, but this time it's not your own, and you are sitting on the edge of your seat, waiting for the last breath to come.

Later, much later, the hospice nurse finally arrives, and gives our mother a shot. She tells the staff to start administering liquid morphine orally, as much as our mother needs. She fades into sleep. The nurse, my sister, and I go into the hall to talk.

"I hate to be blunt, but is she going to die tonight?" I ask.

"I don't think so. It's always hard to tell, but really, I think you should get a good night's rest. I don't think it will be tonight."

"Are you sure?"

"I think so."

"Thanks," I say, relieved.

"But it could be tomorrow," she adds.

Before we leave, I call her social worker Tim and leave a message; I call Cathy too. Cathy has been with me from the beginning of this and I know she'll want to come one more time. I have a bad feeling tomorrow night will be our mother's last. My sister leaves messages for Renée and Cheryl. I call Doug to tell him what is going on. "I love you," he says. "Call me in the middle of the night if you need to. I'll be here."

The following day, everyone comes.

ↄ৵

The red and white amaryllis I bought for her three days before has bloomed three times, one for each day. We keep it on a stand across the room so she can see it. Thanks to Cathy and all her gifts, the room is warm and inviting. I put on a CD of tranquil lute music. One by one people come to stay a short while, then go. My mother appears unconscious the whole time, but who can be sure? We talk to her anyway. Cathy, as always, is still there, the last to leave. I say to her and Natalia, "I know she probably can't hear me but I'm going to play her some Bach."

I go down the hall to the dining room and sit at the blond upright. I play a piece by Purcell and then play one of my mother's and my favorites, "Jesu, Joy of Man's Desiring" by Bach, one of Myra Hess's signature pieces that she played at her free concerts during the Blitz. I first learned to play it at Mr. Benjamin's when I was twelve.

My fingers are clumsy because I'm so tired, and I stumble over some of the notes. Two of the residents come in the room when they hear the music—a woman named Louise, who forgets who I am after every conversation, rolls in on her wheelchair, and the sad man I met the other day who lost his house slowly makes his way over and sits in a chair behind me. I play more Purcell for them and an air by Handel, then go back, leaving them sitting, staring at the keys.

When I return, Natalia says, "When you left, I told her you were going to play some Bach. She smiled."

"It's true," says Cathy. "She really smiled."

After Cathy leaves, my sister says, "I want to spend the night."

I run back to the hotel to get us toiletries and a change of clothes. When I return, we each take one of our mother's hands. We don't know if she can hear us but we talk anyway. They say that the hearing is the last to go. "You are going home," I say. "Everything is there. Don't be afraid."

"We're here," says Natalia. "Don't worry, you're not alone."

We tell her together that when she goes back home, everything in the garden will be there—the dogwood, the magnolia tree, the peonies, and the pink roses. There will be snapdragons and azaleas. Everything will be in bloom. "We'll take care of everything," I say. "Don't worry about the house. We'll take care of it all. We are safe now and we have enough to eat. You can go now. It'll be okay."

Natalia and I kiss our mother good night. I offer my sister the love seat, but she curls up on a blanket on the floor. I lie down and pull a blanket over my head to block out the safety light. I leave a CD on, Pablo Casals playing the Bach Cello Suites.

"Good night, Mommy," I say. "Good night, Rachel," using Natalia's old name.

"Good night," my sister says, and turns on her side. I listen carefully. My mother takes a few labored breaths for a minute or so, barely audible beneath the Bach.

And then she is gone.

That night—after we call the nurses in and bathe her body, after we rub her face and hands and feet with lotion, after we sit beside her and stare at her face for an eternity, then pick out something soft and new and beautiful for her to wear, and then after we call the funeral home, and they carry her away in the middle of the night on a stretcher as if she were still alive, and they take her to the place where she will be purified by fire, and we drive back to our beds at the hotel—I fall asleep and dream about the birds. They keep hurling themselves against a window and falling ten stories down and still they refuse to die. I wake up the next morning with the words forming in my mouth: "Please, can't someone save them?"

I turn on the radio. It's the last movement of Fauré's Requiem: In paradisum.

"Listen," I say to Natalia.

I sit and try to imagine my mother in heaven. But I can't imagine a heaven or a hell, only how the geese gathered outside my mother's room for days, and then the hawk and then the blue heron.

When I return to Massachusetts two days later, I walk in the woods with my little black dog Sadie like I always do. I think about what people say about the dead, how they're always with us. But what exactly do they mean? Do they mean that they turn into ghosts, that their souls becomes part of our body? Or do they mean the rustle of a blue jay's blue-gray wings in winter? How the sound makes you turn so quick and hold your breath? I toss a stick for Sadie, search for redcoats blooming on stumps of rotted pine. Here in the Northeast it is truly winter. The light is different than in Ohio, more lucid and golden. Or is it grief that illuminates each and every thing, the birch I stand beneath, the house through the trees? High above, a pileated woodpecker taps on the bark. *Is that you?* I ask out loud. *Are you there?*

During the day, I retreat to my studio and search through her journals for answers. I am left with so many questions. And my memory of our time together keeps slipping further away. I search my own journals too. In one from a year before, I wrote: "The truth is, I'm not really sure I want to find her, because if I find her, it means I will have to dig up the past. And then, I will have to do something about it. See her, save her, something that requires more than a stamp and postal box in a town where I never lived."

I read some of her old letters again; skim through more diaries. What was this tie that bound us so tightly, across oceans and time? Why couldn't I just let her go, stop writing her, give up? Then I come upon a page from one of my own sketchbooks, eight months before her death. At the top is a small sketch of a trilobite next to a vocabulary list of geological terms, and below that, words she could have easily written herself:

Think about the Cambrian Explosion—a half billion years ago suddenly animals seemed to come out of nowhere … Have you ever noticed how arthropods, such as trilobites, look like aliens? Note to self: Look up the Valley of the Whales in the Sahara. Make a list of specimens. Imagine this: Darwin's Tree of Life has branched out for more than four billion years! As Darwin once said, "… whilst this planet has gone cycling on according to the fixed law of gravity, from so simple a beginning endless forms most beautiful and most wonderful have been, and are being, evolved."

I put the sketchbook down and look around my studio. It's so peaceful, full of plants and books. I'm certain my mother would have liked it here. Above my desk is a bulletin board covered with my Post-its, memory lists, and postcards, several from my mother's many trips to museums. I take down a card that a former student sent me after my car accident. On it she wrote, *No matter what befalls you, may you always be curious.* And then the grandfather of geology, Nicolaus Steno's words come back to me once again: "Beautiful is what we see. More beautiful is what we understand. Most beautiful is what we do not comprehend."

Someplace

Yesterday I was thinking of what I would do if I had an advisor and the money. I would be content to stay for a long period in a first floor level cabana type house in a temperate warm climate where I could step out onto a sandy, clean beach in the a.m., up early of course. The restaurant service would be like Shoney's, where one eats a lighter variety of foods, private, and also a section for those who require service. After breakfast, a half-hour on the clean, sandy beach with sand covering my legs. Very therapeutic. The advisor is needed because off hand, I don't know of any clean beaches anymore. There would be FM radio, I'd rest, continue studying, writing and maybe walk to a well-stocked library with journals, newspapers to bring news of the outer world. Beautiful trees in the distance. Then another half hour sand covering my legs late afternoon. The hot sun is to be avoided. I could pass some pleasant months alone this way. Of course, everything in films and reading is all fiction, but there must be someplace to go.

17

Memory is the enemy of wonder, which abides nowhere else but in the present.
This is why, unless you are a child, wonder depends on forgetting—
on a process, that is, of subtraction.

Michael Pollan, *The Botany of Desire*

A Cabinet of Wonders

Seven months after my mother's death, I am at the Field Museum of Natural History in Chicago, standing in the shadow of Sue, the largest *T. rex* ever found. It's a hot August day and I've come here to meet Dave Willard, the collection manager for the Division of Birds. I am hoping that a tour through the Bird Lab and other behind-the-scenes areas at the museum will jog some old memories from when I worked here. Since my mother died last January, I have been on a quest to visit places from my past.

I am an hour and a half early, so I buy a ticket for the new dinosaur show. I queue up with a horde of schoolkids and their teachers. The museum has gotten very loud since I worked here: exhibits with videos and interactive games, nonstop sound coming out of every corner. For someone with a brain like mine, all that stimulation makes it impossible to think. I stuff earplugs into my ears and wish I owned a soundproof helmet. The earplugs only slightly muffle the noise, though, so I forgo the exhibit and escape to the forgotten halls of dioramas. No rambunctious children, loud movies, computers, or upbeat lectures about paleontology coming out of speakers, just endless cases of dead animals in situ—hunting, sleeping, fighting, and tending to their young.

Sometimes, after work, I used to sit and draw the stuffed animals. The halls were almost always empty. You could live here and no one would know. You could set up house, some furniture, a couple of potted plants. It was always dark and peaceful in the halls of the dead, a good place to eat a sandwich and take a nap. Did my mother draw here when she was homeless in Chicago? Did she lay down her head to sleep? Even here, surrounded by dead antelope and bison, I feel her presence. She sits beside me on this time-worn bench, her cold hand in mine.

When I return to the *T. rex*, a tall, lean man in his fifties approaches, smiling. "Thanks for meeting me," I say.

"My pleasure."

Dave leads me up three flights of stairs to the Bird Lab. He knows from our previous conversation that I had a brain injury and I am trying to piece together memories from Chicago. I had done the same when I was in Cleveland for my high school reunion, three months before my mother died. I drove down West 148th Street with Doug, stopped to see the old apartment buildings on Triskett, visited my old schools. I would have gone to the art museum but it had been closed for renovation.

Dave shows me the main lab where graduate students are preserving bird specimens. "I remember a larger room, with a big vat in the middle. Someone was cooking up something nasty. Could it have been an emu?"

"Not an emu," says Dave. "I've been here thirty years and I don't think we've ever cooked an emu. It could have been an ostrich, though." Dave adds, "That might have been me at the vat."

I know some of my friends would think my visit here macabre, so soon after my mother's death. But I find the idea of being here oddly comforting; the cycle of life so viscerally on display makes her death feel part of some greater and mysterious whole. Maybe it's the same thing that made me draw dead birds when I was a child.

"What did it smell like here nineteen, twenty years ago?" I ask.

"Dead things and mothballs," says Dave.

"I remember formaldehyde and coffee. And the smell of donuts."

Dave smiles when I mention the donuts.

When our olfactory sensors are stimulated, they transmit a signal that cuts a path right to the emotional center of our brain. When I smell mothballs, I'm in my grandparents' closet on West 148th Street, hiding from my grandfather and the sting of his belt. When someone lights up to smoke, my mother's face appears.

The dull fluorescent light and faint sound coming from a room next door reminds me of something but I'm not sure what. I walk to the door, tilt my head, and listen. I can hear the quiet steady sound of carrion beetles having lunch.

"We can go in if you like," says Dave.

The bug room is where the dermestid beetle, bred in fish aquariums, feeds on carcasses in order to pick the bones clean, a most efficient way of preparing skeletons and skulls. I remember the first time I saw them doing their job. I had just started working at the Field. From a distance, the carcass looked like it was vibrating, with all those bugs masticating away.

The room smells putrid, even with the ventilator fan. On the worktable against the wall are boxes of dead birds in various states of decay. A scene from my mother's memorial rises up. I see a woman in a white hat and coat, a troubled black woman in her forties. She had been heartbroken that she wasn't able to visit our mother before she died. She said, "When I saw Miss Norma the first night I came, a woman that old in a place like this, I thought—I could die here too." The beetles and dead birds battle for space with the crying woman inside the small foul-smelling room.

"I think I've seen enough," I say.

Outside the bug room, in the lab, I notice jars of specimens floating in alcohol. This could be any lab—the laboratory I used for my office years ago, or a lab from my biology class in junior high when my mother used to circle the school. I feel nauseous. Ever since my mother died, I don't have the stomach I used to for these kinds of things. Before, I loved to draw just about anything from the natural world, dead or alive. But now I get choked up when I see a deer skeleton in the woods. Even a dead squirrel on the road can bring me to tears. "Can we look at some hummingbirds?" I ask.

"Of course," says Dave.

We walk to a hall of white metal cabinets that go straight up to the ceiling. "I remember long wooden cabinets lining dark hallways. Was it ever like that?"

"Not here. The cabinets used to be black but we changed them to white. Black can be depressing." I think of my mother, who always loved sitting in blackness, who kept the shades drawn, her little radio by her side.

Am I thinking of somewhere else? Another museum? Am I remembering *wunderkammeren*, collector's cabinets of wonders I've never seen? Albertus Seba's drawers of snakes and birds from centuries ago; his plethora of coral, fossils, and shells? King Rudolf's palace in Prague? They say it contained rhinoceros horns encrusted with rubies, astronomical compendia and sundials, an amulet made from toads, arsenic, pearls, emeralds, and medicinal herbs. I think of my mother's own cabinet of wonders, the one at U-Haul that she filled with seventeen years of wandering and loss. *It is important to find the right word*, she wrote me once. *For this, you need a thesaurus. Thesaurus, from the Ancient Greek: thesauros, meaning "storehouse" or "treasury" . . . I need someone with me. Please come home.* We did come home, but perhaps not soon enough.

Inside the cabinets Dave opens for me there are only birds, thousands of them. All of these dead birds, and the birds that gathered outside my mother's room, that were so full of life in the rain. It's hard not to see her face even here, in this cavernous room of stuffed birds, drawers of nests, and rare speckled eggs.

Dave opens a wooden drawer filled with hummingbirds from Peru. "Koepcke's Hermit," says Dave. "In life, it was rather dull."

"Dull as in boring?"

"No." He smiles. "Dull as in it only had a few iridescent feathers. Iridescent green. It's bill was dark—the top part was black, the bottom red. See?" He holds the bird up and touches the tip of its beak.

There are tidy rows of hummingbirds inside the drawer, with a little tag affixed to each bird's leg, a miniature morgue. I remember drawing here years ago. Pulling out drawers of waterbirds and bones. Dave leads me to a cabinet farther down the hall and pulls out another drawer of hummingbirds. I notice a small open box with a skeleton inside. "Can I look?" I ask. Dave nods.

I open up the box. There is a row of numbers written on both sternum and skull. I remember coming into the lab one day and seeing a man hunched over a table, labeling the bones of a minute bird, even the slip of a rib bone. Dave assures me that the most skilled ornithologist would have a hard time labeling every single bone in a hummingbird, especially its rib cage; some are just too small. Could I have dreamt it? I remember thinking, as I watched the ornithologist, how like a Jewish scribe he was, meticulously penning the microscopic scrolls concealed inside the mezuzahs that protect the homes of Jews. I bought my mother a mezuzah when I was in Israel but never sent it. How can you protect your house if you are homeless?

The last thing I ask Dave to show me is the trumpeter swan. I recall them squished into drawers, sometimes three or four together, or a pair with their fuzzy cloud-colored babies. Dave pulls out a drawer labeled *Cygnus buccinator* and there they are, just as I remembered them, their legs folded up next to their heads, a lamentation of swans. I remember holding my mother's hand and watching swans sail across the lagoon in front of the Cleveland Museum of Art. The ones in the drawer look like sleeping birds from a fairy tale, like a story from the book my sister and I found at U-Haul, the one our father gave us. I try to recall the tale, "The Swan-Princess and Tsar Saltan." There is a prince who lives in exile on an island with his mother. One day he falls in love with a swan swimming close to shore. But how does the story end?

On my way out, I take a few pictures of a great auk skeleton on a stand. When Dave and I say goodbye, I realize there's no film left in my disposable camera to take his picture too. I've used up all the film on dead things. This too will fade, I think, this memory of Dave's kind face, and these infinite drawers of birds, their small and tidy bones.

Later, I am in Ancient Egypt. Not much has changed since I worked here years ago. I put in earplugs to drown out the families and ambient sound. I know I will pay for this tomorrow. To talk to someone for a while, then take in so much stimulation, overwhelms me. I feel lava dripping down the back of my head and worry that I might get lost on my way back to my friend

Nancy's house where I am staying. I know I should go but I have to keep on looking, trying to remember things. And maybe I'm here to comfort myself too, my old familiar way of seeking order in the collection and classification of things around me.

I pass through a fake mastaba, fashioned after massive structures slaves built above tombs in Saqqara and Giza. The mastaba provided a home for the deceased's *ka*, or soul, to live in. I descend a tight circular stairway that leads to the rest of the re-created tomb below. I vaguely remember taking students here years ago and talking about the Egyptian *Book of the Dead*.

I walk through a dim corridor, past a coffin decorated with hieroglyphs and the green and black eyes of Horus, falcon son of Osiris, lord of the Underworld, whom Isis put back together after his envious brother tore his body apart. I wonder if I ever got to tell my mother the story, but then, she probably knew it anyway. Was there anything she hadn't studied those seventeen years? Horus's eyes are painted on the side of the coffin so he can gaze out on his journey to the Afterlife. I stop to look at canopic jars carved from stone, where ritual priests placed the organs before they embalmed the body. I remember the jar with jackal-headed Dna-mut-ef on top, which was used to hold the stomach. I forget what the other jars stand for, but recall how the ancient Egyptians believed the heart, not the brain, was the sacred seat of reason.

After circling the exhibit, I end up back where I began. Above my head is a scroll, a painted narrative depicting the Opening of the Mouth Ceremony. There are forty-two gods and goddesses standing by to judge the life of a woman whose name I can't recall. She doesn't beg for forgiveness at her trial after death, or confess the things she feels remorse for. Instead she offers an inventory of sins she denies ever committing. Her list is called the "Negative Confession." The woman recites: "I did not do evil, I did not steal, I never caused anyone to weep, I never abandoned my family in times of need." At my mother's memorial, Steven Friedman, the director of MHS at the time, stood up at the end of the service to thank my sister and me for bringing closure to everyone who knew our mother. He said, "I know of children who have abandoned their parents for much less than you two have gone through." The Egyptian woman on trial in the scroll assures the gods: *I*

never abandoned my family in times of need. Can I say that now with a clear con-
science? Could I have done any more?

Before the memorial service, the shelter manager, Suellen, asked if Natalia and I wanted to go upstairs and see our mother's room. We said yes, and
followed her to the second floor. "This is where she slept," said Suellen. The
room was only big enough to squeeze in two single beds. It opened into a
larger room of bunk beds where many women slept. There was no door to
close between the two rooms. Suellen told us that our mother got a little
more privacy because she was elderly and ill. My sister and I stood in the
entrance and peered in. I thought of us in our grandma's twin beds, and the
trees outside the window that I gazed at each morning. I remembered our
grandma's scratchy blankets, like the one covering our mother's bed at the
shelter, the comforting *plunk-plunk* of rain on the roof drowning out our
mother's nighttime rants. Her shelter room looked like a room in a barracks,
and yet it was her safe house, her refuge, her home. In the end, my mother
had one hundred daughters. They watched over her like my sister and I ultimately couldn't do. We would have had to give up our lives for her, and our
art, the two things she taught us to hold most sacred and dear.

When we walked back downstairs, the community room was already
full of people—women from the shelter; the director and staff from MHS,
social workers, Cathy and her family, Agostino and other old friends, Doug,
his daughter Sianna, my sister's husband, Kerry.

Many women from the shelter spoke, but the most poignant of all was
a woman in her forties whose name I have since forgotten. She had lost her
own mother to cancer, and had a sister who suffered from schizophrenia. "If
you want to get attention for something, whisper," she said. "Miss Norma
had a life of whispering. She taught me to dismiss the noise. Pay attention to
what really matters. The life that Miss Norma had is still going on in all of
you. And I want you to know one more thing—I have walked in your shoes
in sorrow," she said. "But I know that God gives us no more than we can bear."

I'm too tired to walk along the lake back to Nancy's, so I hop the 146 going
north on Michigan. The bus hums with chattering tourists; outside the

open windows the clamoring of Chicago construction and traffic assaults my brain. "Dismiss the noise," I say to myself. I close my eyes and lean back to rest. I see my mother in a room of women talking loudly. She hears every conversation in her head, the radio next door, shouting from the kitchen, cars and dogs outside on the street. My mother says something barely audible above the noise . . . *he says . . . he says . . . he says* . . . the only time in her life that she ever told me what her voices said to her was at her death. My mother, and her sad beautiful life of whispering.

The next morning I take myself out to breakfast. I notice a homeless man outside the restaurant, leaning against the door. He's half asleep or drunk. Should I offer him the rest of my eggs? But I'm too embarrassed. He might be insulted that I'm not offering him a meal of his own. Would my mother have taken the plate from my hands?

I cross the street to sit in the sun in front of the Art Institute. A red van with Jesus stickers all over it stops at the red light in front of the museum; the driver shouts into a loudspeaker, his angry voice spilling out into the street: "Have you received Him? The Man on the cross? The Man who died for your sins?" On the sidewalk nearby, I spot a homeless woman sitting on a milk crate, a cardboard sign saying that she is looking for work and a place to stay. I go up and ask if she needs anything to eat; she tells me she would die for a piece of chocolate cake. I run back to the place where I had breakfast, get her some cake, then return. "My mother was homeless too," I say. "For seventeen years." I suddenly want to tell everyone that she was homeless— friends, acquaintances, strangers. I want them to understand about the thin line, the one between their world and ours. I want to tell them that here too, outside this museum of beautiful things, there are also wonders—this woman on her crate, the brain-injured vet on the corner, the homeless man and his little girl sitting at the entrance to the El. I want to tell them what a woman said at my mother's memorial: "When you die, there are always two dates, the one you were born on and the date you left this earth. The important dates are the ones in between. Whatever you do in this life," she said, "you'll be remembered for something."

———————

Later, on the plane, my head is splitting and my chest feels tight from grief. I
try to summon the Russian fairy tale about the prince in exile and his beautiful swan-princess but all I can see is a drawer of dead trumpeter swans,
smashed into a dark space too small for them to fit. I close my eyes to get
the dead birds out of my head. I think of cerulean-blue waves, a swirling
red skirt and a silver-white moon. A man waiting onshore, the flutter of his
lover's wings approaching. Did my mother read the story to me before she
became too sick? Was my sister the only one who told me stories in the dark
basement, the sun glinting in from the small window above? If only I could
remember the swan, how its feathers turned to flesh, if I could remember
how the swan broke the spell. But then, a swan cannot bring my mother
back, nor can the mummified heart of a cat, a small box of feathers and bones.

When I get home, there is a letter waiting from Dr. Budd, the man who
lived two doors down from our grandparents, whose wife I drew pictures for
when I was a child. Even though he could afford to live in an upscale neighborhood, he never left our street. He always made house calls and treated
our family for free. I feel a pang of regret for never thanking him enough, for
not keeping in touch with Ruth and Army Armstrong and all the others who
helped my sister and me navigate through those troubled years. At U-Haul,
I had found copies of letters my mother wrote to Dr. Budd. I thought it was
only right that he know how her story ended, but I hadn't expected him to
be alive. He wrote:

> Dear Mira,
> This is a brief response to your letter. I am now in the terminal stages of
> life, age 99 years. Same address on W. 148th St. Same friends (Norma
> and others who have not died). I live at home and have daily care. Can-
> not travel and never leave the house. It is sad but familiar to recall the
> old 148th Street address of your family. I'll search for a cassette of Cho-
> pin piano music if it exists and send if it is found. Your mother is play-
> ing on the cassette.
> Yours,
> Dr. John Budd

After reading his letter, I turn on my computer. There is an e-mail from a Dr. Willard Gaylin, the man my mother asked me to find, the psychiatrist she said she used to know. I had no idea if he was real or not, but it turns out he is a well-known doctor and author. I had found his e-mail address online and told him about my mother's death. He wrote back right away:

I had a very fleeting acquaintance with your mother when we were both at Glenville High School in Cleveland. I was seventeen and she was, I believe, a year or two younger. I remembered her then as a lovely and stable person ... Many, many years later ... after I began writing ... she wrote me. It was obvious from her letters that she was having a serious breakdown, but even through the chaos of those communications, a bright, funny and creative personality was apparent ... the enormity of her burdens and her burdens and her struggle for survival and dignity was deeply moving ... Please accept my condolences to you and your sister.

Willard Gaylin

Among the dozens of e-mails are messages from people I don't even know, offering their condolences, and in the post, a pile of letters from strangers and friends. After my mother's death, I had sent an e-mail out about how we had found our mother at the end of her life. I had written about the shelter and the women there, and the people from MHS who roam the streets, looking for mentally ill men and women with no place to stay. I had asked my friends in the letter to please not be afraid and avert their eyes the next time they saw a woman on the street wearing a pile of coats and muttering to herself. Buy a hot chocolate for her, I said, or a sandwich. Tell her where to find the closest shelter. Vote for better legislation. *Do something.* The letter spread on the Internet and people started sending money to the shelter from all over the world—from Israel, Norway, Italy, the U.S., the Bahamas, everywhere.

And still, she is gone.

In my studio, I take down a piece of lichen, a wasp's nest, and mouse skeleton from the top of my bookshelf, put them in a box, and clear a nice clean space. There, I place some of the things I had collected from my mother's *wunderkammer*: a bag of hair, a set of her teeth, my plastic pony with the broken leg, a child's book about owls. I place a framed photograph of her in her favorite red-flowered dress, smiling, her arms outstretched toward the viewer. It was the last picture Doug and I put in the slide show we made for her memorial. The picture reminds me of what a man named Bert said to me that day. He had been her social worker a couple years before Melissa and Tim. She refused to work with him anymore after he took her to see her mother's grave. At the memorial, Bert pulled my sister and me aside and said, "I'm so glad you found her. I was always afraid she'd freeze to death on a park bench. In all my years as a social worker, she was the hardest person I ever tried to help."

If we had had Bert, Melissa, Tim, and MHS when we were growing up, I wonder if things would have turned out they way they did. Maybe our mother still would have taken to the streets. I'll never know. But in the end, as my sister says, we got the best of her back—her sweet essence that not even schizophrenia could take away.

I set my mother's paint box next to her photograph on the shelf. All the greens are gone, and the yellows. I place a prayer card I had found in her purse after she died—a prayer to Saint Jude. It begins: "Saint Jude, patron saint of hopeless and difficult cases." Next to the card, I arrange my mother's sock filled with her seventeen keys. One of them is the key that opened up her storage room at U-Haul. Another is for a safe-deposit box that her bank had neglected to tell me about until after her death. The next time I go back to Cleveland, I will open up the box and see what's inside. After that, there will be fifteen keys left. One, I believe, is the key to her old house. What do the rest of them open?

The last thing I put on the shelf are her ashes. They are still in the white plastic bag I separated from the box my sister has on her shelf in upstate New York. Soon I will make an urn for her, a beautiful Italianate one with painted birds and flowers and, most likely, a tiger and an owl. When the time comes—maybe this summer or next—Natalia and I will spread our mother's ashes across the country. We will scatter them in all the shelters, motels, bus stations, airports, and parks where she slept for seventeen years. We'll scatter them in her old backyard where she spent so many nights, sleeping on the wet grass, waiting to be let in. With whatever of her remains, I will come home and plant a pink azalea, or maybe a tall and sturdy pine.

If memory is a palace, let me live there, forever with her, somewhere in that place between sleep and morning. Without her long nights waiting in the rain, without the weight of guilt I bear when I buy a new pair of shoes. Let me dream a palace in the clear night sky, somewhere between Perseus, the Hero, and Cygnus, the Swan—a dark comforting place. A place lit by stars and a winter moon.

Behold the fields and caves, the measureless caverns of memory, immeasurably full of immeasurable things . . . I pass among them all, I fly from here to there, and nowhere is there any end . . .

St. Augustine, *The Confessions*

Acknowledgments

Grateful acknowledgment is due to the following publications in which some paragraphs, in one form or another, first appeared: *Artful Dodge*, *The Kenyon Review*, *Fourth Genre: Explorations in Nonfiction*, *The Bellingham Review*, and *Another Chicago Magazine*. I am also grateful to the following institutions that have given me financial assistance and/or encouragement: A Room of Her Own Foundation, the American Scandinavian Foundation, The Author's League Fund, The Barbara Deming Money for Women Fund, The Carnegie Foundation, Change, Inc., the Fulbright-Hays Foundation, The Gottlieb Foundation, The Ludwig Vogelstein Foundation, Pen-American, The Pollock Krasner Foundation and the Ragdale Foundation.

An enormous heartfelt thanks to all the people who helped forge this book into its final form: University of Massachusetts writing professors Sabina Murray, Dara Wier, and Chris Bachelder for their dedication, support, and insight; Jeremy Church, Brian Baldi, Andre Kahlil, and all my other wonderful colleagues in the M. F. A. Program at UMass, especially Jedediah Berry, whose deft hand as an editor was invaluable to me, and Rob Morgan, who coaxed me closer to the heart of my story. Thanks to Sylvia Snape and Wanda Bak for their good humor and support and to the great staff at University of Massachusetts's Disability Services. Profound thanks to the following people for championing me at different points along the way: Brenda Miller, Ted Gup, Meredeth Hall, Mary Johnson, Michael McColly, Audrey Niffenegger, Michael Steinberg, and Jody Rein. And much, much gratitude to my dear friends who read parts of or earlier drafts: Ricky Baruc, Alex Chitty, Amy Fagin, Alyssa Dee Krauss, Nancy Plotkin, Jane and Steven Schoenberg, Betsy Scofield and in particular, David Skillicorn, whose insightful editorial suggestions were invaluable to me.

There are several people without whom, this book would not exist:

First and foremost, the Zachary Shuster Harmsworth Literary Agency— in particular, the brilliant Esmond Harmsworth, the sensitive and astute Colleen Rafferty, and last but not least, my agent and dear friend, Jennifer Gates, whose faith in me and whose compassion and dedication carried me through to the completion of this book. I can't imagine having written it without her. I am also very grateful to Jane Rosenman from Algonquin Press for keen editorial assistance, sensitivity and kindness. I owe the deepest gratitude to the entire editorial team at Free Press for their enthusiasm, commitment, and collaborative spirit: Publisher Martha Levin, Associate Publisher Suzanne Donahue, Maura O'Brien, and everyone else who helped on this book. I am particularly indebted to my two incredibly devoted editors, Dominick Anfuso and Leah Miller, for asking the hard questions, for having faith that I could answer them, and for having the imagination, insight, and patience that helped me wrestle this book into its published form. Much thanks also to the Free Press publicity team: Carisa Hays, Meredith Wahl-Jones, Giselle Roig, Laura Cooke, and especially to Nicole Kalian, who was such a joy to work with. Thanks to Claire Kelly and the Free Press marketing team who have been so helpful in getting my book out into the world, and also to the design team that made this book beautiful: Eric Fuenticilla for his stunning cover, and Ellen Sasahara for her beautiful interior design and her collaborative and good-natured spirit.

Special thanks to science writer Alan Cutler, whose extraordinary book *The Seashell on the Mountaintop: How Nicolaus Steno Solved an Ancient Mystery and Created a Science of the Earth*, was the inspiration for the first chapter of my book. And much gratitude to the following people and institutions: The Cleveland Museum of Art, the Jones Library of Amherst, Massachusetts, Janet Poirrier and the Frost Library of Amherst College, illuminator Mary Teichman, photographer extraordinaire Adam Laipson, art history scholars John Varriano and Wendy Watson, Cathy Tedford and the Richard F. Brush Art Gallery at St. Lawrence University, David Willard and the Field Museum of Natural History's Division of Birds, and to Mary Sherman and Transcultural Exchange. Thanks to Risitiina Nystad, Maia Hætta, and the Sámi community in Guovdageaidnu, Norway; Agostino Cerasuolo, Bea-

Britt, Lille Mira, Ida and Michel, Bob Marstall, Zach Lewis, Deb Habib, Levi Baruc, Nick, Gabe, and John Hennessy, Kerry Grant, Lisa Finestone, Mary Ann and Tony Palmieri, Barbara Metz, and the River Valley Illustrators Guild. Boundless thanks to Alex Chitty for technical and artistic advice, and for being the other half of my brain and to Stephen Bauer for putting the bee in my bonnet. To Merrill and Goose for tubeworms and fiddle tunes; to Sadie, Zoe, Topaz, and Sophie; to Mark and Ellie Mesler, David and Barbara Regenspan and all my friends who kept post boxes for me over the years, and to Cathy Oakley Smith and her family for being there at the beginning and at the end.

I am indebted to Dr. Constance Carpenter-Bixler for her support, wisdom and help following my accident and to my amazing attorney, Michael Kaplan without whose assistance I would never have had the funds to write this book, and whose dedication to those suffering from brain injuries goes way beyond the call of duty. Enormous thanks to Diana Smarse from the Massachusetts Rehabilitation Commission, for all her wisdom and support. I am also immensely grateful to the Mental Health Services of Cleveland, Inc., and the PATH Program, the program that found my mother and gave her safe harbor. Thanks to former director of MHS, Inc. Steven Friedman, to Susan Neth, Suellen Saunders, Renée Parks, Pastor Tricia Gilbert, and to Tim Raymond, Melissa Yuhas, and Bert Rahl for helping my mother in her final years. I have no words to express my gratitude to the staff and residents at the Community Women's Shelter of Cleveland (now renamed the Norma Herr Women's Center)—without them my mother might have perished on the streets. And much thanks to the dedicated staff at the Westlake Healthcare Center and the Hospice of the Western Reserve who took such incredible care of my mother in her final weeks. I am also forever grateful to the families who helped my mother throughout her difficult life: The Armstrongs, the Budds, the Bentes, the Brunners, the Cerasuolos, Gloria Johnson and family, the Sewells, the Stincics, the Sullivans, Philip Smith and family, Mike and Perry Drake, and a host of thousands. I apologize if I cannot remember every name.

Profound gratitude to Jya and Sianna Plavin, who read earlier drafts of this book, and who have, over the last ten years, provided me with encouragement, love, understanding and comic relief. Immeasurable thanks to Doug Plavin, my best friend, beloved companion and faithful reader—whose love, honesty and unshakable belief in me kept me going until the very end. And finally, to my sister, Natalia Rachel Singer, who wrote her story first, and whose fierce determination to be a writer, against all odds, will always be an inspiration to me.

The Memory Palace
A Memoir

MIRA BARTÓK

Reading Group Guide
Author Q&A

About This Guide

The following reading group guide and author interview are intended to help you find interesting and rewarding approaches to your reading of *The Memory Palace*. We hope this enhances your enjoyment and appreciation of the book. For a complete listing of reading group guides from Simon and Schuster, visit http://community.simonandschuster.com.

Introduction

When piano prodigy Norma Herr was well, she was the most vibrant personality in the room. But as her schizophrenic episodes became more frequent and more dangerous, she withdrew into a world that neither of her daughters could make any sense of. After being violently attacked for demanding that Norma seek help, Mira Bartók and her sister changed their names and cut off all contact in order to keep themselves safe. For the next seventeen years Mira's only contact with her mother was through infrequent letters exchanged through post office boxes, often not even in the same city where she was living.

At the age of forty, artist Mira suffered a debilitating head injury that leaves her memories foggy and her ability to make sense of the world around her forever changed. Hoping to reconnect with her past, Mira reached out to the homeless shelter where her mother is living. When she received word that her mother is dying in a hospital, Mira and her sister traveled to their mother's deathbed to reconcile one last time. Norma gave them a key to a storage unit in which she has kept hundreds of diaries, photographs, and mementos from the past that Mira never imagined she would see again. These artifacts trigger a flood of memories, and give Mira access to the past that she believed had been lost forever.

Discussion Points

1. The prologue describes a homeless woman on a window ledge, thinking about jumping. The author writes, "Let's call her my mother for now, or yours." (p. 8) How did imagining a loved one of your own in that position change the way you thought about the book? Did it help you connect, or make the situation more personal?

2. Early in the book, Mira sees her mother for the first time in seventeen years. What was your impression of this hospital visit? What impact did it leave on Mira?

3. While their mother is dying at the hospital, Mira and her sister Natalia go through their mom's storage facility. How did it make you feel to be with the two sisters as they rummaged through the collection? Share what discovered or rediscovered items touched you most and why.

4. On page 44, Mira says, "Memory, if it is anything at all, is unreliable." How does Mira's own unreliable memory—a lingering effect of her auto accident—underscore the schizophrenic mind of her mother? Do you think it helps her relate to her mother? Why or why not?

5. Mira turns to art as a way to express herself. On page 69, when she visits a Russian Orthodox Church with her grandfather, she sees the "Beautiful Gate" of painted icons and wonders: "Can a painting save a person's life?" Describe ways in which art is therapeutic in this book.

6. As an illustration of how memory can be unreliable, Mira explains that she vividly remembers seeing the Cuyahoga River burning in Cleveland in 1969, and then admits that she's almost certain she wasn't really there, even though the memory of the event is so clear. Can you think of things that are imprinted in your own memory (perhaps from hearing family stories or seeing images on screen) even though you were not there? Do you think anyone's memory can be an accurate record of truth? Why or why not?

7. In Italy, Mira gets a job making reproductions of old paintings for tourists. She later suspects that they are being sold as authentic antiquities. How does Mira react to this news? What deeper feeling does it evoke in Mira about her life in general? How does this discovery fit into the book's questions about authenticity?

8. After visiting their father's grave in the New Orleans area, Mira and Natalia decide to visit a state park. Their heads and hearts filled with emotion, they get lost along the way. But after they find the park and enjoy some peaceful time in nature, the road away from the park seems clear and simple. Describe the role that nature and meditation play in Mira's life and in this book.

9. On page 285, when Mira's husband William is in a fit of depression, Mira feels like "It's that January day in 1990 all over again." Compare and contrast Mira's characterization of her husband and her mother. How did her experiences with her mother impact the way she responds to William's depression?

10. At her mother's memorial service, the director of MHS (Mental Health Services, Inc.) says to Mira, "I know of children who have abandoned their parents for much less than you two have gone through," but Mira wonders if she and her sister truly did enough. How does this book make you think about the obligations that children have to their parents? Are there limits to what family members owe each other?

11. Mira seems to regard the homeless people she sees on the streets a little differently—as though any one of them could be a mother or father. She wants people to understand the "thin line, the one between their worlds and ours."(p. 351) Has this book helped you see homeless people in a different light? Why or why not? How has it impacted the way you think about mental illness?

Enhance Your Book Club

1. One purpose of this memoir is to show first-hand what it's like to live with (and apart from) a person who suffers from a mental illness. Do a little research to find out more about what it's like to live with this disease. You can start with websites such as schizophrenia.com, nami.org/, and healthyplace.com/thought-disorders/nimh/world-of-people-with-schizophrenia/menu-id-1154. You might also try typing in the search term "schizophrenia documentary" at YouTube.com in order to see a variety of homemade and televised documentaries about people who suffer from this debilitating mental illness.

2. Mira Bartók is a writer, poet, musician and artist. She is also a strong advocate for other people in the arts. She blogs about grants, fellowships, and opportunities for both the established and aspiring. Visit her blog at miraslist.blogspot.com. Are there any opportunities there you may want to explore? Share them with the group—and encourage your fellow readers to pursue their own creative interests.

3. The author wants you to understand how thin the line is between one world and another—between what you may consider a "normal" life and a life on the streets or one plagued with a mind or mood-altering

condition. After reading this book, take a closer look at people you may ordinarily ignore. Look a homeless person in the eye and greet him or her with a salutation as you might any other person. If possible, try volunteering at a local homeless shelter, or better yet, your book club could volunteer as a group. Be sure to share and discuss your experience with your fellow book club members.

Author Q&A

You mention that your mother admired the ability of a person to mix words and art. Do you think she would have been proud of this book, which combines your artwork with your writing? Did your mother's encouragement prompt you to combine words and art, or did you always think you'd be a writer?

I think she would have been very proud of me for writing this book, although I'm sure there are many parts in it that would upset her too. However, I know she would have liked the artwork and she would have appreciated the great effort it took to create a book like this, given my disability. As far as always thinking I would be a writer, I never thought about that and still don't think of myself in that way. Although I always wrote—mostly poetry, essays and short fiction, and also I made artists' book with images and text—I am an artist first, and that means, for me, that I serve the idea. If the idea, which often starts out as an image, needs to be a story, then I will write a story. If it should be a painting or a film, then I have to follow that trajectory. My next project is an illustrated young adult novel/adult fiction crossover. I have also started to explore creating radio documentaries with my husband, musician and producer, Doug Plavin. Can you tell that I don't like labels? ☺

You are an accomplished artist, author, poet, and musician. Do you have a favorite medium?

My first love was music, and still is, although I am hardly an accomplished musician—more of an amateur. And due to some cognitive deficits from my brain injury, it will take a lot of focused practicing to regain much of my former ability to play music.

How do you choose which form to use when expressing an emotion, theme, or story?

I think it chooses me. I have no idea. See my answer to question one!

How did combining art forms using writing and painting help you construct your memoir?

Music informed my use of language, art informed the imagistic way I wrote. And when words failed me, I would draw. When I couldn't draw, I would write. And sometimes, while typing, if words got stuck in my head, I'd bring up an image from my computer to help me along visually.

This book is a very personal and moving testimony to the turbulent and loving relationship between a mother and daughter. Were there certain aspects of your story you were reluctant to share?

Yes, definitely. I withheld certain things that might have appeared sensational, particularly violent episodes with our grandfather. I'm not a huge fan of misery memoirs, ones that relentlessly describe one terrible thing after another without any self-examination on the author's part. I wanted to express beauty as well and I also did not want to contribute to the unfortunate stereotype of a violent schizophrenic; statistically, most schizophrenics are more likely to harm themselves than others. I also decided against sharing a couple very personal drawings, like the one I did of my mother when she was dying.

How has it been sharing your story with others?

It's been quite surprising. I had no idea this story would impact others the way it has. I am extremely moved when people come up to me after a reading with tears in their eyes, telling me that they have a mentally ill family member or they themselves have a brain injury. I am particularly happy when people tell me that the story inspired them and also challenged their assumptions about those less fortunate than themselves. And I am also quite pleased when someone gets the dark humor that comes up from time to time in the book. Believe or not, some passages are actually funny. As my grandma used to say, "Ya gotta laugh to stop from crying!"

Though this is a story about the lasting bond of parental love, it's also very much about the unreliability of memory. What message did you most want to convey to readers about these subjects?

I never intended to get across any kind of message when I wrote the book. I simply set out to explore the connections that I shared with my mother, nothing more, and I set out to do that through pictures, because I am a visual thinker. But yes, the story of mother-daughter love shines through and for me, I think I came to understand that it is a very primal thing, one that is still difficult for me to explain and understand. With memory, the more I researched the subject and explored my own relationship to memory, especially in the light of living with TBI, the more I found all these arguments about so-called "truth" in memory (and thus, memoir) to be silly. I'm not talking about making up some sensational story so that one can sell a fictional book as a memoir (and you know who I mean!) but rather, the idea that just because one remembers something "clearly," it has to be true is simply false. Ask any neuroscientist, any forensic psychologist criminal investigator. Oh, if writers only read a little more science, I'd be so happy! Anyway, I personally think the strongest message in the book is about compassion, and the more times I rewrote the book, the more compassion I discovered within myself.

When you wrote your memoir, how did you feel about scenes that involve your sister or other featured characters who may read it? How does the unreliability of memory come into play in these scenes, given the different perspectives of people who may have experienced the same moments in different ways? What has it been like to share these memories with the people who lived through them with you?

I think that the only person I was worried about was my sister, Natalia Singer, because of her very private nature and her difficult personal choice not to write our mother during those seventeen years of separation. I was just worried about bringing to light, in a public way, a very painful part of our family history. Nevertheless, I felt compelled to write the book and hoped that ultimately, her reading it would be a healing experience for both of us—and I really think it was. After she read it, she called to say that she loved it and that I was very brave to have written this book. And aside from that, she had written her own memoir a few years ago, called *Scraping by in the Big Eighties*, about how she tried to rise above our difficult past to make it as a struggling writer during that decadent era of big hair and junk bonds. She never, to my recollection (ah . . . memory again!) asked me to help her recall any events from that period while she was writing her book, nor do I think she should have.

Basically, I tried hard not to think of anyone reading the book until I was done. At one point, while I was working on an early draft, my sister asked me if I was going to show her the book before I was finished so she could check my memories and make sure they were right. I thought that was pretty funny, given that my book was about how unreliable memory was. I thanked her but told her that I was more interested in what things we miss-remember and why. I was and still am very intrigued by how family members recall things differently. It's the psychology behind what we choose to forget and the neuroscience that I am interested in, not some journalistic approach to memoir. Also, most people who read memoirs know that conversations and scenes are condensed and altered in the interest of time and telling a good story. But what we don't often see in memoir is the exploration of memory itself, how it functions, and how in the retelling of an event, the telling transforms not only the memory but our brain as well.

One thing almost everyone says after reading the book is: how could you write a book like that if you have such a problem with memory? What I think they don't understand is that for many years, from the time I was fourteen, I have been keeping very detailed journals, dream diaries, and sketchbooks. Also, with TBI, much of our long-term memory returns. It's the short-term memory that is most compromised with me (and still is). All that aside, the funny thing is that after certain family members or friends from childhood read the book, they all said how close their memories were to my own. I didn't expect that at all.

There is a difference between the unreliability of memory and the conscious effort to stretch truth into fiction. There have been some high profile allegations in the memoir genre in recent years. Were you at all concerned about this sort of scandal?
Never. My book is hardly scandalous. If anything, it is a story about the transformative power of empathy.

Did you ever consider writing about your experiences in a fictional way?
Actually, before I wrote this book I was writing a novel but the mother character (a minor figure in the novel) kept getting in the way so I thought I would just write about my mother and be done with it! My next book has

some bits and pieces of autobiographical material but more related to place since it is set in Northern Norway where I lived for a time.

Why do you think your mother requested that you contact Willard Gaylin? Have you had any additional contact with him besides the single message in the book?

I think that my mother really respected him and remembered him from her past as a kind, gentle and helpful man. In her journals and her letters to me, she often talked about her need to find an 'advisor' and I think he probably fit the bill in her mind for some reason. And yes, I have had more contact with him! When the hardcover come out, I sent him a signed copy. He wrote back to tell me how much he loved the book.

Your mother wrote, "Everyone is guaranteed the right to be deprived of the pursuit of happiness." (p. 297) Do you think she believed that in the end? Do you?

I don't know. Sometimes she made up these dark funny phrases but I don't know how much she believed in them. I would imagine she was commenting on this American belief that everyone has a right to the pursuit of happiness while for those who are poor and disenfranchised, it is extremely arduous for them to not only find happiness but to even pursue it, especially if they are living on the street. I think that unfortunately, many Americans think happiness means entitlement—being able to drive gas-guzzling cars, and consume as much as we want, usually at the expense of another human being's suffering (i.e. working in sweatshops). Nothing is ever enough and therefore, they can never truly be happy. Personally, I think true happiness comes from trying to alleviate the suffering of others. I also think it comes from always remembering what you love—paying attention to and recreating that sense of wonderment that we experienced in childhood but often forget about as we grow older.

Part three of your memoir is aptly called "Palimpsest." Do you feel as though writing this book was a new beginning for you?

Absolutely!

Did the book's publication create a transitory moment similar to or different from the feeling you had when you finished writing it?

It's a different feeling. Finishing the book felt like a monumental thing for me, but monumental on a personal level. Publishing it makes the story public and creates this odd (and powerful) connection to a larger world, i.e. an audience. I found that after I finished the book I was incredibly relieved and felt like now I can go on and write fiction, make radio documentaries, make prints and paintings, etc. But the reality is that now that the book is out there, I have to go full-steam ahead and promote it—do events, engage with readers, etc. It's a bit overwhelming and stressful, although incredibly exciting too.

As a practiced author and artist, can you briefly describe your creative process? Do you practice daily, or in fits of inspiration? Do you approach visual art differently than writing?

I often start writing when I am walking in the woods with my dog. I bring a hand-held voice recorder with me, and speak/write as I walk. I get some of my best writing ideas in the morning when I'm out in nature but if I don't record them right away they probably will disappear from the memory bank by the time I get home. As far as practicing daily goes, I write every day when I am working on a literary project. However, because I live with a brain injury, if I have dinner with friends the night before, that means I don't write the next day. Or if I speak at a conference and have to travel there and back, I am usually so mentally fatigued that I probably won't write for a couple or few days. I have to measure everything I do very carefully. It goes the other way around too—if I write one day I might not be able to drive my car the next. As for making art though, I find it very hard to start something (starting projects is very difficult for people with TBI) but once I do, it takes less mental energy and can be quite meditative. I approach both art and writing in a similar way though—with strong images. I usually get inspired to write or draw by looking at an image or remembering one. I then write, or draw myself into the discovery of what that image means to me. I also get a lot of ideas from my very wild, mythic and adventurous dreams! I see images I have to write down or I hear the first line in a poem, right before I wake up.

Describe how you came to title this book *The Memory Palace*. Do you feel like writing this memoir was a memory palace in itself? How did you put together the bits and pieces until they made a more sensible whole for you?

I originally thought of structuring this book as a kind of cabinet of curiosities, given my background in museum collections and taxonomy, but then I remembered this ancient Renaissance system of memory recall and bingo—it was perfect. Also, I had been making these pictures for each memory so they all ended up on a giant canvas on my studio wall. And by using the Memory Palace motif as a way to architecturally contain the book, it provided the perfect background to weave in musings about memory itself and the brain. In order to make sense of the whole thing (and not lose my mind in the process!), I created an actual cabinet in my studio, with openings for each chapter. That way, if I wrote something one day or jotted down a note or sketched a picture, I could place it in its drawer (since I probably would forget about it the following day). So in this way, my own creative process was a building of a palace—on my wall, in this cabinet, in the book.

Your memoir is very intense and moving. What do you hope readers will take away from *The Memory Palace*?
I never have an agenda for anything I create. I didn't write this book to teach anyone a lesson about brain injury or mental illness or the plight of the homeless population. I wrote it because I needed to, and also, I knew it was one hell of a good story. That said, if readers walk away from this book with more empathy for those less fortunate or if they gain a more compassionate understanding of mental illness and the other issues I bring up, then that is the icing on the cake. Like I say in the book, there is a thin line between the world of homelessness and "our" world. And each and every woman out there, trying to survive on the street is someone's mother, daughter, sister or friend. I also hope my friends and family will understand my struggles with living with a brain injury a little bit better. Even after over ten years, most people still don't get it when I tell them I need to not talk on the phone or see people for a while in order to rest my brain. I think it's very hard to see someone who looks and sounds normal and accept that there is something seriously wrong. And I certainly hope that friends and family of others living with TBI, as well as those living with other invisible disabilities, such as Lupus, Fibromyalgia, Chronic Fatigue Syndrome, Lyme Disease, etc. will be more understanding toward their loved ones. And last but not least, I hope that, even though I revealed some very dark things about her, my mother's memory is honored in some way, and that readers will go away with the feeling that she was a beautiful, gifted and extraordinary human being. And the best thing is, the shelter that

she lived in the last three years of her life has recently been renamed in her honor. It is now a bright, shiny new facility called The Norma Herr Women's Center! I am now working with the shelter to hopefully raise money to create a community garden near the shelter for the women there to grow their own food. How is that for a happy ending?

How has your life changed since the book was actually published? What responses have you been getting to the book, both from strangers and people you know? Have there been any surprises?
Well, my life certainly has gotten a lot more hectic! I hope things calm down at some point so I can work on something new. But for now, I really need to not only promote this book but also try to reach out to some communities and organizations that might find the book helpful, such as brain injury foundations, and places that help the homeless population and those suffering from mental illness. I recently signed on with a speaker's bureau (Creative Well, Inc.) and already I am getting some requests to talk to groups about the issues raised in the book.

Most responses about the book have been amazing and very positive! Ever since it came out I have been receiving letters and emails from all over the country and even from people overseas. The majority are from people who have a family member who suffers from mental illness or people who have recently experienced the death of someone close to them. I have also gotten beautiful letters from traumatic brain injury survivors. It's a bit overwhelming, I must say. I had no idea I would get this kind of response. These people basically just want to tell me that after reading my book they just didn't feel alone anymore. It's very touching. Some letters have certainly brought tears to my eyes.

As far as responses from people I know, well, the greatest response was from my sister, who loved the book and who finally felt understood for the decisions she had to make. The book has really been great for our relationship because we didn't talk about our mother that much for so many years and now, since my sister has read the book, a door has opened for the both of us and I just feel so much closer to her.

The biggest surprise has been all these people who have appeared out of nowhere who knew my mom! They all heard me talking with Terry Gross on National Public Radio's *Fresh Air*. I have gotten to visit with my mother's best friend from childhood and her younger sister, who actually owns the baby grand piano that my mother grew up playing (but how my grandparents could have afforded a piano like that in the poor neighborhood they lived is still a mystery). These 'girls' knew my mom years before she became sick and remembered her as a kind, talented, vivacious and loving girl—a warm and funny person who was always there for you if you needed her. Margie and Claire (the sisters) told me all kinds of wonderful stories about my mom, and filled in some of the gaps about how she was raised and what she liked to do. One thing I discovered was that no one, not even Margie and Claire, ever met my mom's parents! She always met her friends and boyfriends at their houses because she didn't want anyone to come to her own home, which was a tiny apartment in a run-down building. I am sure it had to do with her father, who was such a difficult, violent and controlling man. Meeting these women has given me a glimpse into who my mother could have been, had schizophrenia not highjacked her mind. I also just heard this past week from my mom's best friend and roommate from music conservatory. My mother had her first psychotic episode while at music school so I am really looking forward to meeting this old friend of hers named Dahlia, who was there at the beginning of my mom's illness and before.

And one of the most surprising things is that the shelter where my mother lived the last three years of her life has been renamed in her honor and is now called The Norma Herr Women's Center. MHS, Inc, the organization that oversees the shelter, received some Obama Stimulus funding to renovate the shelter, along with some other local grants. They decided to not put some big important politician's name on the building but rather, the name of their oldest and dearest resident, a small but well-loved and brilliant woman who had had a very hard life, my mom, Norma Herr.

What have you been up to since you finished writing the book?
Pretty much just promoting the book and traveling around, reading to audiences. I've also been doing a lot of radio shows, which I discovered I love to do! For someone with a brain injury, it's actually a delight to sit in a sound-proofed room alone with no distractions, a headset so I can focus, and just talk. One of the many great things that has come out of doing radio is that after hearing me on the air, our local NPR station asked me to write and record commentaries for them throughout the year. They are letting me write anything I want.

Other than that, when I have a few moments or a couple days break, I try to work on my next big project, titled *Nine Valleys in One Twilight*, which is a Young Adult novel (hopefully the first in a series of three) set above the arctic circle in Northern Norway during World War II. It's the weaving of two true stories—a girl who crosses the tundra to bring her grandmother a gift before she dies and the story of a young Jewish boy, escaping the Holocaust, trying to make his way to Sweden. They meet, hiding in a wolf den during a blizzard, and then the adventure begins! Although there is a lot of real-life stuff in the book there is quite a bit of fantasy too—some time travel, some ancient mythology from the region, some creatures that don't really exist. And it's illustrated of course and might have a few graphic novel sections.

I am also working on a radio documentary about my journey trying to track down an old recording of an interview my father did with Studs Terkel years ago. The piece is called *The Sound of Memory: The Search for My Father's Voice*, and I'm working on it with my husband, musician and music producer Doug Plavin. We recently started a venture called North of Radio (www.northofradio.com) where we create and produce innovative and collaborative multi-media projects. Aside from those two big things, the book and radio documentary, I just try to make weird little drawings and collages at night to keep myself out of trouble.

About the Author

Mira Bartók is a Chicago-born artist and writer and the author of twenty-eight books for children. Her writing has appeared in several literary journals and anthologies and has been noted in *The Best American Essays* series. She lives in Western Massachusetts where she runs Mira's List, a blog (miraslist.blogspot.com) that helps artists find funding and residencies all over the world. *The Memory Palace* is Mira's first book for adults. You can find her at: mirabartok.com